Valeriano **Lencioni**

Dictionary of Cuisine French

Dictionary of Cuisine French

Steve Combes

BA (Hons.) Lond.

Hutchinson

London Melbourne Sydney Auckland Johannesburg

Hutchinson & Co. (Publishers) Ltd

An imprint of the Hutchinson Publishing Group

17-21 Conway Street, London W1P 6JD

Hutchinson Publishing Group (Australia) Pty Ltd
16-22 Church Street, Hawthorn, Melbourne, Victoria 3122

Hutchinson Group (NZ) Ltd
32-34 View Road, PO Box 40-086, Glenfield, Auckland 10

Hutchinson Group (SA) (Pty) Ltd
PO Box 337, Bergvlei 2012, South Africa

First published by Barrie & Rockliff 1962
Reprinted 1967
Reprinted by Barrie & Jenkins Ltd 1974, 1977
First published by Hutchinson 1980
Reprinted 1981, 1984, 1985

Printed and bound in Great Britain by
Anchor Brendon Ltd, Tiptree, Essex

ISBN 0 09 144241 9

FOREWORD

by

J. Vincent, M.B.E., F.H.C.I.
Chevalier de l'Étoile Noire

This dictionary of terms used in the kitchen and the restaurant, in French and English, will prove a great asset to students and teachers at hotel schools all over the country.

There is no doubt that a great deal of work and forethought has been devoted to it, and I feel sure that it will help students to understand kitchen French in all its forms and implications. They will find in it a precise and well-compiled range of words used every day by those engaged in the art and practice of cookery and service.

The English–French section will give students the opportunity of obtaining a very good and very useful vocabulary of French, which will help them considerably in learning the more academic language of the classroom.

I sincerely hope that this dictionary will find its way into the library of every student interested in becoming bilingual, and I wish its author the success he deserves.

CONTENTS

AUTHOR'S PREFACE

The purpose of this dictionary is to carry a stage further the work begun in the text *Restaurant French*. Let it first be understood that this *is* a dictionary and not a bilingual recipe-book. Thus, like any other dictionary, it translates words and phrases, but not whole sentences—or entire recipes. Fortunately, many French recipe-books are phrased in simple, 'telegrammatic' language, composed mostly of nouns, adjectives, verbs and adverbs—a language which, with use, becomes progressively easier to decipher.

For the reader who already has a basic knowledge of French, the aim of the present work is to provide an extensive vocabulary of commodities, equipment, processes, manipulations, etc., and, especially, a more comprehensive French–English coverage of the flora and fauna used in French cookery than the author has so far been able to find in any work of this kind. Indeed, to the best of the author's knowledge, some French names of French flora and fauna given herein have never before been translated or explained in a French–English dictionary published in this country.

Since this book is not encyclopædic, it does not pretend to cover either the culinary implications or the historical origins of proper nouns used as designations in French menus. For an explanation of what is meant to the cook by such names as "Radziwill" and "Rossini", the answer will depend on his choice of recipe-book or on his previous training and professional experience. As to historical origins, the author hopes to explain these in another work in the course of preparation.

When an author trained as a linguist ventures into a technological field, he is very grateful for any advice which may be forthcoming from an authority on the technology concerned. The same author, working in an artistic context, is equally grateful to a master in the relevant art for any lore which the latter may be disposed to pass on. As the practical study of gastronomy and cookery is at once an art and a technology, the author is thereby doubly indebted to A. E. Simms, Esq., F.H.C.I., F.R.S.H., the benefit of whose advice and experience in all matters relating to this text has made the compilation of it possible. Mr. Simms has, by simplifying technical difficulties and by clarifying gastronomic obscurities, greatly assisted not only the author but also the venture as a whole by his invaluable counsel and encouragement.

New technical dictionaries compiled from first principles always present considerable difficulties to the humble author. The editing of the English–French section of the present work has been much helped by J. L. Isherwood, Esq., whose patience and carefulness in sifting and indexing material is much appreciated.

Where a French word or phrase has more than one meaning, the author has given only such English translation or translations as is or are relevant to the scope of the dictionary.

Several references, especially to birds and fishes, are made primarily for purposes of identification and so that the text shall be comprehensive, and do not signify that the birds or fish concerned may not enjoy statutory protection in certain countries (or legally designated parts of them) or at certain times of year.

This book is a new work, and its author offers it with apologies for its shortcomings. Suggestions for eventual improvements will be very welcome, and should be addressed to the publishers, whom the author wishes to thank for their patience.

Portchester, May 1962   STEVE COMBES

ABBREVIATIONS

adj.—adjective.
adv.—adverb.
conj.—conjunction.
dem.—demonstrative.
e.g.—for example.
esp.—especially.
f.—feminine.
i.—intransitive.
ind.—indirect.
int.—interjection.
interr.—interrogative.
inv.—invariable.
lit.—literally.
m.—masculine.
n.—noun.
occ.—occasionally.
opp.—opposite.
phr.—phrase.
pl.—plural.
prep.—preposition.
pron.—pronoun.
qch.—quelque chose.
q.v.—which (please) see.
refl.—reflexive.
sing.—singular.
tr.—transitive.
v.—verb.

VOCABULARY

FRENCH–ENGLISH

French–English

a

à prep. to; with.

abaisse n.f. thinly-rolled paste, for pastry preparations.

abaissé adj. rolled thin, thinly-rolled.

abaisser v.tr. to roll thin (paste, for pastry preparations).

abat(t)is n.m.pl. giblets.

abats n.m.pl. offal.
  entrée d'abats n.f. *entrée* (q.v.) of offal.

abatte n.f. cutlet-bat.

abatteur n.m. slaughterer.

abattoir n.m. slaughterhouse.

abattre v.tr. to slaughter.

abdomen n.m. abdomen.

abdominal, aux adj. abdominal.

abîmé adj. spoiled, ruined.

abîmer v.tr. to spoil, to ruin.

ablette n.f. bleak.

aboyer v.i. to "bark", to relay orders.

aboyeur n.m. "barker" (in kitchen).

abricot n.m. apricot.

abricoté adj. decorated or flavoured with apricots.

abricoter v.tr. to decorate or flavour with apricots.

absinthe n.f. wormwood; absinth(e).

absorbé adj. absorbed.

absorber v.tr. to absorb.

abusseau, -eaux n.m. variety of atherine found off the French Atlantic coast.

acajou n.m. mahogany.
  noix d'acajou n.f. cashew-nut.

accepter v.tr. to accept.

accolé adj. placed together, stuck together (e.g. halves of meringue).

accoler v.tr. to place together, to stick together (e.g. halves of meringue).

accommodé adj. done up; dressed; seasoned.

accommoder v.tr. to do up; to dress; to season.
  accommoder une salade to dress a salad.

accommoder une sauce to do up a sauce.

accompagné adj. accompanied.
  accompagné de accompanied by, accompanied with.

accompagnement n.m. accompaniment, trimming.

accompagner v.tr. to accompany, to go with (sth.).

achard n.m. (variety of) highly-spiced Oriental pickle.

achillée n.f. milfoil, yarrow.

acide adj. acid, sharp.
  n.m. acid.
  acide acétique acetic acid.
  acide salicylique salicylic acid.

acidité n.f. acidity.

acidulé adj. acidulated, acid.

aciduler v.tr. to acidulate (esp. with lemon-juice).

acier n.m. steel.
  acier inoxydable stainless steel, rustless steel.

acore n.m. sweet flag.

additionner v.tr. to add up.
  additionner de v.tr. to augment with.

adhérer v.i. to adhere, to stick.

affranchi adj. (food, e.g. pastry) loosened, detached (from inner surfaces of cooking utensil).

affranchir v.tr. to loosen, to detach (food from inner surfaces of cooking utensil).
  affranchir du dessous v.tr. to loosen on, to detach from, the underside.

agami n.m. trumpeter (bird).

agaric n.m. agaric.
  agaric comestible common edible mushroom.

agité adj. shaken, shaken up.

agiter v.tr. to shake, to shake up.

agneau, -eaux n.m. lamb; wether lamb.
  agneau de lait milk(-fed) lamb.
  agneau de Pauillac Pauillac lamb.

agnelet n.m. lambkin, young lamb.

agnelle n.f. ewe lamb.

agoursi n.m. variety of ridged cucumber, used especially in hors d'œuvre preparations.

agréable adj. pleasant.

   agréable à l'œil pleasant to look at.

aider v.tr. to help, to assist.

aiglefin n.m. haddock.

aigre adj. sour, sharp.

aigrefin n.m. haddock.

aigrelet, -ette adj. sourish, somewhat sharp.

aigu, -uë adj. sharp, pointed.

aiguillat n.m. dogfish.

aiguille n.f. needle.

   aiguille à brider trussing-needle.

   aiguille à piquer larding-needle.

aiguillette n.f. long thin slice, strip (esp. of poultry flesh).

aiguisé adj. sharpened (blade).

aiguiser v.tr. to sharpen (blade).

   pierre à aiguiser n.f. sharpening-stone, whetstone.

ail n.m. garlic.

   gousse d'ail n.f. clove of garlic.

   pointe d'ail n.f. touch of garlic.

aile n.f. wing.

aileron n.m. winglet.

aillade n.f. garlic sauce; any preparation with a garlic base or containing a strong garlic flavouring.

aillé adj. flavoured with garlic; containing garlic.

ailler v.tr. to flavour with garlic.

ailloli n.m. garlic pounded with olive oil and egg-yolk.

aioli n.m. see *ailloli*.

aïoli n.m. see *ailloli*.

airelle n.f.

   airelle myrtille bilberry, whortleberry, "huckleberry".

   airelle rouge cranberry.

ajouter v.tr. to add.

   ajouter qch. à qch. to add something to something.

alambic n.m. still.

albarelle n.f. variety of boletus mushroom which grows on chestnut-trees and white poplars.

alberge n.f. clingstone apricot; clingstone peach.

albumen n.m. albumen.

albumine n.f. albumin.

alcaloïde adj. & n.m. alkaloid.

alcool n.m. alcohol, spirit.

alcoolique adj. alcoholic, alcoholized.

alimentation n.f. nourishment, nutrition.

alkékenge n.f. winter cherry.

allant au feu adj. phr. fire-proof.

allant au four adj. phr. oven-proof.

aller v.i. to go.

alliacé adj. alliaceous; of, pertaining to, garlic.

alliacée n.f. (any) garlic plant.

allongé adj. lengthened (dimension); extended (sauce).

allonger v.tr. to lengthen (dimension); to extend (sauce).

   allonger de to extend with.

allumer v.tr. to light (lamp, fire, etc.).

allumette n.f. (lucifer) match.

alose n.f. shad.

   grande alose allice-shad.

alouette n.f. lark.

aloyau, -aux n.m. sirloin (of beef).

alterné adj. alternate.

alterner v.tr. to alternate.

alvéole n.m. or f. cell (of honeycomb).

alvéolé adj. honeycombed.

amalgamé adj. amalgamated; mixed in.

amalgamer v.tr. to amalgamate; to mix in.

amande n.f. almond.

   amande amère bitter almond.

   amande douce sweet almond.

amélanche n.f. shad-berry.

aménagements n.m.pl. (kitchen) fixtures.

aménager v.tr. to arrange, to dispose.

amener à ébullition v.tr. to bring to the boil.

amer, -ère adj. bitter.

   amer n.m. bitter(s).

amidon n.m. starch.

ammocète n.m. larval lamprey.

amome n.m. amomum, plant from which come grains of paradise.

amourettes n.f.pl. (beef or veal) spinal marrow.

amphibie adj. amphibious. n.m. amphibian.

ampoule n.f. electric-light bulb.

amuse-gueule pl. **amuse-gueules** n.m. cocktail snack.

amygdalin adj. amygdalic; made of almonds.

amygdaline n.f. amygdalin.

analogue adj. analogous, similar.

   analogue à similar to.

ananas n.m. pineapple.

anchois n.m. anchovy.
  anchois de Norvège sprat.
andouille n.f. chitterlings (made into sausages).
andouillette n.f. small chitterling-sausage.
anémone de mer n.f. sea-anemone.
anet(h) n.m. anethum.
  anet(h) doux fennel.
  anet(h) odorant dill.
angélique n.f. angelica.
angelot n.m. angel-fish; angler.
anguille n.f. eel.
  anguille de rivière fresh-water eel, river eel.
animal, -aux n.m. animal.
  animal de basse-cour farmyard animal.
animelles n.f.pl. lamb's fry.
anis n.m. anise; aniseed.
  anis étoilé star anise.
  graine d'anis n.f. aniseed.
anisette n.f. anisette-cordial.
anneau, -eaux n.m. ring, ring-shape.
anone n.f. anona.
  anone écailleuse sweet-sop.
  anone muriquée, anone réti-culée muricate anona, reticulate anona, West Indian custard-apple, sour-sop.
antenne n.f. antenna.
anthyllide n.f. anthyllis.
  anthyllide vulnéraire kidney-vetch, lady's fingers.
août n.m. August.
api n.m. lady-apple.
aplati adj. flattened.
aplatir v.tr. to flatten.
aponévrose n.f. aponeurosis, fascia.
appareil n.m. basic culinary pre-paration comprising two or more ingredients.
appeler v.tr. to call.
  s'appeler v.refl. to be called, to be named.
appellation n.f. appellation, de-nomination, designation.
appétit n.m. appetite.
apporter v.tr. to bring.
apprenti n.m. apprentice.
  apprenti cuisinier apprentice cook.
apprentie n.f. female apprentice.
  apprentie cuisinière female ap-prentice cook.
apprentissage n.m. apprentice-ship.

B

approcher v.tr. to bring near, to draw near.
approprié adj. appropriate.
approprier v.tr. to appropriate.
aqueux, -euse adj. watery.
araignée n.f. wire spider.
  araignée de mer sea-spider; weever.
arbenne n.f. white partridge.
arbouse n.f. arbutus-berry.
arbousier n.m. arbutus.
  arbousier commun strawberry-tree.
arcanette n.f. small non-migrant teal found in Lorraine.
arête n.f. (fish-)bone.
  arête médiane backbone (of fish).
  grande arête backbone (of fish).
argent n.m. silver; money.
  argent massif solid silver.
  argent orfévré silver plate.
argentier n.m. plate-man.
argentine n.f. argentina.
aromate n.m. aromatic; spice.
aromatique adj. aromatic.
aromatisé adj. aromatized.
aromatiser v.tr. to aromatize.
arome n.m. aroma.
arrière-train n.m. hindquarters.
arroche n.f. orach.
arrosage n.m. sprinkling (with liquid); basting.
arrosé adj. sprinkled (with liquid); basted.
arroser v.tr. to sprinkle (with liquid); to baste.
arrow-root n.m. arrow-root.
artichaut n.m. globe artichoke.
  artichaut de Jérusalem squash-melon.
  artichaut d'Espagne squash-melon.
  artichaut des toits houseleek, Jupiter's beard.
  artichaut d'hiver Jerusalem artichoke.
  foin d'artichaut choke (of arti-choke).
  fond d'artichaut base of arti-choke.
article n.m. article.
artocarpe n.m. bread-fruit tree.
asperge n.f. asparagus.
  petites asperges n.f.pl. sprue.
aspergé adj. sprinkled.
  aspergé de sprinkled with.
asperger v.tr. to sprinkle.
  asperger de to sprinkle with.

aspérule n.f. asperula.
   aspérule odorante woodruff.
aspic n.m. aspic(-jelly).
aspiqué adj. set in aspic; coated with aspic.
aspiquer v.tr. to set in aspic; to coat with aspic.
assaisonné adj. seasoned.
assaisonnement n.m. seasoning.
assaisonner v.tr. to season.
   assaisonner de haut goût to season highly, strongly.
assez adv. enough, sufficiently; rather, fairly.
   assez chaud hot enough; fairly hot.
assiette n.f. plate.
   assiette anglaise plate of assorted cold meats, e.g. beef, ham and tongue.
   assiette à potage soup-plate.
   assiette à salade salad-plate.
   assiette creuse soup-plate.
   assiette plate meat-plate.
assiettée n.f. plateful.
assommer v.tr. to kill (esp. eels, by a blow on the head).
astringent adj. & n.m. astringent.
athérine n.f. atherine.
attaché adj. attached.
attacher v.tr. to attach.
attelet n.m. ornate metal skewer (sometimes used to label an item on a cold buffet).
attendre v.i. to wait.
   v.tr. to wait for.
attendri adj. tenderized; softened.
attendrir v.tr. to tenderize; to soften.
attendu adj. (game) left to hang.
attente n.f. wait.
attention n.f. attention.
   faire attention à to pay attention to, to take notice of.
atténué adj. attenuated, toned down.
atténuer v.tr. to attenuate, to tone down.
attereau, -eaux n.m. preparation whose constituents are cooked skewered together.
auberge n.f. inn.
aubergine n.f. egg-plant.
aujourd'hui adv. to-day.
aunée n.f. (strictly) inula; elecampane.
   aunée hélène elecampane.
auparavant adv. before, beforehand, previously.

aurone n.f. southernwood.
autant adv. as much.
   autant de as much (of), as many.
   autant de vin as much wine.
autoclave n.m. pressure cooker.
automne n.m. autumn.
autre adj. & pron. other.
   autre chose something else.
autrement adv. differently; otherwise.
à l'avance adv. phr. in advance, previously.
avancement n.m. promotion, advancement
   avancement par ancienneté promotion by seniority.
   avancement par choix promotion by selection.
avant prep. before.
   avant de (followed by infinitive) prep. phr. before.
   avant que (followed by subjunctive) conj. before.
avec prep. with.
aveline n.f. hazel-nut, filbert, cobnut.
avis n.m. notice; advice, opinion.
aviver v.tr. to revive; to brighten (colour, appearance).
avocat n.m. avocado pear, alligator pear.
avocette n.f. avocet.
avoine n.f. oats.
   farine d'avoine oatmeal.
avoir v.tr. to have.
   avoir besoin de to need, to have need of.
   avoir soin de to attend to, to take care of.
avril n.m. April.
axonge n.f. hog's fat, lard.
azerole n.f. Neapolitan medlar.
azyme adj. unleavened.

b

baba n.m. small individual *entremets* (q.v.) made from fermented paste and soaked in rum.
babeurre n.m. buttermilk.
bac à dégivrage n.m. defreezing-compartment (of refrigerator).
bacon n.m. cured bacon.
bactérie n.f. bacterium.
   bactéries bacteria.
badian n.m. star anise.
badiane n.f. star anise.

badigeonné adj. brushed over (with liquid, esp. egg-wash).

badigeonner v.tr. to brush over (with liquid, esp. egg-wash).

bague n.f. ring, ring-shape; annulus (of mushroom).

en bague in the shape of a ring.

baie n.f. berry.

baie de genévrier juniper-berry.

baie de genièvre juniper-berry.

bâiller v.i. to gape open, to "yawn" (esp. of bivalve molluscs which are not fresh).

bain n.m. bath.

bain-marie pl. **bains-marie** n.m. any combination of two receptacles, one inside the other, the outer one containing hot water, and the whole designed to keep liquids hot but not boiling.

baisure n.f. kissing-crust (of loaf, where it has touched another loaf during baking).

bajoue n.f. chaps, cheeks, chops.

balance n.f. balance, scales.

balane n.f. acorn-shell.

baleine n.f. whale.

ballottine n.f. joint of boned, stuffed, rolled and tied butcher's meat; boned and stuffed whole poultry.

bambou n.m. bamboo.

pousse de bambou n.f. bamboo-shoot.

banane n.f. banana.

bande n.f. band, strip.

banquet n.m. banquet.

baquet n.m. small wooden tub.

bar n.m. sea-perch.

bar commun sea-dace, sea-wolf.

bar noir black bass.

bar rayé striped bass.

barbadine n.f. passion-flower fruit.

barbe n.f. barbel (of fish); gills (of oyster); mildew.

barbeau, -eaux n.m. barbel (fish, as distinct from *barbe*, q.v.).

barbe-de-bouc pl. **barbes-de-bouc** n.f. (variety of) wild salsify.

barbe-de-capucin pl. **barbes-de-capucin** n.f. wild chicory.

barbe-de-chèvre pl. **barbes-de-chèvre** n.f. clavaria, club-top mushroom.

barbillon n.m. barb, barbel (of fish); barbel (fish); wattle (e.g. of cockerel).

barbotine n.f. tansy.

barbue n.f. brill.

bardane n.f. burdock.

barde n.f. strip of uncured fat bacon (for larding).

bardé adj. larded, covered with strips of uncured fat bacon.

barder v.tr. to lard, to cover with strips of uncured fat bacon.

barder de lard to lard, to cover with strips of bacon.

barge n.f. godwit.

baricaut n.m. keg, small barrel, small cask.

baril n.m. barrel, cask.

barillet n.m. keg, small barrel, small cask.

baron n.m. baron, the saddle and the two legs (of beef, lamb).

barquette n.f. boat-shaped pastry-case.

barre n.f. bar, rod.

barriquaut n.m. keg, small barrel, small cask.

barrique n.f. large barrel, containing over two hundred litres and roughly equivalent to a hogshead.

barrot n.m. small barrel containing salted anchovies.

bartavelle n.f. Greek partridge, variety of red partridge.

bas, basse adj. low; low(er), lesser, inferior.

basse venaison n.f. small(er) venison (esp. hares and rabbits).

base n.f. base; basis.

baselle n.f. basella.

basilic n.m. basil.

basse-côte n.f. uncovered cutlet.

basse-cour n.f. farmyard.

bassin n.m. basin, bowl.

bassine n.f. pan.

bassine à confiture(s) preserving-pan.

bat n.m. tail (of fish); length of fish from eye to tail.

bâton n.m. stick, stick-shape.

bâtonnet n.m. small stick, small stick-shape.

batracien n.m. batrachian (esp. frog).

batte n.f. bat.

batte à boucherie cutlet-bat.

batterie n.f. collection, complete set.

batterie de cuisine complete set of kitchen utensils.

battoir n.m. beater.

battoir en bois wooden beater.

battre v.tr. to beat, to whip, to whisk.
  battre à pointe to beat to a point.
  battre en neige to beat stiffly to a fluffy consistency.
battu adj. beaten, whipped, whisked.
baudroie n.f. angler.
bavarois n.m. Bavarian cream. adj. Bavarian.
bavaroise n.f. type of mild punch, usually to a tea or coffee base, and containing egg-yolks, sugar and a liqueur.
bavette n.f. bib.
  bavette d'aloyau skirt of beef.
beau, bel (before masc. nouns beginning with a vowel or an unaspirated h), f. **belle**, pl. **beaux**, f. **belles** adj. beautiful, handsome, fine.
beaucoup n.m.inv. much, a lot. adv. much.
  beaucoup de a lot of.
  beaucoup de patience a lot of patience.
bécasse n.f. woodcock.
  bécasse de mer oyster-catcher.
bécasseau, -eaux n.m. sandpiper; young of the woodcock.
bécassin n.m. jack-snipe.
bécassine n.f. snipe.
bécau, -aux n.m. young snipe.
béchamel n.f. Béchamel sauce.
  béchamel serrée thick Béchamel sauce.
beignet n.m. fritter.
  beignet de maïs corn fritter.
bélier n.m. ram.
Bénédictine n.f. Benedictine liqueur.
bénéfice n.m. profit.
benoîte n.f. herb-bennet.
berceau, -eaux n.m. cradle, cradle-shape.
bergamot(t)e n.f. bergamot (citrus fruit); bergamot (pear).
bernache n.f. barnacle; bernacle (goose), barnacle (goose).
bernacle n.f. barnacle; bernacle (goose), barnacle (goose).
besoin n.m. need.
  au besoin adv. phr. if need be, in case of need.
  avoir besoin de to need, to have need of.
bette n.f. beet, chard.
betterave n.f. beetroot.
beurre n.m. butter.

beurre acidulé softened butter flavoured with lemon-juice.
beurre clarifié clarified butter.
beurre composé compound butter.
beurre d'anchois anchovy butter.
beurre de basilic basil butter.
beurre d'écrevisse(s) crayfish butter.
beurre d'escargot(s) snail butter.
beurre d'estragon tarragon butter.
beurre de laiterie dairy butter.
beurre de persil parsley butter.
beurre de pistaches pistachio butter.
beurre en pommade softened butter.
beurre fondu melted butter.
beurre manié butter and flour thickening.
beurre moutardé mustard butter.
beurre noir black butter.
beurre noisette nut-brown butter.
beurré adj. buttered.
beurrer v.tr. to butter.
bicarbonate de soude n.m. sodium bicarbonate, bicarbonate of soda.
biche n.f. doe, hind.
bident n.m. carving-fork.
bien adv. well; very.
  bien cuit well cooked, well done.
  ou bien or else.
bientôt adv. soon.
bière n.f. beer, ale.
  bière blonde light beer, pale ale.
  bière blonde allemande lager.
  bière brune brown ale.
  bière noire dark beer, dark ale.
  bière noire forte stout.
  bière panachée shandy.
bifteck n.m. beefsteak.
bigarade n.f. Seville orange, bitter orange.
bigarreau, -eaux n.m. white-heart cherry.
  bigarreau confit pickled cherry.
bigorneau, -eaux n.m. periwinkle, winkle.
biscotte n.f. rusk.
biscuit n.m. biscuit.
  biscuit à cuiller finger-biscuit.
  biscuit à l'eau water-biscuit.
  biscuit de mer ship's biscuit.

bisque n.f. thick shell-fish soup.
bistorte n.f. adderwort, bistort, Easter-ledges, snake-root, snake(-)weed.
bitok, bitoque n.m. meat-cake, usually of beef, veal or chicken.
blanc, blanche adj. white.
  blanc n.m. white; blank, space.
  à blanc cooked, prepared, from the raw state.
  blanc de poireau white of leek.
  blanc de poulet white flesh of breast of chicken.
  blanc d'œuf egg-white, white of egg.
  blanc rosé pinkish white.
  un blanc d'œuf the white of an egg.
blanchaille n.f. whitebait.
blanchâtre adj. whitish.
blanchi adj. blanched.
blanchir v.tr. to blanch.
blanc-manger n.m. blancmange.
blanquette n.f. white veal stew, distinct from *fricassée*, q.v.
blé n.m. corn.
  blé froment wheat.
  blé noir buckwheat.
blet, blette adj. sleepy (e.g. pears).
blette n.f. chard.
bleu adj. & n.m. blue.
  au bleu (steak) sealed but hardly cooked, almost raw.
  au bleu (trout) cooked by a process including first sealing the fish in acid liquid, usually vinegar, to give it a blue colour.
bleuâtre adj. bluish.
blinis n.m.pl. buckwheat pancakes.
bloc n.m. block, lump.
  bloc de glace block of ice.
blond adj. fawn (stock); pale, light (beer).
blondi adj. lightly coloured; turned golden brown.
blondir v.tr. & i. to colour lightly; to turn golden brown.
bocal, -aux n.m. (preserving) jar or bottle (for fruit, pickles).
  mettre en bocal v.tr. to bottle (fruit).
bœuf n.m. ox; beef.
boire v.tr. & i. to drink.
bois n.m. wood.
boisson n.f. drink, beverage.
boîte n.f. box; tin, can.
  boîte à charbon coal-box.

boîte à ficelle string-box.
boîte à sel salt-box.
boîte de conserve(s) tin of conserves.
boîte en fer blanc tin, tin can.
bol n.m. bowl.
bolet n.m. boletus mushroom.
bombe n.f. ice pudding.
  bombe glacée ice pudding.
bombé adj. convex; bulging.
bomber v.i. to bulge.
  v.tr. to cause to bulge.
bon, bonne adj. good.
  bon à manger fit to eat.
  bon n.m. voucher, check, chit.
  bon de commande order check.
bonbon n.m. sweet(meat).
bonde n.f. bung, bung-hole; plug, plug-hole.
bonite n.f. bonito.
bonne-bouche n.f. titbit, savoury.
bonnet n.m. second stomach (of ruminant).
bord n.m. edge; border, hem; brim, rim.
bordé adj. bordered, edged.
  bordé de bordered with, edged with.
border v.tr. to border, to edge.
  border de to border with, to edge with.
bordure n.f. edging, border; surround.
botte n.f. bunch, bundle.
bottelé adj. tied up into bunches.
botteler v.tr. to tie up into bunches.
bottillon n.m. small bunch, small bundle.
boucage n.m. pimpinella.
bouche n.f. mouth.
bouché adj. corked, stoppered, stopped; blocked, choked.
bouchée n.f. mouthful; small patty, esp. of puff pastry.
  bouchée mignonne very small *bouchée*, q.v.
boucher v.tr. to cork, to stopper, to stop; to block, to choke.
  n.m. butcher.
boucherie n.f. butchery (department); butchery (work).
boudin n.m. white sausage.
  boudin noir black pudding.
boudinière n.f. sausage-funnel.
boudreuil n.m. angler.
bouillabaisse n.f. (variety of) Mediterranean fish-stew.

bouilleture n.f. *matelote* (q.v.) of eels in red wine, containing, among other ingredients, prunes.

bouilli adj. boiled.
n.m. boiled beef left over from the making of *bouillon*, q.v.
à bouilli perdu adv. phr. see *bouillir à bouilli perdu*.

bouillie n.f. gruel.

bouillir v.tr. & i. to boil.
bouillir à bouilli perdu v.tr. & i. to boil away.
bouillir à gros bouillons to boil vigorously (lit. with large bubbles).
bouillir à petits bouillons to boil gently (lit. with small bubbles).

bouillon n.m. bubble (in liquid); boiling; broth.
donner un bouillon to give a boiling.
donner quelques bouillons to give a few boilings.

boulanger n.m. baker.

boulangerie n.f. bakery (department); bakery (work).

boule n.f. ball, ball-shape.
boule de chou-fleur cauliflower-top.
boule de neige snowball, food preparation resembling a snowball in appearance.

boulet n.m. ball, stage in boiling of sugar.
au grand boulet (cooked) to a large-ball stage.

boulette n.f. small ball, small ball-shape; forcemeat ball.

bouquet n.m. sprig, bunch.
bouquet garni bunch of herbs, usually of parsley, thyme and bay-leaf.

bourcette n.f. corn-salad, lamb's lettuce.

bourgeon n.m. bud.

bourrache n.f. borage.

bourse n.f. purse, purse-shape.

se boursoufler v.refl. to bulge, to swell.

bout n.m. end (in space), extremity; short length (e.g. of string).
bout de ficelle piece, short length, of string.

bouteille n.f. bottle.

bouton n.m. button.
boutons de Bruxelles small Brussels sprouts.

boyau, -aux n.m. gut; sausage-casing.
petit boyau small intestine.

braisage n.m. (the operation of) braising.
braisage à blanc white braising.
braisage à brun brown braising.
fonds de braisage n.m. braising-stock.

braise n.f. braising-fire.
à la braise adv. phr. (cooked) over a braising-fire.

braisé adj. braised.

braiser v.tr. to braise.

braisière n.f. braising-pan.

branche n.f. branch.

branchette n.f. small branch.

branchie n.f. gill (of fish).

branchillon n.m. very small branch, twig.

brandade n.f. Provençal preparation of salt cod, pounded with oil, garlic and cream.

brassage n.m. (operation of) brewing, mashing; (operation of) mixing, stirring.

brassé adj. brewed, mashed; mixed, stirred.

brasser v.tr. to brew, to mash; to mix, to stir.

brebis n.f. ewe.

bréchet n.m. breast-bone (esp. of chicken).

brème n.f. bream.
brème de mer sea-tench.

breuvage n.m. beverage, drink.

bridage n.m. (the operation of) trussing.

bridé adj. trussed.

brider v.tr. to truss.
brider en entrée to truss (chicken) with the legs entered.

brie n.m. Brie cheese.

brigade n.f. brigade, entire personnel (of kitchen, restaurant).
brigade de cuisine kitchen brigade, entire kitchen staff.

brignole n.f. dried plum from Brignoles (Var.).

brillant adj. brilliant.
n.m. gloss, lustre.

briller v.i. to glisten, to shine.

brin n.m. sprig.
brin de sauge sprig of sage.
brin de thym sprig of thyme.

brindille n.f. small sprig.

brioche n.f. brioche.
brioche à tête (true) brioche, shaped like a cottage loaf.

en brioche (shaped) like a cottage loaf.
brionne n.f. chow-chow.
broche n.f. spit.
à la broche (cooked) on the spit.
brochet n.m. pike.
brocheton n.m. small pike, young pike.
brochette n.f. skewer.
brochette à anneau metal skewer with a ring handle.
brochette en bois wooden skewer.
brochette en fer metal skewer.
brosse n.f. brush.
brossé adj. brushed.
brosser v.tr. to brush.
brou n.m. husk (of nut).
brouillé adj. scrambled.
brouiller v.tr. to scramble.
broyé adj. crushed, pounded.
broyer v.tr. to crush, to pound.
brugnon n.m. nectarine.
brûlant adj. burning, on fire.
brûlé adj. burned.
brûler v.tr. & i. to burn.
brun adj. & n.m. brown.
à brun (braising) brown.
brun clair light brown.
brun foncé dark brown.
brunâtre adj. brownish.
brunoise n.f. very fine dice of vegetables.
grosse brunoise coarse *brunoise*, q.v.
bucarde n.f. cockle.
buée n.f. steam, vapour.
buffet n.m. sideboard; buffet.
buffet froid cold buffet.
buglosse n.f. bugloss.
buisson n.m. bush; bush-like arrangement, esp. of small fish.
bureau, -eaux n.m. office.
butyreux, -euse adj. buttery.

C

cabillaud n.m. fresh cod.
cabri n.m. kid, young goat.
cacahouette, cacahuète n.f. peanut, ground-nut.
cacao n.m. cocoa.
cachet n.m. stamp, mark, trade-mark (of manufacture, manufacturer); cachet, hall-mark, stamp, &c. (of regional, special or specialist preparation).

cachir adj. inv. Kosher.
café n.m. coffee; café.
caféine n.f. caffeine.
caille n.f. quail.
caille d'Amérique American partridge.
caillé n.m. curd(s).
adj. clotted, curdled.
caille-lait n.m. rennet.
cailler v.tr. & i. to clot, to curdle.
caillette n.f. fourth stomach (of ruminant).
caillot n.m. clot (e.g. in curdled milk).
caillou, -oux n.m. pebble.
caisse n.f. packing-case; box, chest.
caissette n.f. paper case (e.g. for soufflés); fireproof porcelain dish in which food is both prepared and served.
calendrier n.m. calendar.
calendrier gastronomique gastronomic calendar.
calice n.m. calyx.
calice de fleur de coing calyx of quince-blossom.
calmar n.m. calamary, (type of) squid.
calorie n.f. calorie.
grande calorie large calorie, food calorie, unit of heat required to raise the temperature of one kilogram of water by one centigrade degree.
petite calorie small calorie, unit of heat required to raise the temperature of one gram of water by one centigrade degree.
calorique n.m. heat.
calorique latent latent heat.
calotte n.f. cap, cover; sector, segment (esp. of orange-peel).
calvados n.m. apple-brandy, cider-brandy.
calville n.f. queening, queening apple.
camomille n.f. camomile.
campanule n.f. campanula.
campanule doucette Venus's looking-glass.
campêche n.m. logwood.
canapé n.m. hors d'œuvre or savoury preparation dressed on a slice of toasted bread.
canard n.m. duck; drake.
canard de Barbarie Barbary duck.

canard nantais   duck reared at Nantes (Loire-Atlantique) and weighing about 3–4 lb.; any duck of about this size.

canard rouennais   duck reared at Rouen (Seine-Maritime) and weighing about 5–6 lb.; any duck of about this size.

canard sauvage   (strictly) mallard; wild duck.

canard siffleur   widgeon.

canardeau, -eaux   n.m.   duckling.

cancale   n.f.   oyster from Cancale (Ille-et-Vilaine).

candi   adj.   candied, crystallized.

fruits candis   n.m.pl.   crystallized fruit.

sucre candi   n.m.   sugar candy.

candir   v.tr.   to candy, to crystallize.

cane   n.f.   (female) duck.

canepetière   n.f.   field-duck, little bustard.

caneton   n.m.   duckling; (usual description of) duck (other than wild duck) on restaurant menu.

cannelé   adj.   channelled, fluted, grooved.

canneler   v.tr.   to channel, to flute, to groove.

cannelle   n.f.   cinnamon.

cannelle de Ceylan   Ceylon cinnamon.

cannelle de Chine   China cinnamon, cassia.

cannellone, pl. **cannelloni**   n.m. pasta preparation stuffed with a savoury mince and rolled into cigar-shapes.

cannelure   n.f.   fluting, groove, grooving.

à larges cannelures   (cut, shaped) with wide grooves.

cantaloup   n.m.   cantaloup melon.

canthère   n.m.   sea-bream.

capelan   n.m.   capelin, caplin.

capilotade   n.f.   ragoût, stew.

câpre   n.f.   caper.

câpre capucine   nasturtium seed.

capucine   n.f.   nasturtium.

salade de capucines   n.f.   nasturtium salad.

caque   n.f.   barrel for the pressing of salt herring or smoked herring.

car   conj.   for, because.

carafe   n.f.   decanter; water-jug.

caramel   n.m.   caramel, burnt sugar.

caramélisé   adj.   caramelized.

caraméliser   v.tr.   to caramelize (sugar).

carapace   n.f.   carapace, hard shell (of crab, turtle).

carbonate de soude   n.m.   sodium carbonate, carbonate of soda, washing soda.

carbonnade   n.f.   meat stewed in beer.

carcasse   n.f.   carcass, carcase.

carde   n.f.   chard.

cardon   n.m.   cardoon.

carême   n.m.   Lent; (the) Lenten fast; Lenten fasting. (N.B. This word is not to be confused with the name of the famous French chef Antonin Carême (1784–1833)).

carmin   n.m.   carmine.

carotte   n.f.   carrot.

carpe   n.f.   carp.

carpe (à) miroir(s)   mirror carp.

carpe cuir   leather carp.

carpeau, -eaux   n.m.   young carp.

carpillon   n.m.   very small carp.

carpion   n.m.   (variety of) Alpine river-trout.

carré   adj.   square.

n.m.   square, square-shape; best end.

carré d'agneau   best end of lamb.

carrelet   n.m.   dab; plaice.

carte   n.f.   card; menu, bill of fare.

cartilage   n.m.   cartilage, gristle.

cartilagineux, -euse   adj.   cartilaginous.

cartouche   n.f.   round piece of grease-proof paper.

carvi   n.m.   caraway.

graines de carvi   n.f.pl.   caraway seeds.

caséine   n.f.   casein.

cassant   adj.   brittle; fragile; crisp.

cassave   n.f.   cassava, manioc.

casse   n.f.   breakage, damage; breakages.

cassé   adj.   broken, cracked.

casse-noisette(s)   n.m.inv. in pl. (pair of) nut-crackers.

casse-pierre(s)   n.m.inv. in pl. samphire; saxifrage.

casser   v.tr.   to break; to crack.

casser un œuf   to break an egg.

casserole   n.f.   saucepan; stew, of butcher's meat or poultry, made in a container with a tight-fitting lid.

casserole pour bain-marie   tall saucepan suitable for standing in the *bain-marie*, q.v.

casserole russe (any) saucepan of vertical side, of height at least equal to its diameter, and usually having a single, long handle.

cassis n.m. blackcurrant; blackcurrant cordial; blackcurrant liqueur.

cassolette n.f. small paper case; small fireproof dish.

cassonade n.f. brown sugar.

    cassonade en gros cristaux Demerara sugar.

cassoulet n.m. type of stew, of haricot beans and fillets of meat (esp. goose), made in Languedoc.

catillac n.m. warden, large cooking-pear.

catillard n.m. see *catillac*.

caviar n.m. caviar(e).

    caviar gris grey caviar.

cavité n.f. cavity, hollow.

cayenne n.m. Cayenne pepper.

cayenné adj. condimented, seasoned, with cayenne pepper.

cayenner v.tr. to condiment, to season, with cayenne pepper.

cédrat n.m. citron.

célèbre adj. famous.

céleri n.m. celery.

    céleri cordé stringy celery.

    morceau de céleri n.m. stick of celery.

céleri-rave n.m. celeriac.

celui-ci dem. pron. this, this one; the latter.

celui-là dem. pron. that, that one; the former.

cendre n.f. ash, cinders.

    cendre de bois wood-ash.

    cendre de bois chaude hot wood-ash.

    sous la cendre (cooked) in wood-ash.

centaurée n.f. centaury.

    grand centaurée great(er) centaury.

    petite centaurée erythraea, lesser centaury.

centilitre n.m. centilitre, one hundredth of a *litre*, q.v.

centimètre n.m. centimetre, one hundredth of a *mètre*, q.v.

    centimètre cube cubic centimetre.

central pl. **centraux** adj. central.

centre n.m. centre.

cep n.m. vine-plant, vine-stock.

cèpe n.m. flap mushroom.

céphalopode n.m. cephalopod.

cercle n.m. circle; ring.

    cercle à flan flan-ring.

cerclé adj. circled, encircled.

    cerclé de circled with, encircled by.

cercler v.tr. to circle, to encircle.

    cercler de to circle with, to encircle with.

cercueil n.m. coffin.

    en cercueil (esp. small game bird) cooked in a paste "coffin".

céréale adj.f. & n.f. cereal.

cerf n.m. stag.

cerfeuil n.m. chervil.

    cerfeuil bulbeux bulbous chervil, tuberous chervil.

cerise n.f. cherry.

    cerise d'hiver winter cherry.

    cerise d'ours bearberry.

cerisier n.m. cherry-tree.

    feuille de cerisier n.f. cherry-tree leaf (e.g. for *saumure*, q.v.).

cerné adj. cut round.

cerneau, -eaux n.m. green walnut.

    cerneau confit au vinaigre pickled walnut.

cerner v.tr. to cut round.

cernure n.f. circular scoring (-mark).

cervelas n.m. saveloy.

cervelle n.f. brain(s).

    cervelle(s) de veau calves' brains.

cesser v.tr. & i. to cease, to stop.

    cesser de faire quelque chose to stop doing something.

chaîne n.f. chain.

chair n.f. flesh.

    chair à saucisse sausage-meat.

    chair crue raw flesh; raw meat.

    chair cuite cooked flesh; cooked meat.

    chair de boucherie butcher's meat.

chaleur n.f. heat.

    chaleur douce gentle heat.

champagne n.m. champagne.

    champagne mousseux sparkling champagne.

    champagne non mousseux still champagne.

    fine champagne n.f. liqueur brandy (from the Champagne de Saintonges).

champignon n.m. mushroom; mushroom, puree-presser.

    champignon de couche cultivated mushroom.

champignon de prairie   field mushroom.

chanteau, -eaux   n.m.   hunk (of bread).

   chanteau de pain   hunk of bread.

chanterelle   n.f.   cantharellus mushroom.

chapeau, -eaux   n.m.   hat; pie-crust.

   chapeau de champignon   mushroom head.

chapelure   n.f.   breadcrumbs (for frying, etc.).

chapeluré   adj.   crumbed (before cooking).

chapelurer   v.tr.   to crumb (before cooking).

chapon   n.m.   capon.

chaque   adj.   each.

charcuterie   n.f.   pork-butchery; pork-butcher's meat; pork-butcher's department or shop.

charcutier   n.m.   pork-butcher.

charnu   adj.   fleshy.

chartreuse, Chartreuse   n.f.   Chartreuse liqueur.

   en chartreuse   (bird, e.g. partridge) stewed with quartered or shredded cabbage.

châteaubriand   n.m.   double fillet steak cut from the head of the fillet.

châtré   adj.   castrated, gelded; gutted (e.g. crayfish).

châtrer   v.tr.   to castrate, to geld; to gut (e.g. crayfish).

chaud   adj.   hot.

   tenir au chaud   v.tr.   to keep hot.

chaud-froid   n.m.   (esp.) poultry coated with a *sauce chaud-froid* (q.v.) and set in aspic.

chaudron   n.m.   cauldron.

chauffage   n.m.   heating.

   chauffage central   central heating.

chauffant   adj.   heating, warming.

chauffé   adj.   heated, warmed.

chauffer   v.tr.   to heat, to warm.

chaufroité   adj.   coated with a *sauce chaud-froid*, q.v.

chaufroiter   v.tr.   to coat with a *sauce chaud-froid*, q.v.

chausson   n.m.   turnover.

chef   n.m.   chief, head.

   chef communard   m.   cook in charge of the preparation of staff meals.

   chef de cuisine   head cook (of a large kitchen).

chef de garde   relief *sous-chef*, q.v.

chef de nuit   head night-cook.

chef entremettier   head vegetable-cook.

chef froitier   head cook specializing in cold savoury dishes.

chef garde-manger   head larder cook.

chef grillardin   head grill-cook.

chef hors d'œuvrier   cook in charge of the preparation of hors d'œuvres.

chef de partie   section leader, head of a "corner" in the kitchen.

chef pâtissier   head pastry-cook.

chef poissonnier   head fish-cook.

chef potager   head soup-cook.

chef rôtisseur   head roast-cook.

chef saucier   head sauce-cook.

chef tournant   relief *chef de partie*, q.v.

chélonée   n.f.   chelone.

   chélonée franche   green turtle.

cheminée   n.f.   chimney; "chimney", esp. in the centre of a pastry-crust.

chemise   n.f.   shirt; thin inner coating of jelly in mould; coating of aspic.

chemisé   adj.   (mould) coated with thin inner coating of jelly; coated with aspic.

chemiser   v.tr.   to coat (mould) with thin inner coating of jelly; to coat with aspic.

cher, chère   adj.   dear, expensive.

chercher   v.tr.   to look for, to seek.

chester   n.m.   Cheshire cheese; Chester cheese.

chevaine   n.m.   chub.

cheval, -aux   n.m.   horse.

   à cheval   adj. or adv. phr.   (esp. savouries) "on horseback".

chevalé   adj.   arranged in an overlapping pattern.

chevaler   v.tr.   to arrange in an overlapping pattern.

chevalier   n.m.   name given to some varieties of wading birds, including the sandpiper.

chevesne   n.m.   chub.

chèvre   n.f.   (general name for) goat; she-goat, nanny-goat.

chevreau, -eaux   n.m.   kid, young goat.

chevreuil   n.m.   roebuck.

chevrier   n.m.   green kidney bean.

chicorée   n.f.   endive.

chien de mer   n.m.   dogfish.

chiffon n.m. rag, shred.
chiffonnade n.f. long thin shreds.
  chiffonnade d'oseille shredded sorrel.
chiffonné adj. shredded (lettuce, sorrel).
chiffonner v.tr. to shred (lettuce, sorrel).
chinois n.m. conical strainer.
  chinois fin fine conical strainer.
chipiron n.m. (variety of) small Mediterranean octopus.
chipolata n.f. small sausage; (variety of) onion stew.
chiqueté adj. checkered, having a chessboard pattern.
chiqueter v.tr. to checker, to mark with a chessboard pattern.
chlorophylle n.f. chlorophyll.
chocolat n.m. chocolate.
choisir v.tr. to choose.
choix n.m. choice.
  de choix adj. phr. choice, of best quality.
chorizo n.m. Spanish pork-sausage containing pimentoes.
chou, -oux n.m. cabbage.
  chou de Bruxelles Brussels sprout.
  choux de Bruxelles Brussels sprouts.
  chou de mer sea-kale.
  chou de Milan Savoy cabbage.
  chou de Savoie Savoy cabbage.
  chou frisé borecole, (curly) kale.
  chou marin sea-kale.
  chou palmiste palm-cabbage.
  chou pommé whiteheart cabbage.
  chou rouge red cabbage.
choucroute n.f. pickled white cabbage; sauerkraut.
chou-fleur pl. choux-fleurs, n.m. cauliflower.
chou-navet, pl. **choux-navets** n.m. swede, Swedish turnip.
chou-rave, pl. **choux-raves** n.m. kohl-rabi, turnip cabbage.
chrysanthème n.m. chrysanthemum.
ciboule n.f. spring onion; Welsh onion.
ciboulette n.f. chive.
cidre n.m. cider.
cigale de mer n.f. squill-fish.
ciguë n.f. conium, hemlock.
cimier n.m. haunch (of venison), (rarely) rump (of beef).

cinquième adj. fifth.
  n.m. fifth part.
ciseaux n.m.pl. scissors.
ciselé adj. incised; coarsely shredded.
ciseler v.tr. to incise; to shred coarsely.
citron n.m. lemon.
citronnat n.m. candied lemon-peel.
citronné adj. flavoured with lemon.
citronnelle n.f. citronella; lemon-balm, melissa.
citronner v.tr. to flavour with lemon.
citrouille n.f. pumpkin.
cive n.f. chive.
civet n.m.
  civet de lièvre jugged hare.
civette n.f. chive.
claie n.f. hurdle.
  claie en osier wicker hurdle.
clair adj. clear; light (in colour).
clarification n.f. clarification.
clarifié adj. clarified.
clarifier v.tr. to clarify.
classique adj. classical.
clavaire n.f. clavaria, club-top mushroom.
clayette n.f. grape-sorting hurdle.
clayon n.m. wicker draining-tray; pastry drying-rack.
cloche n.f. bell-shaped fire-proof glass cover placed over a fire-proof glass cooking-dish.
clou n.m. nail; clove.
  clou de girofle clove.
clouté adj. studded (esp. with cloves).
clouter v.tr. to stud (esp. with cloves).
clovisse n.f. cockle.
clupe n.f. any fish of the family which includes herrings, sardines and anchovies.
cochenille n.f. cochineal.
cochon n.m. pig.
  cochon de lait sucking-pig.
cochonnet n.m. young pig, piglet.
coco n.m. coco-nut.
cocotte n.f. fire-proof earthenware dish for cooking and service.
  cocotte à oreilles eared *cocotte* q.v.
  cocotte ovale oval *cocotte*, q.v.
cœur n.m. heart; (stylized) heart-shape.

cœur de chou cabbage-heart.

cœur de laitue lettuce-heart.

cœur de romaine cos lettuce-heart.

en cœur (shaped) like a stylized heart.

coffre n.m. trunk (of body of lobster).

coiffe n.f. caul.

coiffe de veau caul of veal.

coin n.m. corner.

un coin de torchon the corner of a cloth (e.g. for squeezing out).

coing n.m. quince.

fleur de coing n.f. quince-blossom.

colin n.m. hake; American partridge.

colle n.f. glue, paste.

colle de poisson isinglass.

collé adj. pasted, stuck.

coller v.tr. to paste, to stick.

collerette n.f. annulus, annulus-shape.

collet n.m. neck, scrag.

collet de veau neck of veal, scrag of veal.

colonne n.f. column, column-shape, pillar, pillar-shape.

colorant adj. colouring.

n.m. colouring agent.

coloré adj. coloured.

colorer v.tr. to colour.

se colorer v.refl. to colour, to take colour.

combien adv. how many, how much.

combien? how many? how much?

combien de carottes? how many carrots?

combien de farine? how much flour?

commande n.f. order (from customer to waiter).

commander v.tr. to order (food, drink).

comment adv. how.

comment? how?

commerce n.m. trade; (a) business.

commis n.m. assistant; clerk.

commis de cuisine cook, commis.

premier commis first commis, in rank immediately below a *chef de partie*, q.v.

compacte adj. compact.

complément n.m. complement.

complémentaire adj. complementary.

compléter v.tr. to complete.

compote n.f. compote of fruit, stewed fruit.

compotier n.m. compote-dish; fruit-dish.

comprendre v.tr. to understand; to comprise; to include.

comprimé adj. compressed.

comprimer v.tr. to compress.

compris adj. understood; included.

compter v.tr. to count.

concassé adj. coarsely broken up with a knife or in a mortar.

concasser v.tr. to break up coarsely with a knife or in a mortar.

concentré adj. concentrated.

concentrer v.tr. to concentrate.

concombre n.m. cucumber.

concombre brodé ridged cucumber.

condiment n.m. condiment.

condimentation n.f. (the action of) condimenting, seasoning.

condimenté adj. condimented, seasoned.

condimenter v.tr. to condiment, to season.

cône n.m. cone, cone-shape.

cône tronqué truncated cone.

confiserie n.f. confectionery.

confiseur, -euse n. confectioner.

confit adj. preserved.

n.m. conserve.

confit d'oie savoury conserve of fillets of goose.

confiture n.f. jam.

confiturier n.m. jam-dish; jam-pot.

congélation n.f. (action of) congelation, freezing.

congelé adj. congealed, frozen.

congeler v.tr. to congeal, to freeze.

congre n.m. conger eel.

connaissance n.f. knowledge, acquaintance.

connaisseur n.m. connoisseur, expert.

connaître v.tr. to know, to be acquainted with.

conserve n.f. preserved food.

conserves preserves.

de conserve adj. phr. preserved, esp. in tin(s).

tomates de conserve tinned tomatoes, canned tomatoes.

consistance n.f. consistency.

à consistance de with the consistency of, having the consistency of.

à consistance de potage of soupy consistency, having the consistency of soup.

consistance moelleuse soft consistency.

consistance sirupeuse syrupy consistency.

consistance voulue desired, required, consistency.

consommé n.m. clarified soup.

consommé blanc white unclarified *consommé*, q.v.

consommé de bœuf clarified beef soup.

consommé de volaille clarified chicken soup.

consommé double clarified soup of double strength.

consommé ordinaire clarified beef soup.

consommé tomaté tomato-flavoured clarified soup.

consommer v.tr. to consume; to use up.

se consommer v.refl. to boil down.

constituer v.tr. to constitute.

contenant n.m. container, receptacle.

contenir v.tr. to contain, to hold.

contenu adj. contained.
n.m. content, contents.

contisé adj. (fillets of fish, etc.) decorated, encrusted, with small pieces of truffle stuck on with egg-white.

contiser v.tr. to decorate, to encrust (fillets of fish, etc.), with small pieces of truffle stuck on with egg-white.

contraste n.m. contrast.

contre prep. against.

contrefilet n.m. boned sirloin of beef.

contrôle n.m. control, direction; control, checking.

contrôle de service duty-roster.

convenable adj. appropriate, suitable.

convenablement adv. appropriately, suitably.

copeau, -eaux n.m. shaving (esp. of cheese).

copeaux de gruyère shavings of Gruyère cheese.

copie n.f. copy (from original, not copy of book, &c.).

copié adj. copied.

copier v.tr. to copy.

coprin n.m. edible mushroom with black spores.

coq n.m. cockerel.

coq au vin young cockerel cooked in wine.

coq de Bantam bantam-cock.

coq de bruyère black game.

coq des bouleaux blackcock.

coq des marais hazel-grouse, hazel-hen.

petit coq de bruyère blackcock.

coque n.f. (familiar name for) cockle; shell (of egg); husk (of fruit, nut).

coque de melon melon-husk.

coquelicot n.m. corn poppy, red poppy.

coquemar n.m. kettle (usually of copper).

coquerelle n.f. winter cherry.

coqueret n.m. winter cherry.

coqueret du Pérou Cape gooseberry.

coquetier n.m. egg-cup.

coquetière n.f. egg-boiler.

coquillage n.m. shell-fish; empty shell; preparation cooked and served in a scollop-shell.

coquille n.f. shell (of oyster, snail, etc.).

coquille creuse deep shell (of oyster).

coquille d'argent (simulation of) scollop shell (in silver or silver plate).

coquille de meringue meringue shell.

coquille (de) Saint-Jacques scollop; scollop-shell.

coquillettes n.f.pl. farinaceous paste shaped like shells.

corail, -aux n.m. coral (of lobster).

corbeille n.f. (open) basket.

corde n.f. rope.

cordé adj. stringy (celery).

céleri cordé stringy celery.

cordial, -aux n.m. cordial.

cordon n.m. thin line of sauce or thickened gravy surrounding a finished preparation.

cordon-bleu, pl. **cordons-bleus** n.m. highly-skilled woman cook.

cordonné adj. surrounded with a *cordon*, q.v.

cordonner v.tr. to surround with a *cordon*, q.v.

coriace adj. (meat) hard, leathery.

coriandre n.m. coriander.

corne n.f. horn, horn-shape.

  corne de pâtissier horn scraper.

cornet n.m. cornet, cornet-shape; slice of ham rolled into a cornet shape.

  cornet de ris de veau stinted end of *ris de veau*, q.v.

cornichon n.m. gherkin.

cornouille n.f. dogberry.

corossol n.m. custard-apple.

  corossol écailleux sweet-sop.

  corossol hérissé sour-sop.

corriger v.tr. to correct, to rectify.

  se corrompre v.refl. to deteriorate, to spoil; to taint.

corsé adj. thickened, tightened (sauce).

corser v.tr. to thicken, to tighten (sauce).

  se corser v.refl. to thicken, to tighten (sauce).

cosse n.f. pod, shuck (of beans, peas).

  cosses de haricots bean-pods, bean-shucks.

  cosses de pois pea-pods, pea-shucks.

côte n.f. rib.

  basse côte uncovered cutlet.

  côte découverte uncovered cutlet.

  côte première loin chop.

  plate côte flat rib.

côté n.m. side.

  à côté de beside, next to.

  côté bombé convex side (esp. of flat fish).

  côté creux concave side.

  côté droit white side, underside (of flat fish).

  côté gauche dark side, topside (of flat fish, i.e. side on which both eyes are found).

  côté peau noire "black skin" side, dark side, topside (of flat fish).

  sur le côté du feu on the side of the flame (as in simmering).

côtelette n.f. cutlet; chop.

  côtelette d'agneau lamb cutlet.

  côtelette de filet loin chop.

  côtelette de gigot chump chop.

  côtelette de porc pork chop.

  côtelette de veau veal cutlet.

côtelette de volaille chicken cutlet.

côtelettes premières best end of neck.

cotignac n.m. quince jam; quince marmalade.

cotriade n.f. Breton version of *bouillabaisse*, q.v.

cou n.m. neck.

  cou d'agneau neck of lamb.

couche n.f. layer; base, such as a *lit d'épinards*, q.v.

couché adj. laid, spread; piped (e.g. through piping-tube).

coucher v.tr. to lay, to spread; to pipe (e.g. through piping-tube).

  coucher à la poche to pipe through a piping-tube.

coucou n.m. cowslip.

coucoumelle n.f. (variety of) edible white agaric.

coudre v.tr. to sew, to sew up.

couenne n.f. pork-rind; bacon-rind; crackling (of roast pork).

  couenne grasse fat rind.

couler v.i. to flow, to run (liquid); to leak (barrel).

couleur n.f. colour.

coulis n.m. fundamental preparation including juices extracted (e.g.) from lobster, herbs, &c.

  coulis d'écrevisse(s) crayfish *coulis*, q.v.

  coulis de homard lobster *coulis*, q.v.

  coulis d'herbes mixed herb *coulis*, q.v.

coup n.m. blow.

  coup de feu firing, exposure to heat.

  coup de main helping hand.

  Donnez-moi un coup de main Give me a hand.

coupe n.f. made-up *entremets* (q.v.) of fruit, cream, ice-cream, &c., served in a crystal glass; cup awarded as a trophy.

coupé adj. cut.

coupe-pâte n.m.inv. in pl. paste-cutter.

couper v.tr. to cut.

  couper en julienne to cut to the shape and size of a *julienne*, q.v.

couperet n.m. chopper, cleaver.

courge n.f. gourd.

courgette n.f. vegetable marrow.

courlieu n.m. curlew.

  courlieu de terre great plover.

courlis n.m. curlew.
  courlis de terre great plover.
couronne n.f. crown; annulus, corona, ring; crown-shape; annulus-, corona-, ring-shape.
  en couronne (arranged, dressed) in the shape of an annulus, corona, ring.
court adj. short (dimension).
  julienne courte short *julienne*, q.v.
court-bouillon n.m. short cooking-liquor.
court-bouillonné adj. moistened with a short cooking-liquor.
court-bouillonner v.tr. to moisten with a short cooking-liquor.
couscous n.m. couscous, couscoussou.
couscoussière n.f. special pot in which *couscous* (q.v.) is prepared.
cousu adj. sewn, sewn up.
couteau, -eaux n.m. knife.
  couteau à canneler channelling-knife, fluting-knife, grooving-knife.
  couteau à conserves tin-opener.
  couteau à décorer les citrons channelling-knife, fluting-knife, grooving-knife.
  couteau à découper carving-knife.
  couteau à désosser boning-knife.
  couteau à dessert dessert-knife.
  couteau à filets de sole sole-knife.
  couteau à huîtres oyster-knife.
  couteau à jambon ham-knife.
  couteau à pain (de mie) bread-knife.
  couteau à poisson fish-knife.
  couteau à zester (les citrons) zesting-knife.
  couteau de boucher butcher's knife.
  couteau de cuisine kitchen-knife.
  couteau (d')économe vegetable-peeler.
  couteau de table table-knife.
  couteau d'office small vegetable-knife.
coutellerie n.f. cutlery.
couvercle n.m. lid, cover.
  couvercle à anse lid with handle in the centre.
  couvercle à queue saucepan-lid with long handle projecting from its edge and fitting over the handle of the saucepan itself.
  couvercle de casserole saucepan-lid.
couvert n.m. fork and spoon, etc.; cover, place at table.
  adj. covered.
  couvert de covered with.
  à couvert (cooked) while covered (with a lid).
couverture n.f. cover, covering.
couvrir v.tr. to cover.
crabe n.m. crab.
crambe n.m. sea-kale.
crambé n.m. sea-kale.
crâne n.m. cranium, skull.
crapaud n.m. toad.
  crapaud de mer angler.
crapaudine n.f.
  à la crapaudine adj. phr. spatch-cocked.
  poulet à la crapaudine spatch-cocked chicken.
craquelin n.m. (variety of) crisp cake.
crémant adj. creaming (e.g. wine).
crème n.f. cream; custard.
  à la crème with cream.
  crème aigre sour cream.
  crème aigrie sour(ed) cream.
  crème anglaise egg-yolk custard.
  crème de menthe peppermint liqueur.
  crème de riz cream of rice.
  crème épaisse thick cream.
  crème fouettée whipped cream.
  crème fraîche fresh cream.
  crème frite made-up *entremets* (q.v.) of egg-yolk custard blended with flour, flavoured with liqueur, coated with bread-crumbs or batter, and deep fried.
  crème glacée ice-cream.
  crème pâtissière pastry cream.
  crème renversée egg-yolk custard *entremets*, q.v.
crémé adj. creamed.
crémer v.tr. to cream.
crémeux, -euse adj. creamy.
crêpe n.f. pancake.
  crêpe flambée flamed pancake.
  crêpe fourrée filled pancake.
  crêpe sans sucre savoury pancake.
crépine n.f. caul.
crépinette n.f. meat-cake wrapped in caul.
cresson n.m. cress.

cresson alénois   garden cress.
cresson de fontaine   watercress.
cresson de jardin   garden cress.
cressonnière   n.f.   watercress bed.
crête   n.f.   crest, crest-shape.
  crête de coq   cockscomb.
cretons   n.m.pl.   rendered lard.
creusé   adj.   hollowed, hollowed out.
creuser   v.tr.   to hollow, to hollow out.
creux, -euse   adj.   hollow.
  assiette creuse   soup-plate.
  côté creux   concave side.
  creux   n.m.   hollow.
crevette   n.f.
  crevette grise   shrimp.
  crevette rose   prawn.
  crevette rouge   prawn.
crible   n.m.   sieve, riddle.
crin   n.m.   horsehair.
  tamis de crin   n.m.   hair sieve.
cristal, -aux   n.m.   crystal; crystal glass.
cristallisé   adj.   crystallized.
cristalliser   v.tr.   to crystallize.
criste-marine, pl. **cristes-marines**   n.f.   rock-samphire.
croc de boucherie   n.m.   butcher's hook.
croissant   n.m.   horse-shoe-shaped roll made of fermented fancy bread.
croix   n.f.   cross, cross-pattern, cross-shape.
cromesqui(s)   n.m.   kromesky.
croquant   adj.   crisp.
  n.m.   gristle; variety of brittle, dry *petit four*, q.v.
croquembouche   n.m.   crisp or hard *entremets*, q.v.
croque-monsieur   n.m. inv. in pl. hot hors d'œuvre, in the form of a sandwich or a *canapé* (q.v.), including ham and grated cheese.
croquet   n.m.   dry *petit four*, q.v.
croquette   n.f.   croquette, cylinder-shape.
croquignol(l)e   n.f.   small, hard, glazed biscuit, usually shaped like a button or a stick.
crosne   n.m.   Chinese artichoke, "Japanese" artichoke.
  crosne du Japon   Chinese artichoke, "Japanese" artichoke.
crosse   n.f.   knuckle (of leg).
croupion   n.m.   "parson's nose" (of chicken); tail-base.
croustade   n.f.   empty pastry-case.

croustadine   n.f.   small *croustade*, q.v.
croustillant   adj.   crisp, crunchy, crusty.
croustilles   n.f.pl.   game chips, potato crisps.
croûte   n.f.   crust; slice of toast for *canapé*, q.v.; pastry-crust.
  croûte à flan   flan-crust.
  croûte au pot   soup with toast or sippets in it.
  croûte de pâte feuilletée   puff-pastry case.
croûté   adj.   covered with a crust.
croûtelette   n.f.   small crust.
croûter   v.tr.   to cover with a crust.
croûton   n.m.   piece of crust; sippet; slice of fried or toasted bread.
  croûton de gelée   piece of meat-jelly, shaped like a triangle, rectangle, &c., used to decorate *chaud-froid*, q.v.
  croûton en brioche   sippet in the shape of a *brioche*, q.v.
  croûton en cœur   heart-shaped piece of fried bread, usually served with feathered game.
croûtonné   adj.   garnished with sippets.
croûtonner   v.tr.   to garnish with sippets.
cru   adj.   raw, uncooked.
  à cru   (cooked, prepared) from the raw state, i.e. without initial parboiling or other cooking.
cruchon   n.m.   small jug.
crudité   n.f.   crudity, indigestibility.
  crudités   pl.   raw fruit, raw vegetables, esp. as hors d'œuvre.
crustacé   n.m.   crustacean, crustacean shell-fish.
cube   n.m.   cube.
  adj.   cubic.
  centimètre cube   cubic centimetre.
cucurbitacée   n.f.   (any) plant of the cucurbitaceous family, which includes gourds, marrows, pumpkins and cucumbers.
cuiller   n.f.   spoon.
  cuiller à bouche   soup-spoon; table-spoon.
  cuiller à café   coffee-spoon.
  cuiller à dessert   dessert-spoon, sweet-spoon.
  cuiller à entremets   dessert-spoon, sweet-spoon.

cuiller à légumes spoon for turning vegetables.

cuiller à moutarde mustard-spoon.

cuiller à œufs egg-spoon.

cuiller à pomme noisette small round-bowled spoon for cutting out *pommes noisettes* (q.v.), spoon cutter.

cuiller à printanier spoon for cutting out *printanier*, q.v.

cuiller à racines spoon for turning root vegetables.

cuiller à soupe soup-spoon.

cuiller à thé tea-spoon.

cuiller de table table-spoon.

cuiller ovale oval-bowled spoon, e.g. table-spoon.

cuillère n.f. spoon.

N.B. This word may be used as an alternative to *cuiller* for all entries under the heading of *cuiller*, q.v.

cuillerée n.f. spoonful; tablespoonful.

cuillerée à bouche tablespoonful.

cuillerée à café coffeespoonful.

cuillerée à thé teaspoonful.

une forte cuillerée a good spoonful; a good tablespoonful.

cuilleron n.m. bowl (of spoon).

cuir n.m. leather.

cuire v.tr. & i. to cook.

faire cuire v.tr. to cook.

(faire) cuire à demi dans (de) l'eau to parboil.

(faire) cuire au four to bake.

(faire) cuire bleu to cook (meat) just enough to seal it, but so that it is still *saignant*, q.v.

(faire) cuire vert see *(faire) cuire bleu*.

cuiseur à pression n.m. pressure cooker.

cuisine n.f. kitchen; cookery; cooking; high-class cookery.

cuisine bourgeoise middle-class French family cookery.

cuisine maigre meatless cookery, i.e. cookery containing no elements which are forbidden to Catholics on Fridays.

haute cuisine high-class cookery.

cuisiné adj. cooked, treated by cooking.

cuisiner v.tr. & i. to cook, to pass through a process of cooking.

cuisinier n.m. (male) cook.

cuisinière n.f. (female) cook; (electric, gas) cooker.

cuisinière à électricité electric cooker.

cuisinière à gaz gas cooker.

cuisse n.f. leg.

cuisse de grenouille frog's leg.

cuisse de poulet chicken leg.

cuisseau, -eaux n.m. fillet of the leg (of veal).

cuisson n.f. (operation or process of) cooking; cooking-liquor; cooking-time.

jus de cuisson n.m. cooking-liquor.

temps de cuisson n.m. cooking-time.

cuissot n.m. leg (of pork); haunch (of venison).

cuit adj. cooked.

cuit à point medium (steak).

pas assez cuit underdone, i.e. not cooked enough.

trop cuit overdone, i.e. cooked too much.

cuivre n.m. copper.

cuivre étamé tinned copper.

cul-blanc, pl **culs-blancs** n.m. wheatear, white-tail.

culinaire adj. culinary; of, pertaining to, cookery.

culotte n.f. rump (of beef).

cumin n.m. cumin.

cumin des prés caraway.

curaçao n.m. curaçao, orange-flavoured liqueur.

curcuma n.m. curcuma, turmeric, condiment used in curry-powder.

curette n.f. scraper, scraping-out implement.

curry n.m. curry.

cylindre n.m. cylinder, cylinder-shape.

d

dague n.f. dagger, dirk.

dague d'honneur "dirk of honour", with an ornate garnish impaled on the haft end of its blade, stuck, as a decoration, esp. into a dressed boar's head.

daim n.m. fallow deer; buck.

dame-jeanne, pl. **dames-jeannes** n.f. demijohn.

damier n.m. chess-board pattern (strictly draught-board pattern).

dans prep. in, inside.

dard n.m. dace.

dariole n.f. small mould, esp. in the shape of a truncated cone.

darne n.f. thick slice (of fish), including the central bone, and thinner than a *tronçon*, q.v.

date n.f. date (day).

datte n.f. date (fruit).

daube n.f. stew of meat steamed in red wine in a closed container.

daubière n.f. container, receptacle, used in the preparation of a *daube*, q.v.

daurade n.f. chrysophrys.

de prep. of; from; (after infinitive, past participle) by, with.

dé n.m. die; die-shaped piece (e.g. of vegetable).

   en dés (cut, shaped) in dice.

déballer v.tr. to unpack, to untie.

débarder v.tr. to remove strips of larding bacon from (after cooking).

débarrasser v.tr. to clear (e.g. table).

   débarrasser de v.tr. to rid of.

débité adj. cut up.

débiter v.tr. to cut up.

déborder v.i. to overflow; to boil over.

déboucher v.tr. to uncork; to clear of obstruction (e.g. pipe, tube).

débrider v.tr. to remove binding, trussing, from.

débris n.m.pl. remains, left-overs (after cooking or other culinary preparation) which may be used for some other cooking purpose.

débrocher v.tr. to remove from skewer or spit.

décalotté adj. stripped of outer covering, e.g. peel, rind.

décalotter v.tr. to strip of outer covering (e.g. cooked ham of its rind).

décantation n.f. (the operation of) decanting.

décanté adj. decanted.

décanter v.tr. to decant.

décembre n.m. December.

déchet(s) n.m.(pl.) inedible *débris*, q.v.; secondary offal.

déchiré adj. torn, torn apart, torn up.

déchirer v.tr. to tear, to tear apart, to tear up.

déchirure n.f. laceration, tear.

décigramme n.m. decigram, one tenth of a *gramme*, q.v.

décilitre n.m. decilitre, one tenth of a *litre*, q.v.

décongélation n.f. defrosting, thawing (e.g. of chilled meat).

décongelé adj. defrosted, thawed (chilled meat).

décongeler v.tr. to defrost, to thaw (chilled meat).

décoquillé adj. removed from (its) shell (e.g. mollusc, snail).

décoquiller v.tr. to remove from (its) shell (e.g. mollusc, snail).

décor n.m. décor.

décoratif, -ive adj. decorative.

décoré adj. decorated.

décorer v.tr. to decorate.

décortiqué adj. decorticated; (of shrimps' tails) having had the cortical exterior removed.

décortiquer v.tr. to decorticate; to remove the cortical exterior of (e.g. shrimps' tails).

découpage n.m. carving; cutting up.

découpé adj. carved; cut up.

découper v.tr. to carve; to cut up.

découvert adj. uncovered; discovered.

   à découvert adv. phr. (cooked) uncovered, (cooked) in a receptacle without a lid.

découvrir v.tr. to uncover; to discover.

décuire v.tr. to add water to (e.g. jam, syrup) to decrease the degree of cooking.

dedans adv. in, inside, within.

défaire v.tr. to undo; to dismantle.

défait adj. undone; dismantled.

défaut n.m. defect, fault; lack, absence.

   à défaut adv. phr. if not available.

   à défaut de prep. phr. in the absence of.

déformé adj. having lost (its, their) shape.

déformer v.tr. to deform; to ruin, to spoil, the shape of (esp. carved or moulded preparation).

   se déformer v.refl. to lose (its, their) shape.

se dégager v.refl. to come off, to come up, to rise (aroma of cooking).

dégivrage n.m. (the operation of) defreezing.

   bac à dégivrage n.m. defreezing-compartment (of refrigerator).

déglaçage n.m. (the operation of) deglazing.
déglacé adj. deglazed.
déglacer v.tr. to deglaze.
dégorgé adj. cleaned by soaking in cold water; (meat) soaked in cold water to whiten it; (shell-fish) purged in salt water.
dégorgeage n.m. cleaning by soaking in cold water; soaking (of meat) in cold water to whiten it; purging (of shell-fish) in salt water.
dégorger v.tr. to clean by soaking in cold water; to soak (meat) in cold water to whiten it; to purge (shell-fish) in salt water.
faire dégorger v.tr. to purge (fish).
dégraissage n.m. (operation of) skimming.
dégraissé adj. skimmed, freed of surface fat.
dégraisser v.tr. to skim, to free of surface fat.
dégraissi(s) n.m. skimmings.
 dégraissi(s) de marmite stock-pot skimmings.
déguisé adj. disguised, masked.
déguiser v.tr. to disguise, to mask.
dehors adv. outside.
 en dehors prep.phr. outside, outside of; away from (heat).
déjà adv. already.
déjeuner v.i. to lunch, to take luncheon; to breakfast.
 n.m. lunch, luncheon.
 le petit déjeuner breakfast.
délayé adj. (e.g. flour) mixed with liquid.
délayer v.tr. to mix (e.g. flour) with liquid.
 délayer de la farine dans de l'eau to mix flour with water.
délicat adj. delicate.
délicatement adv. delicately.
délicieux, -euse adj. delicious; delightful.
demande n.f. request.
 une demande d'emploi a request for work.
 "demandes d'emploi" "situations wanted".
demandé adj. asked for, requested.
demander v.tr. to ask; to ask for, to request.
demi- adj. demi-, half-.
 demi-bouteille n.f. half-bottle.
 demi-carapace n.f. half-shell (esp. of lobster).

à demi-cuisson adv. phr. at the halfway point, stage (in cooking-process).
demi-deuil n.m. "half-mourning", contrast between black and white, effect of coating of white sauce decorated with black truffles.
demi-douzaine n.f. half-dozen. half a dozen.
demi-feuilletage n.m. half-puff pastry.
demi-glace n.f. half-glaze.
demi-glace tomatée half-glaze flavoured with tomato.
demi-heure n.f. half-hour, half an hour.
demi-homard n.m. half-lobster.
demi-litre n.m. half-litre.
demi-lune n.f. half-moon (-shape).
demi-selle n.f. half-saddle.
demi-solide adj. semi-solid.
demi-sphérique adj. hemi-spherical.
demi-tomate n.f. half-tomato.
demi-verre n.m. half-glass.
demi-zeste n.m. zest of half a lemon or half an orange.
démoulé adj. turned out from (its) mould.
démouler v.tr. to turn out from (its) mould.
dénervé adj. (meat) having had sinews, tendons, &c., removed.
dénerver v.tr. to remove sinews, tendons, &c., from (meat).
dénomination n.f. denomination, appellation, designation.
dénommé adj. named, designated.
dénommer v.tr. to name, to designate.
dénoyauté adj. stoned (fruit).
dénoyauter v.tr. to stone (fruit).
denrée n.f. commodity; foodstuff.
 denrées alimentaires food products.
densité n.f. density.
dent n.f. tooth.
dent-de-loup, pl. **dents-de-loup** n.f. triangular *croûton*, q.v.
dentelé adj. indented; serrated.
denteler v.tr. to indent; to serrate.
départ n.m. departure.
 au départ adv.phr. (finished, garnished, inspected) at the point of leaving (the kitchen).
département n.m. department.
dépasser v.tr. to exceed.

dépeçage n.m. (the operation of) cutting up, cutting into pieces.

dépecé adj. cut up, cut into pieces.

dépecer v.tr. to cut up, to cut into pieces.

se dépêcher v.refl. to hurry, to hurry up.

dépenser v.tr. to spend (money).

dépôt n.m. deposit, sediment; depot, store.

dépotage n.m. decanting (of liquid); turning out (of food, from saucepan).

dépoté adj. decanted (liquid); (food) turned out (from saucepan).

dépoter v.tr. to decant (liquid); to turn out (food from saucepan).

dépouille n.f. skin (of eel).

dépouillé adj. skinned (eel); skimmed (sauce); freed of skin and bone (fish).

dépouillement n.m. skinning (of eel); skimming (of sauce); (operation of) freeing (fish) of skin and bone.

dépouiller v.tr. to skin (eel); to skim (sauce); to free (fish) of skin and bone.

dernier, -ère adj. last.
   au dernier moment at the last moment, at the last minute.

dérobé adj. blanched (almonds); skinned (broad beans).

dérober v.tr. to blanch (almonds); to skin (broad beans).

dés n.m. plural of *dé*, q.v.

se désagréger v.refl. to break up, to disintegrate.

désarêté adj. boned, filleted (fish).

désarêter v.tr. to bone, to fillet (fish).

description n.f. description.

déshuilé, adj. having had excess oil removed.

déshuiler v.tr. to remove excess oil from.

désossage n.m. (the operation of) boning.

désossé adj. boned (fish).

désosser v.tr. to bone (fish).

dessablé adj. having had sand removed, freed of sand.

dessabler v.tr. to remove sand from, to free of sand.

dessalé adj. having had salt removed, freed of salt; rendered less salt(y), e.g. by soaking.

dessaler v.tr. to remove salt from, to free of salt; to render less salt(y), e.g. by soaking.

desséché adj. dried; dried thoroughly; desiccated.

dessécher v.tr. to dry; to dry thoroughly; to desiccate.

dessert n.m. dessert.

desserte n.f. left-overs, remains, of food.
   desserte de poisson left-overs, scraps, of fish.

dessiccation n.f. desiccation, drying.

dessous prep. under.
   n.m. underneath, underside.

dessus prep. on, above.
   n.m. top; upper side.

détaché adj. detached.

détacher v.tr. to detach; to remove stains, spots, from.

détacheur n.m. stain-remover.

détail n.m. detail; retail; cutting, cutting up.
   prix de détail n.m. retail price.
   détails de cornichons n.m.pl. cuttings of gherkins.

détaillé adj. detailed; cut up.

détailler v.tr. to detail, to enumerate; to cut up.

détendre v.tr. to loosen, to slacken (e.g. consistency).

détendu adj. loosened, slackened (e.g. consistency).

détrempe n.f. mixture of flour and water for the making of a paste.

détrempé adj. (flour) mixed with water (or, e.g., egg-yolk) for the making of a paste.

détremper v.tr. to mix (flour), esp. with water, for the making of a paste.

devant prep. in front of.

développé adj. developed; unwrapped; unfolded (cloth).

développer v.tr. to develop; to unwrap; to unfold (cloth).

dextrine n.f. dextrin.

dextrose n.m. or f. dextrose.

diable n.m. devil.
   diable de mer angler.

diablé adj. devilled.

diabler v.tr. to devil.

diablotin n.m. garnished and condimented roundel of bread (cut from a flute-shaped loaf), sprinkled with grated cheese and gratinated, used as an accompaniment esp. to *consommé*, q.v.

diamétral, -aux adj. diametrical.
diamètre n.m. diameter.
différence n.f. difference.
différent adj. different.
digéré adj. digested.
digérer v.tr. to digest.
digestion n.f. digestion.
dilué adj. diluted; watered down (liquid).
diluer v.tr. to dilute; to water down.
dilution n.f. dilution; watering down.
dimanche n.m. Sunday.
dimension n.f. size.
diminué adj. lessened, reduced.
diminuer v.tr. to lessen, to reduce.
  diminuer le feu to turn down the flame.
dinde n.f. turkey-hen.
dindon n.m. turkey, turkey-cock.
dindonneau, -eaux n.m. young turkey; (usual description of) turkey on restaurant menu.
dîner v.i. to dine, to have dinner. n.m. dinner.
dire v.tr. to say, to tell.
disposer v.tr. to arrange, to place, to set out.
  disposer de v.tr. to have available, to have at one's disposal.
se dissocier v.refl. to dissociate (e.g. liquid mixture).
dissoudre v.tr. to dissolve; to melt in liquid.
  se dissoudre v.refl. to dissolve.
dissous adj. dissolved.
divers adj.pl. various.
divisé adj. divided.
  divisé en quatre divided into four.
diviser v.tr. to divide.
  diviser en quatre to divide into four.
doigt n.m. finger.
doigtier n.m. finger-stall.
dôme n.m. dome, dome-shape.
  en dôme (shaped) in the form of a dome.
dominant adj. dominant, predominating.
  couleur dominante predominating colour.
dominer v.i. to predominate.
donner v.tr. to give.
donzelle n.f. ophidium.
doré adj. golden; coloured golden; glazed with whipped egg or egg-yolk.

dorer v.tr. to colour golden; to glaze with whipped egg or egg-yolk.
doroir n.m. pastry-brush.
dorure n.f. golden colouring; glaze of whipped egg or egg-yolk.
  pinceau à dorure n.m. pastry-brush.
dos n.m. back.
double adj. double.
  n.m. part comprising the two hindquarters.
  double d'agneau part of the lamb comprising the two hindquarters.
doucette n.f. corn-salad, lamb's lettuce.
  doucette de Paris corn-salad, lamb's lettuce.
douille n.f. piping-tube.
  douille unie round, smooth, piping-tube.
  petite douille small piping-tube.
  petite douille cannelée small corrugated, grooved, piping-tube.
doux, douce adj. sweet; soft.
douzaine n.f. dozen.
dragée n.f. almond covered with hard sugar.
draine n.f. missel-thrush.
drèche n.f. draff.
drêche n.f. draff.
drenne n.f. missel-thrush.
dressé adj. set up; dished up; arranged.
dresser v.tr. to set up; to dish up; to arrange.
  dresser en couronne to arrange in the shape of an annulus, corona, ring.
droit adj. straight; right (side). n.m. right, privilege.
droite n.f. right side, right hand side.
  à droite to the right, on the right.
drupe n.f. (any) fleshy fruit containing a single kernel (e.g. apricot, cherry).
dur adj. hard.
  œuf dur hard-boiled egg.
durci adj. hardened.
durcir v.tr. & i. to harden.
durée n.f. length, duration.
durer v.i. to last.
duvet n.m. down (on bird, fruit).
duxelles n.f. fundamental preparation containing chopped mushrooms and shallots cooked together.
  duxelles sèche dry *duxelles*, q.v.

e

eau, eaux n.f. water.
  eau bouillante boiling water.
  eau chaude hot water.
  eau de fleurs d'oranger orange-flower water.
  eau de mer sea water.
  eau de seltz soda-water.
  eau de vaisselle dish-water.
  eau douce fresh water, e.i. water from river or lake; soft water.
  eau dure hard water.
  eau fraîche fresh water, i.e. water straight from tap; cool water; cold water.
  eau froide cold water.
  eau gazeuse aerated water.
  eau grasse dish-water.
  eau minérale mineral water.
  eau potable drinking water.
  eau salée salt water, salted water.
  eau savonneuse soapy water.
  eau tiède tepid water, lukewarm water.
  eaux grasses pl. swill.
  grande eau water in large quantity; good depth of water.
  laver à grande eau to wash in plenty of water; to swill out.
  laver le plancher à grande eau to swill the floor.
eau-de-vie, pl. **eaux-de-vie** n.f. brandy; spirits.
ébarbé adj. (vegetable) trimmed of root-hairs; (oyster) bearded, trimmed of gills.
ébarber v.tr. to trim (vegetable) of root-hairs; to beard, to remove gills from (oyster).
ébouillanté adj. dipped in boiling water; scalded (person); scalded out (saucepan).
ébouillanter v.tr. to dip in boiling water; to scald (person); to scald out (saucepan).
ébouilli adj. boiled away.
ébouillir v.i. to boil away.
ébullition n.f. (action of) boiling, ebullition.
  en ébullition boiling, in a boiling state.
  petite ébullition gentle boiling.
  point d'ébullition boiling point.
écaille n.f. scale (of fish).
écaillé adj. scaled (fish); opened (oyster).

écailler v.tr. to scale (fish); to open (oyster).
écailleux, -euse adj. scaly (animal, fruit).
  corossol écailleux n.m. sweet-sop.
écale n.f. husk (of walnut); pod, shuck (of pea).
écalé adj. husked (walnut); shucked (pea).
écaler v.tr. to husk (walnut); to shuck (pea).
écarlate n.f. & adj. scarlet.
  à l'écarlate (coated) with brown aspic.
écarté adj. separated, set apart; drawn away, moved away.
écarter v.tr. to separate, to set apart; to draw away, to move away.
  écarter du feu to move away from the flame, to withdraw from the flame.
échalote n.f. shallot.
écharbot n.m. water caltrop(s).
échassier n.m. wader, wading bird.
échaudé adj. scalded; scalded out. n.m. canary bread.
échauder v.tr. to scald (hand); to scald out (saucepan).
échine n.f. spine; chine.
échinée n.f. chine, griskin, of pork.
éclair n.m. long, individual bun, made of *pâte à chou* (q.v.), filled with fresh cream or pastry cream and covered with chocolate or coffee fondant.
éclairage n.m. lighting, illumination.
éclairé adj. lit, illuminated.
éclairer v.tr. to light, to illuminate.
éclanche n.f. shoulder of mutton.
économe adj. economical, thrifty. n.m. & f. (kitchen) storekeeper.
économie n.f. economy, thrift; economy, economic system.
économique adj. economical, inexpensive.
écorce n.f. peel, rind.
  écorce d'orange orange-peel.
écorcé adj. peeled (orange).
écorcer v.tr. to peel (orange).
écorché adj. skinned (eel); flayed (ox).
écorcher v.tr. to skin (eel); to flay (ox).
écossé adj. shucked (pea).
écosser v.tr. to shuck (pea).

écourté adj. shortened, trimmed.

écourter v.tr. to shorten, to trim.

écouter v.tr. to listen to.
v.i. to listen.

écrasé adj. crushed, squashed.

écraser v.tr. to crush, to squash.

écrémage n.m. creaming; separating (of milk); skimming (of milk).

écrémé adj. creamed; separated (milk); skimmed (milk).
lait écrémé skim milk.

écrémer v.tr. to cream; to separate (milk); to skim (milk).

écrémeuse n.f. creamer; separator.

écrevisse n.f. (fresh-water) crayfish.
écrevisse châtrée gutted crayfish.

écrire v.tr. to write.

écu n.m. shield, shield-shape.

écumage n.m. (the operation of) scumming, skimming (esp. of jam).

écume n.f. scum; froth.

écumé adj. scummed, skimmed.

écumer v.tr. to scum, to skim.

écumoire n.f. skimmer, skimming-ladle.

édulcoré adj. edulcorated, sweetened.

édulcorer v.tr. to edulcorate, to sweeten.

effeuillé adj. stripped of (its) leaves.

effeuiller v.tr. to strip of (its) leaves.

effilé adj. (beans) stripped of their strings; shredded (almonds); unravelled.

effiler v.tr. (beans) to strip of their strings, to string; to shred (almonds); to unravel.

effiloché adj. shredded; unravelled.

effilocher v.tr. to shred; to unravel.

égal n.m. & adj. equal.

égalé adj. equalled.

également adv. equally; also, similarly.

égaler v.tr. to equal.

églefin n.m. (incorrect spelling of) *aiglefin*, q.v.

égouttage n.m. (the operation of) draining; draining (of cheese).

égoutté adj. drained.

égoutter v.tr. to drain; to drain (cheese).

égouttoir n.m. draining-board; draining-rack.

égrappé adj. stalked (grapes).

égrapper v.tr. to stalk (grapes).

égrefin n.m. (incorrect spelling of) *aigrefin*, q.v.

égrené adj. stalked (grapes).

égrener v.tr. to stalk (grapes).

égrugeoir n.m. mortar.

égruger v.tr. to pound in the mortar.

électricité n.f. electricity.

électrique adj. electric.

élément n.m. element.
élément nutritif nutritive element.

éliminer v.tr. to eliminate.

élixir n.m. elixir.

elliptique adj. elliptical.

émail n.m. enamel.

émaillé adj. enamelled.

émailler v.tr. to enamel.

emballé adj. wrapped, wrapped up.

emballer v.tr. to wrap, to wrap up.

embroché adj. spitted, impaled on the spit.

embrocher v.tr. to spit, to impale on the spit.

émietté adj. crumbled, reduced to crumbs (bread).

émietter v.tr. to crumble, to reduce to crumbs (bread).

émincé adj. thinly sliced (meat); cut up into small pieces.
n.m. thin slice (of meat); dish prepared from thinly-sliced meat.

émincer v.tr. to slice thinly (meat); to cut up into small pieces.

émondé adj. skinned (almonds, tomatoes) by blanching.

émonder v.tr. to skin (almonds, tomatoes) by blanching.

empêcher v.tr. to prevent.

empilé adj. piled (up), stacked.

empiler v.tr. to pile (up), to stack.

empli adj. filled.

emplir v.tr. to fill.

emploi n.m. employment, occupation.
demande d'emploi request for employment.
"demandes d'emploi" "situations wanted".
offre d'emploi offer of employment.
"offres d'emploi" "situations vacant".

employé, -ée n. employee.
employé adj. employed, used (method, utensil).

employer v.tr. to employ (staff); to employ, to use (method, utensil).

empois n.m. light paste made of starch.

emporte-pièce n.m.inv. in pl. (paste-)cutter.

  emporte-pièce cannelé channelled cutter, grooved cutter; wheeled cutter.

  emporte-pièce carré square cutter.

  emporte-pièce uni smooth round cutter.

emporter v.tr. to carry away, to take away; to cut out, to remove (with a cutter).

empotage n.m. (operation of) potting (jam, pickles).

empoter v.tr. to pot (jam, pickles).

émulsion n.f. emulsion.

encaqué adj. barrelled (salt herring or smoked herring).

encaquer v.tr. to barrel (salt herring or smoked herring).

encastré adj. embedded, set (in).

encastrer v.tr. to embed, to set (in).

endive n.f. chicory (salad, vegetable), "endive".

  endive belge Belgian "endive".

endroit n.m. place, spot.

enduire v.tr. to smear.

  enduire de to smear with.

enduit adj. smeared.

  enduit de smeared with.

enduit n.m. coating.

enfermer v.tr. to enclose.

  enfermer dans to enclose in.

enfilé adj. strung; threaded (e.g. on a spit or skewer); threaded (needle).

enfiler v.tr. to string; to thread (e.g. on a spit or skewer); to thread (needle).

enfin adv. at last.

engrais n.m. manure.

engraissant adj. fattening (food).

engraissé adj. fattened, fattened up (animal, fowl).

engraissement n.m. (process of) fattening (animal, fowl).

engraisser v.tr. to fatten, to fatten up (animal, fowl).

enlevé adj. removed, taken away.

enlever v.tr. to remove, to take away.

  enlever les filets de to fillet.

  enlever les filets d'un poisson to fillet a fish.

enrobé adj. coated.

  enrobé de coated with.

enrober v.tr. to coat.

  enrober de to coat with.

enroulé adj. rolled, rolled up.

enrouler v.tr. to roll, to roll up.

ensemble adv. together.

  n.m. ensemble, whole.

ensuite adv. then; after(wards).

entaille n.f. notch.

entaillé adj. notched.

entailler v.tr. to notch.

entassé adj. heaped up, piled up.

entasser v.tr. to heap up, to pile up.

entendre v.tr. to hear.

entendu! int. understood! all right! O.K!

  bien entendu naturally, of course.

entier, -ière adj. whole, entire.

entièrement adv. wholly, entirely.

entonné adj. barrelled, casked; filled (sausage).

entonner v.tr. to barrel, to cask; to fill (sausage).

entonnoir n.m. funnel (for decanting, pouring).

entouré adj. surrounded.

  entouré de surrounded by.

entourer v.tr. to surround.

  entourer de to surround with.

entre prep. between.

entrecôte n.f. steak cut from the ribs (of beef).

entrée n.f. entree, dish (usually) served between fish and joint; entrance; entry, admission.

  entrée d'abats—*entrée* (q.v.) of offal.

  entrée de boucherie—*entrée* (q.v.) of butcher's meat.

  entrée volante light *entrée*, q.v.

  à l'entrée du four (cooked) just inside the oven.

  brider en entrée to truss (chicken) with the legs entered.

entrelardé adj. larded.

  entrelardé de larded with.

entremets n.m. sweet course; (originally) any minor dish served between more important ones.

  entremets de légume vegetable (e.g. asparagus) served as a separate course.

entremettier n.m. vegetable-cook.

  chef entremettier head vegetable-cook.

entrer v.i. to enter, to come in, to go in.
  entrer dans la cuisine to come into, to go into, the kitchen.
entretemps (or **entre-temps**) adv. meanwhile.
enveloppe n.f. casing, covering, wrapping; outer skin (e.g. of vegetable, left intact when centre has been removed).
enveloppé adj. wrapped.
envelopper v.tr. to wrap.
en envoyant adv. phr. (of garnish, sauce, &c., added to the dish, or of other operation carried out) at the moment of sending up (from the kitchen).
envoyer v.tr. to send; to send up (from the kitchen).
épais, -aisse adj. thick.
épaisseur n.f. thickness; layer.
épaissi adj. thickened.
épaissir v.tr. to thicken.
épaule n.f. shoulder.
épépiné adj. seeded (e.g. raisins).
épépiner v.tr. to seed (e.g. raisins).
éperlan n.m. smelt.
épice n.f. spice.
  quatre épices (not to be confused with *quatre-épices*, q.v.) allspice.
épicé adj. spiced.
épicer v.tr. to spice.
épiderme n.m. epidermis.
épigramme n.f. epigram.
  épigramme d'agneau compressed breast of lamb, cut into a diamond-shape, covered with egg and breadcrumb, and jumped in butter.
épinard n.m. spinach.
  épinards en branches, épinards en feuilles leaf spinach.
épine-vinette, pl. **épines-vinettes** n.f. barberry.
épluchage n.m. (the operation of) paring, peeling (fruit, vegetables).
épluché adj. pared, peeled (fruit, vegetables).
éplucher v.tr. to pare, to peel (fruit, vegetables).
épluchures n.f.pl. parings, peelings.
éponge n.f. sponge.
épongé adj. sponged, wiped with (or as with) a sponge.
éponger v.tr. to sponge, to wipe with (or as with) a sponge.
épuration n.f. (the operation of) cleansing, purifying.

épuré adj. cleansed, purified.
épurer v.tr. to cleanse, to purify.
équeuté adj. stalked (e.g. strawberries).
équeuter v.tr. to stalk (e.g. strawberries).
équilibre n.m. equilibrium, balance.
équilibré adj. balanced.
  bien équilibré well-balanced.
équilibrer v.tr. to balance (menu).
équille n.f. sand-eel.
équivalent adj. & n.m. equivalent.
erreur n.f. error, mistake.
escalope n.f. scollop (of veal); slice cut on the bias.
escalopé adj. cut, sliced, on the bias.
escaloper v.tr. to cut, to slice, on the bias.
escarbilles n.f.pl. clinker.
escargot n.m. snail; edible snail.
  escargot comestible edible snail.
escargotière n.f. snail-dish.
escarole n.f. Batavian endive.
espadon n.m. swordfish.
esprot n.m. sprat.
essai n.m. sample, taste (of food, wine).
essayer v.tr. to test, to try; to taste (e.g. before correcting seasoning).
  essayer de faire quelque chose to try to do something.
essence n.f. essence.
essuyer v.tr. to wipe; to wipe dry; to wipe clean.
estomac n.m. stomach.
estouffade n.f. brown meat stock.
estragon n.m. tarragon.
  estragon en branches leaf tarragon.
  estragon haché chopped tarragon.
esturgeon n.m. sturgeon.
étain n.m. tin; pewter.
étalé adj. laid out, set out; displayed.
étaler v.tr. to lay out, to set out; to display.
étamage n.m. (the operation of) tinning (esp. of copper).
étamé adj. tinned (copper).
  cuivre étamé tinned copper.
étamer v.tr. to tin (copper).
étamine n.f. cloth strainer.
  passer à l'étamine to pass through a cloth strainer.

été n.m. summer.

éteindre v.tr. to extinguish, to put out; to switch off; to turn off.

étiquette n.f. label, tag; etiquette, ceremony.

étoile n.f. star, star-shape.

étoilé adj. star-shaped; starred.

étouffé adj. stewed, slowly cooked.

étouffée n.f. stew of slowly-cooked meat.

étouffer v.tr. to stew, to cook slowly.

étranger, -ère adj. foreign.
  un potage étranger a foreign (to France) soup.

être v.i. to be.

étudiant, -iante n. student.
  étudiant hôtelier (male) catering student.
  étudiante hôtelière (female) catering student.

étuve n.f. (any) closed container for stewing.

étuvé adj. stewed, slowly cooked.

étuvée n.f. stew of slowly-cooked meat.
  à l'étuvée (cooked) by stewing.

étuver v.tr. to stew, to cook slowly.

évaporation n.f. evaporation.

évaporé adj. evaporated.

évaporer v.tr. to evaporate.
  s'évaporer v.refl. to evaporate.

évasé adj. opened out; widened (opening).

évaser v.tr. to open out; to widen (opening).

évidé adj. hollowed, hollowed out; scooped out.

évider v.tr. to hollow out, to scoop out.

éviter v.tr. to avoid.
  éviter de faire quelque chose to avoid doing something.

excellence n.f. excellence.

excellent adj. excellent.

excès n.m. excess.

excipient n.m. excipient.

exocet n.m. flying-fish, sea-swallow.

exotique adj. exotic.

exprimé adj. squeezed, squeezed out (lemon); expressed (idea, opinion).

exprimer v.tr. to squeeze, to squeeze out (lemon); to express (idea, opinion).

externe adj. external, outer.

extraire v.tr. to extract.

extrait adj. extracted.
  n.m. extract.

f

facile adj. easy.

facilement adv. easily.

façon n.f. manner, way.
  à la façon ordinaire in the usual way.
  de façon à so as to.

façonné adj. fashioned, moulded, shaped.

façonner v.tr. to fashion, to mould, to shape.

facultatif, -ive adj. optional.

facultativement adv. optionally, if desired.

fagoue n.f. sweetbreads.

faïence n.f. earthenware, stoneware.
  faïence fine china.

faim n.f. hunger.
  avoir faim to be hungry.

faine n.f. beechnut.

faine n.f. see **faine**.

faire v.tr. to do; to make.
  faire bouillir v.tr. to boil.
  faire cuire v.tr. to cook.
  faire cuire à demi dans l'eau to parboil.
  faire cuire au four to bake.
  faire prendre sur glace to set on ice.
  faire s'ouvrir v.tr. to open (shellfish, esp. by boiling).
  faire tomber à glace to cook to a glaze.

faisan n.m. pheasant; cock-pheasant.

faisandage n.m. hanging (of meat esp. game).

faisande n.f. hen-pheasant.

faisandé adj. high, well hung (meat, esp. game).

faisandeau n.m. pheasant-poult, young pheasant.

faisander v.tr. to hang (meat).
  se faisander v.refl. to get high (meat, esp. game).

faisane n.f. hen-pheasant.

faisselle n.f. basket (or other container) or surface in or on which cheese is drained.

famille n.f. family.
  cuisine de famille simple family cookery.

faon n.m. fawn; young roebuck.

farce n.f. stuffing; forcemeat.

farci adj. stuffed.

farcir v.tr. to stuff.

  farcir de to stuff with.

farinacé adj. farinaceous; flour-like.

  pâte farinacée farinaceous paste.

farinage n.m. farinaceous food, farinaceous preparation.

farine n.f. flour.

  farine d'avoine oatmeal.

  farine de sarrasin buckwheat flour.

  farine tamisée sieved flour.

fariné adj. floured, coated with flour.

fariner v.tr. to flour, to coat with flour.

farineux, -euse adj. farinaceous; floury, covered with flour.

farinière n.f. flour-bin.

fauve n.m. any game animal of the deer family.

faux, -ausse adj. false, "mock".

  fausse tortue mock turtle (soup).

faux-filet n.m. boned and trimmed sirloin of beef.

fécule n.f. starch.

  fécule de pommes de terre potato starch.

fendre v.tr. to crack, to split.

  fendre en deux to split in two down the middle (esp. lobster).

fendu adj. cracked, split.

fêne n.f. see *faine*.

fenouil n.m. fennel.

  fenouil tubéreux tuberous fennel, bulbous fennel.

fenouillet n.m. fennel-apple.

fenouillette n.f. fennel-apple; fennel-liqueur.

fente n.f. crack, split.

fenugrec n.m. fenugreek.

fer n.m. iron.

  fer blanc (or **fer-blanc**) tin (metal).

  boîte en fer blanc tin can, can, tin.

féra n.f. fera, variety of Swiss lake fish.

ferme adj. firm.

  ferme sous le doigt firm to the touch.

fermé adj. closed.

ferment n.m. ferment.

fermentation n.f. fermentation.

fermenté adj. fermented.

fermenter v.tr. to ferment.

fermer v.tr. to close, to shut.

fermeté n.f. firmness.

fermeture n.f. closing, shutting.

festin n.m. banquet.

fête n.f. feast; celebration, party.

feu, -feux n.m. fire (as distinct from *incendie*, q.v.); light (for oven, cigarette, etc.).

  à feu doux adv. phr. (cooked) over a gentle flame, over a low flame, over a slow fire.

  à feu vif adv.phr. (cooked) over a brisk flame, over a quick fire.

  à petit feu adv.phr. (cooked) over a gentle flame, over a low flame, over a slow fire.

  donner du feu to give a light.

  feu de braise braising-fire.

  feu doux gentle flame, low flame, slow fire.

  feu vif brisk flame, quick fire.

  prendre feu to catch fire.

feuillantine n.f. (variety of) small puff-pastry cake.

feuille n.f. leaf; sheet (e.g. of paper).

  feuille à fendre cleaver.

  feuille de gélatine sheet of gelatine.

  feuille de laurier bayleaf.

  feuille de papier sheet of paper.

  feuille de vigne vine-leaf.

  feuilles extérieures outer leaves.

  feuilles extérieures dures hard, tough, outer leaves.

feuillet n.m. third stomach (of cow), fardel; small sheet of paper.

feuilletage n.m. (the operation of) making puff pastry; puff paste.

feuilleté adj. laminated (e.g. puff paste).

  pâte feuilletée puff paste.

feuilleter v.tr. to roll and fold several (usually six) times (paste, in order to make puff paste).

feuilleton n.m. fillet of veal, sliced lengthwise almost through its thickness, then stuffed between the slices and cooked in a pig's caul.

  feuilleton de veau *feuilleton* (q.v.) of veal.

feuillette n.f. small leaf; barrel, cask, containing between 112 and 140 litres.

fève n.f. bean.

  fève de(s) marais broad bean.

  fève de haricot French bean, kidney bean.

fève verte green kidney bean.
féverol(l)e n.f. horse-bean.
fèverol(l)e n.f. horse-bean.
février n.m. February.
fibre n.f. fibre.
ficaire n.f. (lesser) celandine.
ficelage n.m. (operation of) tying (up) with string.
ficelé adj. tied (up) with string.
ficeler v.tr. to tie (up) with string.
ficelle n.f. string.
fiel n.m. gall.
  poche de fiel n.f. gall-bladder (of fish).
fiéla n.f. (Provençal name for) conger eel.
fiella n.f. (Provençal name for) conger eel.
figé adj. congealed; fixed.
figer v.tr. to congeal; to fix.
figue n.f. fig.
  figue de Barbarie prickly pear.
figue-caque, pl. **figues-caques** n.f. persimmon.
fil n.m. thread; grain (of meat).
filament n.m. filament.
filandre n.f. fibre; stringy, fibrous matter (esp. in meat, vegetables).
filandreux, -euse adj. stringy, tough (meat, vegetables).
filé adj. spun (thread); poured out (in a thin trickle).
  œufs filés n.m.pl. beaten eggs poured in a thin trickle through a *chinois* (q.v.) into boiling liquid (e.g. *consommé*, q.v.).
filer v.tr. to pour out (in a thin trickle).
filet n.m. fillet (of meat, fish) free from bone; thin trickle (of liquid); net (for catching fish in *vivier*, q.v.).
  filet d'huile thin trickle of oil.
  filet mignon tenderloin.
filtre n.m. filter.
filtré adj. filtered.
filtrer v.tr. to filter.
fin n.f. end (in time).
  adj. fine, choice.
  fine champagne liqueur brandy (from the Champagne de Saintonges).
  fines herbes mixed herbs.
finement adv. finely.
  finement haché finely chopped.
finir v.tr. & i. to finish.
  finir de faire quelque chose to finish doing something.
finissage n.m. (the process of) finishing, finishing off.

fixé fixed, set.
fixer v.tr. to fix, to set.
  fixer au repère to seal (pie) with semi-liquid sealing-agent.
flageolet n.m. small kidney bean.
flambage n.m. (the operation of) singeing.
flambé adj. flamed; singed.
flambée n.f. blaze, blazing fire.
flamber v.tr. to flame; to singe.
flamme n.f. flame.
flan n.m. flan; open pastry-case.
  flan au lait milk flan.
  flan au lait sans sucre savoury milk flan.
  flan sans sucre savoury flan.
flanchet n.m. flank (of beef).
flanqué adj. flanked.
  flanqué de flanked by, flanked with.
flanquer v.tr. to flank.
  flanquer de to flank with.
flèche n.f. flitch.
  flèche de lard flitch of bacon.
flet n.m. flounder.
flétan n.m. halibut.
fleur n.f. flower; blossom; flower-shape.
  fleur de farine pure wheaten flour.
  fleur d'oranger orange-blossom.
fleurette n.f. floweret, small flower.
  fleurettes de chou-fleur cauliflower tops.
fleuron n.m. small puff-pastry crescent used as garnish.
flocon n.m. flake.
  flocons d'avoine corn-flakes.
fluide adj. & n.m. fluid.
flûte n.f. flute-shape; long and slender bottle, glass, loaf.
foie n.m. liver.
  foie de volaille chicken's liver.
  foie gras fatted liver (of goose).
foin n.m. hay; choke (of artichoke).
fois n.f. time (occasion).
  beaucoup de fois many times.
  deux fois twice.
  une fois once.
follette n.f. orach.
foncé adj. dark (colour); (container) lined (esp. with paste).
  bleu foncé dark blue.
foncer v.tr. to line (esp. with paste).
  foncer une casserole to line (the bottom of) a saucepan.
  pâte à foncer n.f. lining-paste.

fond n.m. base, bottom (not to be confused with *fonds*, q.v.).
  à fond épais adj.phr. (of pan) with a thick base.
  fond d'artichaut artichoke-base.
  fond de plat bread base on which a made-up preparation is laid.
fondant adj. melting.
  n.m. fondant.
fondre v.tr. to dissolve; to melt.
fonds n.m. base, basis; (cooking-) stock.
  fonds blanc white stock.
  fonds brun brown stock.
  fonds brun clair clear brown stock.
  fonds de braisage braising-stock.
  fonds de déglaçage deglazing stock.
  fonds de gibier game stock.
  fonds de poisson fish stock.
  fonds de veau veal stock.
  fonds de volaille chicken stock.
  fonds maigre stock containing no meat or meat derivatives.
fondu adj. melted.
fondue n.f. (any) preparation based on the melting of a vegetable, cheese, &c.
  fondue au fromage made-up preparation of melted cheese.
fontaine n.f. bay, well (in mixing pastry ingredients).
forme n.f. form, shape.
  forme abricot apricot-shape (esp. of pommes Berny).
  forme bouchon cork-shape.
formé adj. formed, shaped.
former v.tr. to form, to shape.
fort adj. strong; loud.
  adv. strongly; loudly.
fortement adv. strongly; highly.
  fortement assaisonné highly seasoned.
  fortement épicé strongly spiced.
fouet n.m. whip, whisk.
fouetté adj. whipped, whisked.
fouetter v.tr. to whip, to whisk.
foulé adj. pressed, pressed down (esp. in passing sauce).
fouler v.tr. to press, to press down (esp. in passing sauce).
foulque n.f. coot.
  foulque noire bald coot.
four n.m. oven.
  four à électricité electric oven.
  four à gaz gas oven.
  four doux low oven.

four modéré moderate oven.
four moyen medium oven.
four vif brisk oven.
four de campagne field oven.
au four (cooked) in the oven.
à l'entrée du four (cooked) just inside the oven.
(petit) four, pl. **petits fours** n.m. (general name for) several varieties of small pastry preparations, glazed fruits, etc.
fourchette n.f. fork; wish-bone (of chicken).
  fourchette à découper carving-fork.
fourneau, -eaux n.m. furnace.
  fourneau de cuisine kitchen-range.
fournée n.f. batch, cooking (of loaves); ovenful (of cooked food).
fourré adj. filled (omelette).
  omelette fourrée filled omelette (as distinct from *omelette garnie*, q.v.).
fourrer v.tr. to fill (esp. omelette, during folding).
fragment n.m. fragment, piece.
fragon n.m. ruscus.
  fragon épineux butcher's broom.
frai n.m. spawn; spawning; spawning-season.
  l'époque du frai n.f. (the) spawning-season.
fraie n.f. spawning-season.
fraieson n.f. spawning-season.
frais, fraîche adj. fresh; cool.
frais n.m.pl. expense(s).
  à mes frais at my expense.
fraisage n.m. kneading with a downward pressure of the palm of the hand.
fraise n.f. strawberry; crow, membrane enveloping intestines of calf, lamb, etc.; wattle (of turkey).
  fraise des bois wild strawberry.
  fraise de veau calf's crow.
fraisé adj. kneaded with a downward pressure of the palm of the hand.
fraiser v.tr. to knead with a downward pressure of the palm of the hand.
framboise n.f. raspberry.
framboisé adj. decorated with raspberries; raspberry-flavoured.
framboiser v.tr. to decorate with raspberries; to flavour with raspberries.

franc, franche adj. real, true.
  chélonée franche green turtle.
franc n.m. franc.
  le nouveau franc français the
  new French franc.
  vingt nouveaux francs twenty
  new francs.
francolin n.m. francolin (a kind of
  partridge).
frangipane n.f. frangipane.
frappé adj. chilled, put on ice;
  struck, hit.
frapper v.tr. to chill, to put on ice;
  to strike, to hit.
fraye n.f. sprawning-season.
frémir v.i. to simmer (water).
frémissement n.m. (the action of)
  simmering (water).
fréquemment adv. frequently.
fréquent adj. frequent.
fressure n.f. pluck (of animal, comprising heart, spleen, liver and lungs).
friand n.m. (variety of) puff-pastry
  sausage roll.
friandise n.f. small sweet delicacy.
fricadelle n.f. fried meat-ball, made
  from veal or beef.
fricandeau, -eaux n.m. joint cut
  from silverside of veal, larded and
  braised.
fricassé adj. fricasseed.
fricassée n.f. white *ragoût*, q.v.
fricasser v.tr. to fricassee.
frigorifié adj. freezing, frozen.
frigorifier v.tr. to refrigerate.
frigorifique adj. refrigerating.
  appareil frigorifique n.m. refrigerator.
frire v.tr. & i. to fry.
  faire frire v.tr. to fry.
  (faire) frire à la (grande) friture
  to fry in (deep) fat.
frisé adj. curly.
  chou frisé n.m. borecole, (curly)
  kale.
frise-beurre n.m.inv. in pl. butter-
  shaper.
frissonnant adj. gently simmering (liquid).
frissonner v.i. to simmer gently
  (liqud).
frit adj. fried.
  frit à la (grande) friture fried in
  (deep) fat.
fritons n.m.pl. greaves, cracklings.
fritot n.m. made-up preparation of
  small deep-fried meat or offal frit-
  ters.

fritôt n.m. see *fritot*.
friture n.f. frying; frying-fat, batter; fried food; small fried fish, e.g.
  whitebait.
  à grande friture (fried) in deep
  fat.
  grande friture deep fat.
  panier à friture n.m. frying-
  basket.
friturier n.m. cook in charge of
  frying.
froid adj. & n.m. cold.
  avoir froid to be cold (of a person).
  buffet froid n.m. cold buffet.
froitier n.m. cook specializing in
  cold savoury dishes.
fromage n.m. cheese; brawn.
  fromage de brebis ewe's milk
  cheese.
  fromage de chèvre goat's milk
  cheese.
  fromage de porc pork brawn.
  fromage de vache cow's milk
  cheese.
  fromage maigre skim-milk
  cheese.
fromagé adj. flavoured with cheese;
  sprinkled with cheese, for gratination.
fromager v.tr. to flavour with
  cheese; to sprinkle with cheese, for
  gratination.
froment n.m. wheat.
  faux froment false oat.
fromental, -aux n.m. false oat.
frotté adj. rubbed.
  frotté de rubbed with.
frotter v.tr. to rub.
  frotter de to rub with.
  frotter d'ail to rub with garlic.
  frotter une allumette to strike
  a match.
frugal, -aux adj. frugal.
fruit n.m. fruit.
  fruit à pain bread-fruit.
  fruits candis crystallized fruit.
  fruits de mer (ensemble of)
  various shellfish.
  fruits frais fresh fruit.
fruitier n.m. fruiterer.
fumage n.m. (the operation of)
  smoking, curing by smoking (e.g.
  meat).
fumaison n.f. (the operation of)
  smoking, curing by smoking (e.g.
  meat).
fumant adj. smoking; steaming.

fumé adj.   smoked, cured by smoking.
fumée n.f.   smoke; fumes; steam.
fumer v.tr.   to smoke.
fumet n.m.   light essence; scent (of food cooking); bouquet (of wine).
 fumet de poisson   light fish-essence.
fusil n.m.   sharpening-steel.

g

gade n.m.   (any) fish of the cod family.
gagner v.tr.   to earn; to win.
gaillet n.m.   cheese-rennet (plant).
gaine n.f.   pouch, sheath (for kitchen-knives).
gainier n.m.   Judas-tree.
gal n.m.   sea-cock (fish).
galanga n.m.   galingale.
galantine n.f.   boned poultry or game bird, stuffed, cooked and pressed, glazed with *chaud-froid* (q.v.) and served cold.
galette n.f.   small round flat cake.
 galette des Rois   twelfth-cake.
 galette feuilletée   puff-pastry *galette*, q.v.
ganga n.m.   pintailed grouse, Pyrenean hazel-hen.
garance n.f.   madder, madder-wort.
garbanzo n.m.   chick pea.
garbure n.f.   rich soup, originating from the Béarn district, and usually containing cabbage, ham, bacon and conserve of goose.
garçon n.m.   boy; waiter.
garde n.f.   guard; relief staff.
 en garde   on guard; on relief duty.
garde-manger n.m.inv.   in pl. larder; cook working in the larder; cold meat-safe.
 chef garde-manger   head larder cook.
garder v.tr.   to keep; to keep back, to keep in reserve; to mind, to look after.
gardon n.m.   roach.
garenne n.f.   rabbit-warren.
 lapin de garenne n.m.   wild rabbit.
 garenne n.m.   wild rabbit.
gargouillette n.f.   goglet, porous container for cooling water.
gargoulette n.f.   goglet, porous container for cooling water.

garni adj.   garnished; decorated.
 bouquet garni n.m.   bunch of herbs, usually of parsley, thyme and bayleaf.
garnir v.tr.   to garnish; to decorate.
 garnir en dôme   to garnish in a dome-shape.
garniture n.f.   garnish.
garrot n.m.   garrot; golden-eye.
gaspillage n.m.   wastage.
gaspillé adj.   wasted.
gaspiller v.tr.   to waste.
gastéropode adj.   gast(e)ropodous. n.m.   gast(e)ropod.
gastrique adj.   gastric.
gastronome n.m.   gastronome(r).
gastronomie n.f.   gastronomy.
gastronomique adj.   gastronomic.
 calendrier gastronomique n.m.   gastronomic calendar.
gatangier n.m.   spotted dogfish.
gâteau, -eaux n.m.   cake; any one of certain types of tart and pudding.
gauche adj.   left, left hand (side); clumsy.
 n.f.   left hand (side).
 à ma gauche   on my left.
gaufre n.f.   waffle.
gaufrette n.f.   wafer biscuit.
 pommes gaufrettes   lattice-perforated potato chips.
gaufreuse n.f.   embossing-block (for pastry).
gaufrier n.m.   waffle-iron.
gave n.f.   crop (of bird).
gaz n.m.   gas.
gazéifié adj.   aerated (liquid).
gazéifier v.tr.   to aerate (liquid).
gazelle n.f.   gazelle.
gélatine n.f.   gelatin(e).
gélatineux, -euse adj.   gelatinous.
gelé adj.   frozen; solidified.
gelée n.f.   jelly.
 gelée d'aspic   aspic jelly.
 gelée de groseille(s)   (red-)currant jelly.
 gelée de pied de veau   calves' foot jelly.
geler v.tr.   to freeze.
 v.i.   to become frozen.
gelinotte n.f.   hazel-grouse, hazel-hen.
gélose n.f.   agar-agar, vegetable gelatine obtained from seaweed.
gendarme n.m.   synonym of *hareng saur*, q.v.
général, -ale, -aux adj.   general.
généralement adv.   generally.

genévrier n.m. juniper(-tree).
   baie de genévrier n.f. juniper-berry.
genièvre n.m. juniper(-berry); gin.
   baie de genièvre n.f. juniper-berry.
génisse n.f. heifer.
génoise n.f. Genoese paste; (any) *entremets* (q.v.) made with Genoese paste.
genou, -oux n.m. knee.
gens n.m.pl., occ.f.pl. people.
   beaucoup de gens a lot of people.
gentiane n.f. gentian; gentian-bitters.
gérant n.m. manager.
gérante n.f. manageress.
germe n.m. germ; eye (of potato); cicatricule, tread (of egg).
   germe d'(un) œuf tread of (an) egg.
germon n.m. albacore.
   germon commun albacore.
gésier n.m. gizzard.
gesse n.f. vetch.
gibelotte n.f. hare or rabbit *fricassée* (q.v.) with red or white wine.
gibier n.m. (wild) game.
   gibier à plume(s) feathered game; "feather".
   gibier à poil furred game; "fur".
   gibier noir black game animal (e.g. boar).
gigot n.m. leg (of lamb, mutton).
   gigot d'agneau leg of lamb.
gigue n.f. haunch (of venison, esp. roebuck).
gingembre n.m. ginger.
   gingembre confit preserved ginger.
giraumon(t) n.m. variety of pumpkin, found in the Antilles.
girelle n.f. rainbow wrasse, small brilliantly-coloured Mediterranean fish used in *bouillabaisse* (q.v.) or fried like whitebait.
girofle n.m. clove.
   un clou de girofle a clove.
giroflée n.f. gillyflower.
girol(l)e n.f. cantharellus mushroom.
gîte n.m. leg of beef, shin of beef.
   gîte à la noix silverside (of beef).
   au gîte (hare, rabbit, trussed and cooked) in a crouching position.
gîte-gîte n.m. leg of beef, shin of beef.

glaçage n.m. (the operation of) icing; (the operation of) glazing.
glace n.f. ice; ice-cream; sugar-icing; glaze; meat-jelly.
   glace broyée broken ice.
   glace panachée mixed ice (-cream).
   sur glace on ice.
glacé adj. iced; glazed.
glacer v.tr. to ice; to glaze.
   glacer vivement to glaze quickly.
glacerie n.f. department of kitchen in which iced *entremets* (q.v.) are prepared.
glacier n.m. *chef de partie* (q.v.) in charge of iced *entremets* (q.v.).
glacière n.f. ice-cave; dredger for icing-sugar.
glaçon n.m. ice-cube.
gland n.m. acorn.
   gland de mer acorn-shell.
   gland de terre earth-nut, pig-nut.
glande n.f. gland.
glisser v.tr. & i. to slide, to slip.
   glisser sur le plat v.tr. to slide onto the dish.
glycérine n.f. glycerin(e), glycerol.
gnoki n.m.pl. (incorrect spelling of) *gnocchi*, q.v.
gobie n.m. goby.
godiveau, -eaux n.m. kidney-suet forcemeat.
   godiveau maigre meatless force-meat.
gombo n.m. gombo, okra.
gomme n.f. gum.
   gomme arabique gum-arabic.
gommé adj. gummed.
gommer v.tr. to gum; to cover with gum.
gommeux, -euse adj. gummy.
gonflé adj. inflated; swollen; puffed (rice).
   riz gonflé n.m. puffed rice.
gonfler v.tr. to inflate; to swell; to puff (rice).
goret n.m. piglet.
gorge n.f. throat; gullet.
   gorge de ris long, thin part of the *ris* (q.v.).
gorgée n.f. mouthful (of liquid); gulp.
   petite gorgée sip.
gosier n.m. gullet; windpipe.
goudale n.f. *garbure* (q.v.) with the addition of red or white wine.
gouet n.m. wild arum, "lords and ladies".

goujon n.m. gudgeon.
  goujon de mer goby.
goulach n.m. goulash.
goulache n.f. goulash.
goulot n.m. neck (of bottle).
gourgane n.f. horse-bean.
gourmand adj. greedy.
  gourmand, gourmande n. gourmand, glutton.
gourmet n.m. gourmet, esp. good judge of wines.
gousse n.f. pod, shuck (of leguminous vegetable).
  gousse d'ail clove of garlic.
  gousse de pois pea-pod.
goût n.m. taste (in all senses); style, mode, manner.
  dans le goût espagnol in the Spanish style.
  au goût adv. phr. to taste.
  assaisonner de haut goût to season highly, strongly.
goûter v.tr. to taste; to taste, to try; to enjoy, to relish.
  v.i. to have a snack.
  n.m. afternoon snack.
goutte n.f. drop (of liquid); gout.
gouttelette n.f. droplet.
goyave n.f. guava.
  confiture de goyave n.f. guava jelly.
grain n.m. grain; corn; bean.
  grain de café coffee-bean.
  grain de poivre peppercorn.
  grain de raisin grape.
  grain d'orge barleycorn.
graine n.f. seed.
  graine d'anis aniseed.
  graine de tomate tomato-pip.
  graines de carvi caraway seeds.
  graines de paradis grains of paradise, Guinea grains.
graisse n.f. grease; fat; cooking-fat; ropiness (of wine).
  graisse à friture frying-fat.
  graisse de bœuf beef dripping; beef fat.
  graisse de porc (hog's) lard.
  graisse de rognon suet.
  graisse de rôti dripping.
  graisse franchement fumante strongly smoking fat.
  graisse légèrement fumante gently smoking fat.
  graisse verte (de la tortue de mer) green fat (of the turtle).
graissé adj. greased, oiled.

graisser v.tr. to grease, to oil.
  v.i. to become ropy (wine).
gramme n.m. gram (unit of weight).
grand adj. large, big; great; tall (person).
granité n.m. water-ice flavoured with liqueur but without Italian meringue.
granulation n.f. granulation.
granule n.m. granule.
granulé adj. granulated.
granuler v.tr. to granulate.
grappe n.f. bunch (e.g. of grapes).
  grappe de raisin bunch of grapes.
  grappe d'oignon string of onions.
gras, grasse adj. fat; fatty; fattened; rich; plump; containing meat or meat derivatives.
  au gras (prepared) with meat or meat derivatives.
  eau grasse n.f. dish-water.
  eaux grasses n.f.pl. swill.
  foie gras n.m. fattened liver.
  matières grasses n.f.pl. fats.
  gras n.m. fat (of meat).
  gras de cuisse top of leg (e.g. of chicken).
gras-double n.m. tripe.
grassement adv. thickly, liberally.
grasset n.m. thin flank (of beef).
grassouillet, -ette adj. plump.
gratin n.m. burnt food adhering to the utensil in which it was cooked; thin crust of breadcrumbs or grated cheese.
  au gratin (covered) with breadcrumbs or grated cheese.
gratinage n.m. gratination.
gratiné adj. gratinated.
gratiner v.tr. to gratinate.
  v.i. to adhere to the bottom and sides of the cooking-utensil.
gratis adv. free of charge, gratis.
gravenche n.f. Swiss lake fish similar to, but smaller than, the dace.
grèbe n.m. grebe.
  (grand) grèbe huppé great(er) crested grebe.
  petit grèbe dabchick, little grebe.
gremille n.f. ruff (fish).
grenade n.f. pomegranate.
grenadin n.m. small larded slice of fillet of veal.
grenadine n.f. grenadine syrup.
grenouille n.f. frog.

cuisses de grenouille n.f.pl. frogs' legs.

grès n.m. stone, stoneware.

pot en grès n.m. stoneware jug.

grésiller v.tr. to shrink, to shrivel (by heat).

v.i. to sizzle.

gressins n.m.pl. Italian grissini.

grianneau, -eaux n.m. young of the black game.

griblette n.f. thin slice of meat wrapped in bacon and grilled or roasted.

gril n.m. grid, grill.

gril à feu dessus grill with overhead heat.

gril double double grill.

grillade n.f. grill, grilled meat.

grillage n.m. (the operation of) grilling; (the operation of) toasting; lattice-pattern, trellis-pattern.

grillagé adj. having the pattern or shape of a lattice or trellis.

grillager v.tr. to shape like a lattice or trellis; to overlay with a lattice- or trellis-pattern.

grillardin n.m. grill-cook.

grille n.f. grating; trellis-pattern.

en grille (arranged) in a trellis-pattern.

grillé adj. grilled, toasted.

grille-pain n.m.inv. in pl. bread-toaster (esp. for toast Melba).

griller v.tr. & i. to grill; to toast.

grilse n.m. grilse.

griotte n.f. morello, bitter cherry.

gris adj. & n.m. grey.

grive n.f. thrush.

grog n.m. punch, toddy.

groin n.m. snout (of pig).

grondin n.m. gurnard, gurnet.

gros, grosse adj. big (in bulk); large; thick; coarse.

gros n.m. bulk; wholesale.

en gros in bulk.

prix de gros n.m. wholesale price.

groseille n.f.

groseille à maquereau (verte) gooseberry.

groseille blanche white-currant.

groseille noire black-currant.

groseille rouge red-currant.

groseille tigrée dessert gooseberry.

groseille verte gooseberry.

grosseur n.f. dimensions, size; thickness.

grosseur doigt, adj. phr. having the thickness of a finger.

grosseur œuf de moineau adj. phr. having the size of a sparrow's egg.

grossier, -ière adj. coarse.

grossièrement adv. coarsely, roughly.

grossièrement haché coarsely chopped.

groupe n.m. group.

grouse n.f. grouse. N.B. This word is merely a borrowing from the English, since the French translation of *grouse* (*lagopède rouge d'Écosse*, q.v.) is too long to figure on the restaurant menu.

gruau, -aux n.m. fine wheat flour; gruel; young crane.

gruau d'avoine oatmeal.

gruau de sarrasin buckwheat flour.

grumeau, -eaux n.m. curd.

grumeaux pl. clots, lumps (caused by careless mixing, e.g. of flour and liquid).

former des grumeaux to curdle.

se mettre en grumeaux to curdle.

gruyère n.m. Gruyère cheese.

gryphée n.f. Portuguese oyster.

guignard n.m. dotterel.

guigne n.f. heart-cherry.

guignette n.f. (another name for) *chevalier*, q.v.; periwinkle, winkle.

guimauve n.f. marsh-mallow (plant).

gurneau, -eaux n.m. (type of) gurnard.

guyave n.f. guava.

confiture de guyave n.f. guava jelly.

h

N.B. All words beginning with aspirate h are marked thus: *

habile adj. adept, skilful.

habileté n.f. ability, skill.

habillage n.m. (complete operation of) preparing for cooking, e.g. drawing and trussing (of poultry), cleaning (of fish), etc.

habillé adj. prepared for cooking, e.g. drawn and trussed (poultry), cleaned (fish), etc.

habiller v.tr. to prepare for cooking, e.g. to draw and truss (poultry), to clean (fish), etc.

habitude n.f. habit, custom.
  d'habitude adv. usually.

*__hachage__ n.m. (operation of) chopping (up), cutting (up).

*__hache__ n.f. hatchet.

*__haché__ adj. chopped (up), cut (up).

*__hache-légumes__ n.m.inv. in pl. vegetable-mincer.

*__hacher__ v.tr. to chop (up), to cut (up).
  hacher grossièrement to chop (up) coarsely.
  hacher menu to chop (up) finely.

*__hache-viande__ n.m.inv. in pl. mincer, mincing-machine.

*__hachis__ n.m. mince.

*__hachoir__ n.m. chopping-knife; mincer; mincing-machine; four-bladed chopper; chopping-board, chopping-block.

*__haddock__ n.m. smoked haddock.

*__halbran__ n.m. young (of the) mallard.

*__halicot de mouton__ n.phr.m. (type of) mutton stew, with turnips, potatoes and onions.

*__halle__ n.f. market, esp. under cover.
  Les Halles centrales the Central Market of Paris.

*__hampe__ n.f. thin flank (of beef).

*__hanche__ n.f. haunch.

*__hareng__ n.m. herring.
  hareng saur (smoked and salted) red herring.

*__harenguet__ n.m. sprat.

*__haricot__ n.m.
  haricot blanc haricot bean.
  haricot de Lima sugar-bean.
  haricot de mouton (incorrect version of) *halicot de mouton*, q.v.
  haricot de Soissons Soissons bean.
  haricot d'Espagne scarlet runner, runner bean.
  haricot noir French nigger bean.
  haricot vert French bean.
  haricots verts panachés French beans mixed with small kidney beans.

*__harle__ n.m. merganser.
  harle huppé hooded merganser.
  harle piette smew.

*__hase__ n.f. doe-hare.

*__hâtelet__ n.m. metal skewer.

*__hâtelette__ n.f. small item, esp. bird, roasted on a metal skewer.

*__hâtelle__ n.f. (variant of) *hâtelette*, q.v.

*__hâtier__ n.m. spit-rack.

*__hâtiveau, -eaux__ n.m. early fruit (esp. early pear); early vegetable (esp. early pea).

*__haut__ adj. high; high-class; higher, upper (reach of river, &c.).
  haut n.m. top part, upper part.
  haute cuisine n.f. high-class cookery.

*__hauteur__ n.f. height.
  à hauteur adv. phr. (container, filled) to the top.

hebdomadaire adj. weekly.

herbe n.f. herb.
  fines herbes mixed herbs.
  herbes à tortue turtle herbs.
  herbes potagères "pot herbs" (orach, spinach, sorrel, &c.).

*__hère__ n.m. young stag.

*__hérissé__ adj. prickly.
  corossol hérissé n.m. sour-sop.

hermétique adj. hermetic.

hermétiquement adv. hermetically.

heure n.f. hour; time.
  l'heure exacte the right time, the correct time.
  heures hors cloche pl. overtime.
  heures supplémentaires pl. overtime.

hier adv. yesterday.

hippophagie n.f. hippophagy, eating of horse-meat.

hirondelle n.f. swallow.

historié adj. decorated, embellished (with figures, motifs, &c.).

historier v.tr. to decorate, to embellish (with figures, motifs, &c.).

hiver n.m. winter.
  artichaut d'hiver n.m. Jerusalem artichoke.
  cerise d'hiver n.f. winter cherry.

*__hocco__ n.m. (type of) curassow, equatorial American bird resembling the turkey.

*__hochepot__ n.m. stew of various meats and vegetables.

holothurie n.f. sea-cucumber.

*__homard__ n.m. lobster.
  homard de Norvège Norway lobster; Dublin Bay prawn.

homme n.m. man.

homogène adj. homogeneous; smooth, uniform.
  pâte homogène n.f. smooth, uniform, paste.

homogénéisé adj. smoothed, rendered uniform.

homogénéiser v.tr. to smooth, to render uniform.

***hors de** prep.phr. outside (of); away from.

hors du feu adv.phr. away from the flame.

hors d'œuvre n.m.inv. in pl. hors d'œuvre(s).

hors d'œuvre chaud(s) hot hors d'œuvre(s).

***hors d'œuvrier** n.m. cook who prepares hors d'œuvre(s).

hôte n.m. host; guest.

table d'hôte n.f. set meal, at fixed price, described on table d'hôte menu.

hôtel n.m. hotel.

hôtelier, -ière n. hotelier; innkeeper.

hôtelier, -ière adj. of, appertaining to, the hotel and catering industry.

hôtesse n.f. hostess.

***hotte** n.f. (woven) basket (esp. made of noodle paste).

***houblon** n.m. hop.

jets de houblon n.m.pl. hop shoots.

***houx** n.m. holly.

***huguenote** n.f. earthenware *marmite* (q.v.) with short legs or no legs.

huile n.f. oil.

huile d'amande almond oil.

huile de cuisine cooking oil.

huile de noix walnut oil.

huile d'olive olive oil.

huile fumante smoking oil.

huilé adj. oiled; dressed with oil.

huiler v.tr. to oil; to dress with oil.

huilier n.m. oil and vinegar cruet.

huîtrier n.m. oyster-catcher (bird).

humecté adj. damped, moistened.

humecter v.tr. to damp, to moist.

humide adj. moist.

huppe n.f. crest (of bird); hoopoe.

***huppé** adj. crested, tufted (bird).

grèbe huppé n.m. crested grebe.

***hure** n.f. head (of boar); jowl (of salmon).

hure de sanglier boar's head.

hure de saumon salmon's jowl.

hydrate n.m. hydrate.

hydrate de carbone carbohydrate.

hygiène n.f. hygiene.

hygiène alimentaire nutrition.

hygiénique adj. hygienic.

hysope n.f. hyssop.

i

icaque n.f. coco-plum.

ichtyocolle n.f. isinglass.

ichtyocolle en cœur leaf isinglass.

ichtyocolle en livre book isinglass.

ichtyocolle en lyre lyre isinglass.

identique adj. identical, identically similar.

igname n.f. yam.

imbibé adj. imbued, impregnated.

imbibé de imbued with, impregnated with.

imbiber de v.tr. to imbue with, to impregnate with.

imbriqué adj. arranged in overlapping pattern (like roof-tiles).

imbriquer v.tr. to arrange in overlapping pattern (like roof-tiles).

imperméable adj. impermeable.

imperméable à l'eau waterproof.

imperméable à la graisse greaseproof.

importance n.f. importance, significance.

important adj. important.

improvisé adj. improvised.

improviser v.tr. to improvise.

impur adj. impure, tainted.

impureté n.f. impurity.

incendie n.m. (accidental) fire, as distinct from *feu*, q.v.

incisé adj. incised.

inciser v.tr. to incise, to make an incision in.

incolore adj. colourless.

incomplet, -ète adj. incomplete.

incomplètement adv. incompletely.

incorporé adj. incorporated.

incorporer v.tr. to incorporate.

incrusté adj. encrusted, incrusted.

incruster v.tr. to encrust, to incrust.

indigène adj. indigenous, native.

indispensable adj. essential, absolutely necessary.

indiqué adj. indicated, pointed out; mentioned.

indiquer v.tr. to indicate, to point out; to mention.
    indiquer du doigt to point to (with the finger).
industrie n.f. industry; industriousness.
    l'industrie hôtelière the hotel and catering industry.
industriel, -elle adj. industrial.
inférieur adj. inferior; lower.
infusé adj. infused.
infuser v.tr. to infuse.
infusion n.f. infusion.
    légère infusion weak infusion.
ingrédient n.m. ingredient, constituent.
inoxydable adj. rustless, stainless.
    acier inoxydable n.m. stainless steel.
instant n.m. moment, instant.
instantané adj. instantaneous.
instantanément adv. instantaneously.
insuffisamment adv. insufficiently.
insuffisance n.f. insufficiency, deficiency; inadequacy.
insuffisant adj. insufficient; inadequate.
intercalé adj. intercalated, interspersed.
intercaler v.tr. to intercalate, to intersperse.
intéressant adj. interesting.
intérieur adj. & n.m. interior, inside.
interne adj. internal.
interstice n.m. interstice.
intestin n.m. intestine.
    gros intestin large intestine.
    intestin grêle small intestine.
introduire v.tr. to introduce, to insert.
inutile adj. useless; pointless; unnecessary.
inventaire n.m. inventory; stocklist; balance-sheet.
invité, -ée n. guest.
isard n.m. wild Pyrenean goat.
isomère adj. isomeric, having identical properties.
issue n.f. offal of butcher's meat.
izard n.m. wild Pyrenean goat.

j

jabot n.m. crop (of bird).
jalousie n.f. (variety of) small puff-pastry cake.

jamais adv. never; ever.
    jamais (used conjunctively) ever.
    ne ... jamais (used conjunctively) never.
jambon n.m. ham.
    jambon fumé smoked ham.
    jambon non fumé unsmoked ham.
    jambon salé cured ham.
jambonneau, -eaux n.m. small ham.
jambonnière n.f. ham-cooker.
jambose n.f. rose-apple.
jamerose n.f. rose-apple.
janvier n.m. January.
jaque n.f. jack-fruit.
jardin n.m. garden.
    jardin potager kitchen garden.
jarret n.m. knuckle.
    jarret de veau knuckle of veal.
jars n.m. gander.
jasmin n.m. jasmine.
jaunâtre adj. yellowish.
jaune adj. & n.m. yellow; yolk.
    jaune d'œuf egg-yolk, yolk of egg.
    un jaune d'œuf an egg-yolk, the yolk of an egg.
jauni adj. turned yellow, yellowed.
jaunir v.i. to turn yellow.
Jean-doré n.m. John Dory.
jet n.m. jet (of liquid, steam); shoot (of plant).
    jets de houblon hop shoots.
jeter v.tr. to throw.
jeudi n.m. Thursday.
joindre v.tr. to join.
jointure n.f. join, joint.
joli adj. pretty.
joubarbe n.f. houseleek, Jupiter's beard, sempervivum.
joue n.f. cheek.
    joue de bœuf ox-cheek.
    joue de veau calf's cheek.
jour n.m. day.
journal, -aux n.m. newspaper; day-book.
journalier, -ière adj. daily; every-day.
    livre journalier n.m. day-book.
journée n.f. day (usually with the idea of duration of time).
juillet n.m. July.
juin n.m. June.
jujube n.f. jujube.
julienne n.f. (ensemble of) fine strips, e.g. of meat, vegetables.
    julienne courte short *julienne*, q.v.
    grosse julienne large, coarse, *julienne*, q.v.

jus n.m. juice.
   jus coloré coloured juice.
   jus de citron lemon-juice.
   jus de limon lime-juice.
   jus d'orange orange-juice.
   jus de réglisse liquorice.
   jus de rôti gravy accompanying roast.
   jus de viande natural meat-juice.
   jus lié thickened meat-gravy (of veal).
jusqu'à prep. until.
   jusqu'à ce que conj. until.
   jusqu'à siccité adv.phr. until completely dry, dried out.
juteux, -euse adj. juicy.

k

kaki n.m. persimmon.
kangourou n.m. kangaroo.
kari n.m. curry.
kebab n.m. Turkish preparation on skewers, basically grilled mutton or lamb.
ketmie n.f. ketmia; gombo, okra.
   ketmie comestible gombo, okra.
kirsch n.m. Kirschwasser.
kola n.m. cola.
   noix de kola n.f. cola-nut.
kummel n.m. Kümmel.

l

labre n.m. wrasse.
lactique adj. lactic.
lagopède n.m. lagopus.
   lagopède alpin ptarmigan.
   lagopède des Alpes ptarmigan.
   lagopède rouge d'Écosse red grouse, moor-fowl.
   lagopède rouge d'Écosse mâle moor-cock.
laisser v.tr. to let; to leave.
   laisser lever v.tr. to allow to rise.
   laisser mijoter v.tr. to allow to simmer (on the side of the stove).
   laisser mitonner v.tr. to allow to simmer (in a closed container in the oven).
   laisser prendre v.tr. to allow to set; to allow to harden.
   laisser prendre couleur v.tr. to allow to colour.
   laisser tomber v.tr. to drop.

laisser tomber à glace v.tr. to allow to glaze.
laisser tomber en pluie v.tr. to rain in (e.g. powder).
lait n.m. milk.
   lait clair whey.
   lait d'amandes infusion of crushed or pounded almonds in milk.
   lait d'âne milk-weed.
   lait de beurre butter milk.
   lait de coco coco-nut milk.
   lait écrémé skim-milk.
   petit lait whey.
laitance n.f. soft roe.
laite n.f. soft roe.
laité adj. soft-roed (fish).
laiteron n.m. milk-weed.
laiteux, -euse adj. milky.
laitue n.f. lettuce.
   laitue pommée cabbage lettuce.
   laitue romaine cos lettuce.
lambeau, -eaux n.m. scrap, shred (e.g. of flesh, skin).
lame n.f. fine slice; blade of knife.
   lame de couteau knife-blade.
   lame de truffe fine slice of truffle.
   couteau à quatre lames n.m. four-bladed cutter.
lamelle n.f. small lame (q.v.).
lamprillon n.m. larval lamprey.
lamproie n.f. lamprey.
   lamproie d'alose river lamprey.
   lamproie de mer sea lamprey.
   lamproie fluviale river lamprey.
   lamproie marine sea lamprey.
lamproyon n.m. larval lamprey.
lançon n.m. sand-eel.
langouste n.f. spiny lobster, craw-fish.
langoustine n.f. Norway lobster; Dublin Bay prawn.
langue n.f. tongue; tongue-shape (esp. of pastry).
   langue de bœuf ox-tongue.
   langue de chat pastry preparation, shaped like a long tongue.
   langue de renne reindeer's tongue.
   langue de veau calf's tongue.
   langue écarlate, langue à l'écarlate tongue coated with brown aspic.
languette n.f. small tongue-shape.
languier n.m. smoked pig's tongue and throat.
lanière n.f. thin strip.

lapereau, -eaux n.m. young rabbit.

lapin n.m. rabbit.
  lapin de clapier tame rabbit.
  lapin de garenne wild rabbit.
  lapin domestique tame rabbit.
  lapin mâle buck rabbit.

lapine n.f. doe of tame rabbit.

larcin n.m. petty theft; act of pilfering.

lard n.m. bacon.
  lard à piquer larding bacon.
  lard maigre streaky bacon.

lardé adj. larded (meat).

larder v.tr. to lard (meat).

lardoire n.f. larding-needle.
  lardoire à manche larding-needle fitted with a handle.

lardon n.m. lardoon, strip of larding bacon.

large adj. broad, wide.

largeur n.f. breadth, width.

larme n.f. "tear", very small quantity of liquid (esp. squeeze of lemon).

lasagna, pl. **lasagne** n.f. pasta preparation consisting of ribbons of noodle-paste.

latent adj. latent.

laurier n.m. laurel; bay.
  feuille de laurier n.f. bayleaf.

lavabo n.m. wash-basin; wash-room; lavatory.

lavage n.m. (operation of) washing.
  lavage à grande eau (operation of) washing in plenty of water; swilling out.

lavandière n.f. wagtail.

lavaret n.m. lavaret.

lavé adj. washed.
  bien lavé washed well.

laver v.tr. to wash.
  laver à grande eau to wash in plenty of water; to swill out.
  laver le plancher à grande eau to swill the floor.
  se laver v.refl. to wash (oneself).
  se laver les mains to wash one's hands.

lavette n.f. dish-cloth; dish-mop; saucepan-brush.

lèche n.f. thin slice (esp. of bread or meat).

lèchefrite n.f. dripping.

léger, -ère adj. light (food, weight); slight; weak (infusion).

légèrement adv. lightly; slightly.

légume n.m. vegetable; leguminous vegetable.
  légumes de (la) marmite pot vegetables.
  légumes secs dried (leguminous) vegetables.
  légumes verts greens.

légumier n.m. vegetable-dish.

légumine n.f. legumin.

lendemain n.m. next day.
  le lendemain adv. phr. on the next day.

lent adj. slow.

lentement adv. slowly.

lentille n.f. lentil.

lésiner v.i. to be close-fisted, stingy (in measuring out ingredients, portions).

letchi n.m. litchi.

levage n.m. (action of) rising (of dough).

levain n.m. leaven.
  levain de bière barm.
  levain léger light ferment.

lever v.tr. to lift, to raise; to remove. v.i. to rise (pastry).
  lever en filets v.tr. to fillet.
  lever les filets de v.tr. to fillet.
  lever les filets d'un poisson to fillet a fish.

levraut n.m. leveret, young hare.

lèvre n.f. lip.

lévulose n.f. laevulose, levulose.

levure n.f. yeast.
  levure artificielle baking-powder.
  levure de bière barm.

liaison n.f. (action of) binding (e.g. sauce); binding, thickening-agent.

libre adj. free, unrestricted; vacant, unoccupied.

lie n.f. lees, dregs.
  lies de vin n.f. lees of wine.

lié adj. bound; tied; bound, coagulated.
  légèrement lié lightly bound (sauce).

liège n.m. cork (material, as distinct from *bouchon*, q.v.).

lier v.tr. to bind; to tie; to bind, to coagulate, to thicken.
  lier légèrement to bind lightly (sauce).

lieu, -eux n.m. place; pollack.
  avoir lieu v.i. to take place.
  en dernier lieu last of all, at the last stage.

en premier lieu   first of all, to begin with.

s'il y a lieu   if there is any call (for it, for them).

lièvre   n.m.   hare.

ligne   n.f.   line.

limaçon   n.m.   (any) snail (as distinct from *escargot*, q.v.).

limaçon de mer   periwinkle, winkle.

limande   n.f.   dab.

lime   n.f.   sweet lime.

limon   n.m.   sour lime.

jus de limon   n.m.   lime-juice.

lin   n.m.   flax.

huile de lin   n.f.   linseed oil.

limoner   v.tr.   to free of outer layer (skin, pellicule, scales, viscous coating) by scalding; to scale (fish) by scalding.

linge   n.m.   linen; cloth.

linge de cuisine   kitchen cloth.

lingue   n.f.   ling.

linot   n.m.   linnet.

linotte   n.f.   linnet; hen-linnet.

liqueur   n.f.   liqueur.

liquide   adj. & n.m.   liquid.

lire   v.tr.   to read.

liséré   adj.   bordered, edged. n.m.   border, edging.

lisérer   v.tr.   to border, to edge.

lisse   adj.   smooth.

lissé   adj.   smoothed.

lisser   v.tr.   to smooth.

lisser au couteau   to smooth with the knife.

lisser des amandes   to sugar almonds.

liste   n.f.   list.

lit   n.m.   bed, layer.

lit d'épinards   bed of spinach.

litchi   n.m.   litchi.

litière   n.f.   "litter", bed (esp. of spinach).

litorne   n.f.   fieldfare.

litre   n.m.   litre (1,000 c.c. or approx. 1·76 pints).

littorine   n.f.   periwinkle, winkle.

livèche   n.f.   lovage.

livre   n.m.   book.

livre journalier   day-book.

livre   n.f.   pound (weight); pound (sterling).

loche   n.f.   loach.

loche de mer   rockling.

loche de rivière   groundling.

loche franche   common loach.

loi   n.f.   law.

long, longue   adj.   long.

longe   n.f.   loin (of pork, veal).

longitudinal, -aux   adj.   lengthwise, longitudinal.

longitudinalement   adv.   lengthwise, longitudinally.

longueur   n.f.   length.

loriot   n.m.   oriole.

lorsque   conj.   when.

losange   n.f.   lozenge-shape.

lotier   n.m.   bird's-foot trefoil.

lotte   n.f.   burbot.

lotte de mer   angler.

lotte de rivière   burbot.

louche   n.f.   ladle, soup-ladle.

loup   n.m.   wolf.

loup de mer   sea-perch.

lourd   adj.   heavy (food, weight).

lumière   n.f.   light.

lundi   n.m.   Monday.

lunette   n.f.   wish-bone (of chicken).

lustré   adj.   glazed; polished.

lustrer   v.tr.   to glaze; to polish.

lut   n.m.   sealing-paste.

luté   adj.   sealed with a sealing-paste.

luter   v.tr.   to seal with a sealing-paste.

luxe   n.m.   luxury.

de luxe   adj. phr.   luxury, luxurious.

luxueux, -euse   adj.   luxurious; sumptuous.

m

macaron   n.m.   macaroon.

macaroni   n.m.pl.   macaroni, pasta preparation in tube-shapes.

macédoine   n.f.   dice of a mixture of vegetables or fresh or conserved fruits.

macération   n.f.   maceration.

macéré   adj.   macerated.

macérer   v.tr.   to macerate.

macérer au rhum   to macerate in rum.

maceron   n.m.

maceron potager   alexanders, horse-parsley.

mâche   n.f.   lamb's lettuce, corn-salad.

machine   n.f.   machine.

machine à beurre   butter-machine.

machine à éplucher les pommes de terre   potato-peeling machine.

machine à hacher   mincer, mincing-machine.

mâchoire n.f. jaw.

macis n.m. mace.

macle n.f. water caltrop(s).

macre n.f. water caltrop(s).

macreuse n.f. scoter, scoter-duck.

madeleine n.f. (type of) light, plain cake.

madère n.m. Madeira (wine).

mai n.m. May.

maigre adj. thin, lean; fatless, lean (meat); meatless (meal); containing no meat or meat derivatives.
  fromage maigre, n.m. skim-milk cheese.
  repas maigre n.m. meatless meal.
  au maigre (prepared) without meat or meat derivatives.
  maigre n.m. lean (of meat); meagre (fish).
  maigre de jambon lean of ham.

main n.f. hand.
  la main droite the right hand.
  la main gauche the left hand.

maintenant adv. now.

mais conj. but.

maïs n.m. maize, Indian corn.
  maïs blanc white corn.
  maïs jaune yellow corn.
  farine de maïs n.f. corn-flour.

maison n.f. house; business, firm.

maître n.m. master.

maître-chef n.m. master chef.
  maître-chef de(s) cuisine(s) head chef (in a large establishment).
  maître d'hôtel head waiter.

majoration n.f. increase (in wages, prices).

mal adv. badly.
  mal, pl. **maux** n.m. hurt, harm.
  se faire mal v.refl. to hurt oneself.

malade adj. ill.

maladie n.f. illness.

malaguette n.f. grains of paradise, malaguetta pepper.

malard n.m. mallard.

malart n.m. mallard.

malaxé adj. kneaded (dough); worked (butter).

malaxer v.tr. to knead (dough); to work (butter).

malgré prep. in spite of.

malvoisie n.m. Malmsey (wine).

manche n.f. sleeve; exposed end of cutlet-bone.

manchette n.f. cutlet-frill.

manchon n.m. muff-shaped confection In flaky pastry and with open ends; muff-shaped *petit four* (q.v.).

mandarine n.f. tangerine.

mandoline n.f. mandolin cutter.

manger v.tr. to eat.
  n.m. food.

mange-tout n.m.inv. in pl. sugar-pea.

mangue n.f. mango.

manié adj. (e.g. butter) softened, worked.
  beurre manié n.m. butter and flour thickening.

maniement n.m. (operation of) softening, working.

manier v.tr. to soften, to work (e.g. butter).

maniguette n.f. grains of paradise, malaguetta pepper.

manioc n.m. manioc, cassava.

manque n.m. lack; shortage.

manqué adj. unsuccessful.

manquer v.i. to lack, to be deficient; to fail.

maquereau, -eaux n.m. mackerel.

marante n.f. maranta, plant from which arrow-root is prepared.

marasquin n.m. maraschino.

marbre n.m. marble.

marbré adj. decorated in imitation of marble, marbled.

marbrée n.f. lamprey.

marbrer v.tr. to decorate in imitation of marble.

marc n.m. marc (of grapes).
  eau-de-vie de marc, eau-de-vie-de-marc n.f. marc-brandy.

marcassin n.m. young wild boar.

marche n.f. step, stair (of staircase, flight of steps).
  Attention à la marche! Mind the step!

marché n.m. market; dealing.
  à bon marché cheap; cheaply.

marcher v.i. to walk; to work, to function (machine).

mardi n.m. Tuesday.
  mardi gras Shrove Tuesday.

maréca n.m. widgeon.

marée n.f. tide; (general term for) fresh sea-water fish (including shell-fish).

marennes n.f. oyster from Marennes (Charente-Maritime).

margarine n.f. margarine.

marinade n.f. marinade; pickle.
  marinade crue raw marinade.
  marinade cuite cooked marinade.

marinage n.m. marinading, marinating; pickling.

mariné adj. marinaded, marinated; pickled.

mariner v.tr. to marinade, to marinate; to pickle.

marjolaine n.f. sweet marjoram.

marmelade n.f. compote; marmalade.

　marmelade de pommes apple puree.

marmite n.f. stock-pot.

　marmite à conserves preserving-pan.

　marmite sous pression pressure cooker.

　petite marmite small earthenware pot in which individual portions of soup are served.

marque n.f. mark; trade mark; brand.

　marque déposée registered trade mark.

　une bonne marque a good make, a good brand.

marqué adj. marked; prepared (for cooking); placed into liquid or onto a base (e.g. of vegetables).

marquer v.tr. to mark; to prepare (for cooking); to place into liquid or onto a base (e.g. of vegetables).

　marquer à l'eau to place into water.

marquise n.f. marquise pear.

marron n.m. large, sweet chestnut having only one large kernel in each husk, the other two being atrophied during growth.

　marron d'Inde horse-chestnut.

　marron glacé chestnut preserved in sugar.

mars n.m. March.

marsala n.m. Marsala (wine).

marteau, -eaux n.m. hammer.

martin-sec, pl. **martins-secs** n.m. (variety of) late-maturing pear.

martin-sire, pl. **martins-sires** n.m. (variety of) yellow pear.

masqué adj. masked, coated.

　masqué de masked with, coated with.

masquer v.tr. to mask, to coat.

　masquer de to mask with, to coat with.

　masquer une cuiller to coat a spoon.

massepain n.m. marzipan.

masser v.tr. to work (substance).

masser à la spatule to work (substance) with a spatula.

massette n.f. bulrush.

mastic n.m. mastic resin.

maté n.m. maté, Paraguayan tea.

matelote n.f. fish stew with red or white wine.

matériel n.m. material, equipment.

　matériel de cuisine kitchen equipment.

matière n.f. material; subject-matter.

　matières grasses fat(ty) content (e.g. of cheese).

　matières premières raw materials.

matignon n.f. base of vegetables, used mainly for braising.

maubèche n.f. sandpiper.

mauvais adj. bad.

mauve n.f. mallow.

mauviette n.f. lark (in season).

mauvis n.m. redwing.

mayonnaise n.f. mayonnaise.

mazagran n.m. (hot or cold) coffee served in a glass.

mazout n.m. fuel oil.

médaillon n.m. medallion; medallion-shape.

meilleur adj. better.

　le meilleur the better (of two); the best.

mélange n.m. mixing; mixture; blend.

　mélange hétéroclite unusual mixture, strange mixture.

mélangé adj. mixed; mixed together; blended.

mélanger v.tr. to mix; to mix together; to blend.

mélasse n.f. molasses, treacle.

　mélasse raffinée golden syrup.

melet n.m. sprat.

melette n.f. sprat.

mélilot n.m. melilot.

méli-mélo, pl. **mélis-mélos** n.m. unusual mixture (esp. of several contrasting elements in a compound salad).

mélisse n.f. balm.

　mélisse officinale lemon-balm.

mellier n.m. third stomach (of ruminant).

melon n.m. melon.

　melon d'eau water-melon.

　melon sucrin sugary melon.

melongène n.f. egg-plant.

membrane n.f. membrane.
membrané adj. webbed (feet, e.g. of duck).
membre n.m. limb.
même adj. same.
adv. even.
ménagère n.f. housewife; housekeeper; cruet-set, cruet.
mendiant n.m. mendicant, esp. mendicant friar.
(**les quatre**) **mendiants** n.m.pl. "the four mendicants", dessert of almonds, hazel-nuts, figs and raisins, representing the colours of the habits worn by the four orders of mendicant friars.
menthe n.f. mint.
menu adj. small, minute.
menus détails n.m.pl. small details.
adv. small, fine(ly).
hacher menu v.tr. to chop finely.
menu n.m. menu.
menu gastronomique gastronomic menu; luxury menu.
menu touristique tourist menu; "economy" menu.
mer n.f. sea.
fruits de mer n.f.pl. (ensemble of) various shell-fish.
mercanette n.f. teal.
merci adv. thanks; thank you; no, thank you.
mercredi n.m. Wednesday.
meringage n.m. (operation of) decorating with meringue; decoration with meringue.
meringue n.f. meringue.
meringué adj. decorated with meringue.
meringuer v.tr. to decorate with meringue.
merise n.f. wild cherry.
mérite n.m. merit, worth.
mériter v.tr. to deserve, to merit.
merlan n.m. whiting.
merlan bleu mackerel.
merlan jaune pollack.
merlan en colère whole whiting, with tail in mouth, dipped in egg and breadcrumb and deep fried.
merle n.m. blackbird.
merluche n.f. hake; dried cod.
merlus n.m. hake; dried cod.
mesure n.f. measure.
mesuré n.f. measured.
mesurer v.tr. to measure.

métal, -aux n.m. metal.
métallique adj. metallic.
métier n.m. trade, craft; craftsmanship.
mets n.m. dish of food; article of food.
mets spécial special dish.
mettre v.tr. to put.
mettre à point to adjust (e.g. consistency).
mettre à point de consistance to adjust for consistency.
mettre au point to adjust.
mettre de côté to put aside, to put to one side.
mettre en bocal to bottle (fruit).
meuble n.m. item of furniture.
meublé adj. furnished (room, etc.).
meubler v.tr. to furnish (room, etc.).
meule n.f. millstone; millstone-shape (esp. of cheese).
meule de fromage round (of) cheese.
meunier n.m. chub.
meurette n.f. Burgundy version of *matelote* (q.v.).
miche n.f. cob (of bread).
microbe n.m. microbe.
midi n.m. midday, noon.
mie n.f. crumb (as distinct from crust).
mie de pain breadcrumb(s).
mie de pain bis brown breadcrumb(s).
mie de pain rassis stale breadcrumbs, crumbs from stale bread.
miel n.m. honey.
miette n.f. crumb (of crumbed bread.)
mieux adv. better.
le mieux adv.phr. (the) best.
mignon, -onne adj. small; delicate.
bouchée mignonne very small *bouchée* (q.v.).
filet mignon tenderloin.
mignonnette n.f. mignonette pepper, coarse-ground pepper.
mi-hauteur n.f. half-height.
à mi-hauteur adv.phr. (container, filled) halfway.
mijoté adj. simmered (on the side of the stove).
mijoter v.tr. & i. to simmer (on the side of the stove).
faire mijoter v.tr. to simmer (on the side of the stove).

laisser mijoter v.tr. to allow to simmer (on the side of the stove).

milandre n.m. dogfish.

milieu, -eux n.m. middle.

mille n.m.inv. & adj.inv. thousand.

millefeuille (or **mille-feuille**) n.f. milfoil, yarrow.

milouin n.m. pochard.

minéral, -aux adj. & n.m. mineral.
   eau minérale mineral water.

minuscule adj. tiny, very small.

minute n.f. minute.

minutieux, -euse adj. careful, thorough.

mirabelle n.f. mirabelle plum.

mirepoix n. usually f., occ. m. large dice of vegetables.
   mirepoix d'appui supporting *mirepoix* (q.v.).

miroir n.m. mirror.

miroité adj. glazed (esp. to produce reflection).

miroitement n.m. glazing (esp. to produce reflection).

miroiter v.tr. to glaze (esp. to produce reflection).

miroton n.m. stew of left-overs of beef, flavoured with onions.

mis adj. put, placed.
   mis de côté put aside, put to one side.

mise n.f. (action of) putting, placing.
   mise à point, mise au point adjustment (of consistency, etc.).
   mise à point de consistance, mise au point de consistance adjustment of consistency.
   mise en place mise en place, (ensemble of) advance preparations for cooking.

mitonné adj. simmered (in a closed container in the oven).

mitonner v.tr. & i. to simmer (in a closed container in the oven).
   faire mitonner v.tr. to simmer (in a closed container in the oven).
   laisser mitonner v.tr. to allow to simmer (in a closed container in the oven).

moderne adj. modern.

moelle n.f. bone-marrow.
   à la moelle (garnished) with bone-marrow.
   moelle allongée medulla oblongata.
   moelle épinière spinal cord, medulla spinalis; spinal marrow.

moelleux, -euse adj. marrowy (esp. bone).

moignon n.m. stump (esp. of chicken-wing).

moins adv. less.
   prep. minus, less.
   au moins adv. at least (in quantity).
   du moins adv. at least, at any rate, at all events.
   le moins adv. least, the least.
   moins de less (of).
   moins de farine less flour.
   moins de (followed by numeral) less than.
   moins de deux litres less than two litres.
   moins que prep. less than.
   moins que nous less than us.

mois n.m. month.

moitié n.f. half.
   à moitié adv. phr. half.
   à moitié vide half empty.

mollet, -ette adj. fairly soft.
   œuf mollet n.m. fairly soft-boiled egg.

moment n.m. moment, instant.
   au dernier moment at the last minute.

mondé adj. skinned (almonds, tomatoes) by blanching.

monder v.tr. to skin (almonds, tomatoes) by blanching.

monté adj. worked up; brought up (e.g. from cellar).
   monté au beurre worked up with butter.
   monté au fouet worked up with a whisk.
   pièce montée n.f. built-up preparation, esp. of pastry and sugar.

monte-charge n.m.inv. in pl. service-lift, goods-lift.

monte-plats n.m.inv. in pl. plate-hoist.

monter v.tr. to work up; to bring up (e.g. from cellar).
   monter au beurre v.tr. to work up with butter.
   monter au fouet v.tr. to work up, to bring up, with a whisk.
   monter du vin to bring up (some) wine (from the cellar).

montmorency n.f. (variety of) cherry with sharp flavour.

montre n.f. watch.
   montre de poignet wrist-watch.

montrer v.tr. to show; to display.

morceau, -eaux n.m. piece, bit, fragment; lump (of sugar).
  bas morceaux pl. inferior cuts (of meat).
  morceau de céleri stick of celery.
  sucre en morceaux n.m. lump sugar.

morille n.f. morel.

morillon n.m. morillon, variety of black grape; tufted duck.

mornay n.f. Mornay sauce.

mort adj. dead. n.f. death.

mortadelle n.f. mortadella.

mortier n.m. mortar.

mortifié adj. tenderized by hanging (meat); hung (game).

mortifier v.tr. to tenderize (meat) by hanging; to hang (game).

morue n.f. (general word for) cod, as distinct from *cabillaud*, q.v.; salt cod.
  morue fraîche fresh cod.
  morue franche fresh cod.
  morue verte (salée) salt cod.

mosaïque n.f. mosaic, mosaic-pattern.

mot n.m. word.

motelle n.f. rockling.

motolaveur n.m. washing-up machine.

motteux n.m. wheatear, white-tail.

motton n.m. lump (esp. in porridge).

mou, molle adj. soft (to the touch).
  fromage mou soft cheese.
  mou n.m. lights, lungs (of offal).

moudre v.tr. to grind, to mill.

mouillage n.m. (operation of) moistening.
  mouillage à blanc moistening with white stock.

mouillé adj. moistened.

mouillement n.m. moistening (liquid).
  court mouillement short, shallow, moistening.

mouiller v.tr. to moisten.

mouillette n.f. finger of bread (esp. for dipping into soft-boiled egg).

moule n.f. mussel. n.m. mould.
  moule à baba baba-mould.
  moule à bordure uni smooth mould.

moule à brioche brioche-mould.

moule à charlotte charlotte-mould.

moule à charnière hinged mould.

mould à colonne column-mould.

moule à couronne turban-mould.

moule à dariole dariole-mould.

moule à dôme dome-mould.

moule à douille piping-tube.

moule à fromage cheese-tub.

moule à griffe hinged mould.

moule à madeleine madeleine-mould.

moule annulaire annulus-shaped mould.

moule à parfait parfait-mould.

moule à pâté pie-mould.

moule cannelé channelled mould, grooved mould.

moule hexagonal hexagonal, six-sided, mould.

moule madeleine madeleine-mould.

moule madeleine à griffe hinged madeleine-mould.

moule uni smooth mould.

moulé adj. moulded.

mouler v.tr. to mould.

moulin n.m. mill.
  moulin à café coffee-mill.
  moulin à poivre pepper-mill.

moulu adj. ground, milled.
  fraîchement moulu freshly ground, freshly milled.

mourir v.i. to die.

moussache n.f. manioc flour.

mousse n.f. (any) very light made-up preparation into which air has been incorporated; froth, foam.
  mousse du Japon agar, agar-agar.

mousseau, -eaux n.m. finest wheaten bread.
  pain mousseau finest wheaten bread; loaf of finest wheaten bread.

mousseline n.f. lighter version of *mousse* (q.v.) incorporating whipped cream.

mousseron n.m. small edible mushroom.

mousseux, -euse adj. frothy, foamy; sparkling (wine).

moussoir n.m. whisk.

moussot n.m. finest wheaten bread.
  pain moussot finest wheaten bread; loaf of finest wheaten bread.

moût n.m. must (of grapes).

moutarde n.f. mustard.
  moutarde allemande German mustard.
  moutarde anglaise English mustard.
  moutarde blanche white mustard.
  moutarde blanche et cresson alénois mustard and cress.
  moutarde d'estragon tarragon mustard.
  moutarde ordinaire ordinary (i.e. French) mustard.
moutardé adj. flavoured with mustard.
moutardelle n.f. (variety of) horse-radish.
moutarder v.tr. to flavour with mustard.
moutardier n.m. mustard-pot.
mouton n.m. mutton.
mouture n.f. (operation of) grinding, milling.
mouvette n.f. wooden spoon stirrer.
moyen, -enne adj. middle; medium; average.
  moyen n.m. means.
  au moyen de prep.phr. by means of.
  moyenne n.f. average.
moyeu, -eux n.m. (old name for) egg-yolk, yolk of egg.
mucilagineux, -euse adj. mucilaginous, viscous.
mufle n.m. (forward part of) muzzle (e.g. of ox).
  mufle de bœuf muzzle of ox.
muge n.m. mullet.
  muge à grosse tête striped mullet.
  muge capitan, muge capiton grey mullet.
mulet n.m. grey mullet.
  mulet de mer striped mullet.
mulle n.m. mullet.
  mulle barbu red mullet.
mur n.m. wall.
mûr adj. ripe; mature.
mûre n.f. (strictly) mulberry; (loosely) blackberry.
  mûre de ronce blackberry.
  mûre sauvage blackberry.
murène n.f. black conger.
muriqué adj. muricate.
  anone muriquée n.f. muricate anona, reticulate anona, West Indian custard-apple, sour-sop.

muscade n.f. nutmeg.
  fleur de muscade n.f. mace.
  noix muscade n.f. nutmeg.
muscadelle n.f. winter musk-pear.
muscat n.m. muscat; musk-pear.
muscle n.m. muscle.
musculaire adj. muscular.
museau, -eaux n.m. muzzle, snout.
  museau de bœuf muzzle of ox.
myrte n.m. myrtle.
myrtille n.f. bilberry.

n

à la nage adj.phr. or adv.phr. (esp. crustaceans, sent up for service) in the *court-bouillon* (q.v.) in which they were cooked.
nageoire n.f. fin (of fish); flipper (of turtle).
  nageoire de tortue turtle-flipper.
nantais adj. of, from, Nantes (Loire-Atlantique).
  canard nantais see under *canard*.
napiforme adj. napiform, turnip-rooted.
nappe n.f. table-cloth; coating.
nappé adj. coated.
  nappé de coated with.
napper v.tr. to coat.
  napper de to coat with.
napperon n.m. tray-cloth; slip-cloth; tea-cloth.
natatoire adj. natatory.
  vessie natatoire n.f. swimming-bladder (of fish).
nard n.m. spikenard.
national, -aux adj. national.
natte n.f. plait-shape, esp. as applied to a plait-shaped long loaf.
nature n.f. nature.
  adj. inv. plain.
  pommes nature plain-boiled potatoes.
naturel, -elle adj. natural.
  au naturel adj.phr. & adv.phr. (e.g. liver) cooked plain (i.e. without being passed through flour).
navet n.m. turnip.
  navet de Suède swede.
  navet jaune swede.
  navet suédois swede.
nécessaire adj. necessary.
  s'il est necessaire if necessary.
nectar n.m. nectar.

nectarine n.f. nectarine, free-stone peach with a thin, downless skin.

nèfle n.f. medlar.

    nèfle d'Amérique sapodilla, sapodilla plum, naseberry.

    nèfle du Japon loquat.

négociant, -ante n. dealer, trader; (wholesale) merchant.

neige n.f. snow; (any) substance or preparation resembling snow.

    neige carbonique dry ice.

    battre en neige to beat stiffly (egg-white) to a fluffy consistency.

nerf n.m. nerve; sinew.

    nerf dorsal dorsal nerve.

néroli n.m. neroli, volatile oil extracted from orange-blossom.

nervure n.f. sinew, tendon.

net, nette adj. clean; pure, un-adulterated; net (weight).

    poids net n.m. net weight.

nettoyage n.m. cleaning.

    nettoyage à sec dry cleaning.

nettoyé adj. cleaned.

    nettoyé à sec dry cleaned.

nettoyer v.tr. to clean.

    nettoyer à sec to dry clean.

neuf, neuve adj. new; unused; mint.

neutre adj. neuter; neutral.

nid n.m. nest; nest-shape.

    nid d'hirondelle swallow's nest

    nid en pommes pailles nest of straw potatoes.

nigelle n.f. nigella, fennel-flower.

nitrate n.m. nitrate.

    nitrate de potasse potassium nitrate.

niverolle n.f. snow finch.

noce n.f. wedding.

    repas de noces n.m. wedding breakfast; (in France) wedding feast (formerly of up to three days' duration).

Noël n.m. Christmas.

    bûche de Noël n.f. yule log.

nœud n.m. knot.

noir adj. black.

noirâtre adj. blackish.

noirci adj. blackened.

noircir v.tr. to blacken.

noisette n.f. hazel-nut.

    beurre noisette n.m. nut-brown butter.

    beurre de noisette hazel-nut butter.

    pommes noisettes potatoes of the shape and size of hazel-nuts.

noix n.f. walnut; nut; cushion (e.g. of veal).

    noix d'acajou cashew-nut.

    noix de coco coco-nut.

    noix de gigot pope's eye (lymphatic gland in leg) of mutton.

    noix de ris round part of the *ris*, q.v.

    noix de terre earth-nut, pig-nut.

    noix de veau cushion of veal.

    noix du Brésil Brazil nut.

    noix muscade nutmeg.

nom n.m. name.

    nom déposé registered trade name.

    du nom adj.phr. of the (same) name.

nombre n.m. number (as distinct from *numéro*, q.v.); number (plural quantity).

    nombre pair even number.

    nombre impair odd number.

nombreux, -euse adj. numerous.

    peu nombreux few.

nommé adj. named, designated.

nommer v.tr. to name; to name, to designate.

non adv. no; not.

nonat n.m. small Mediterranean fish (of apparently indeterminate species) usually fried like whitebait.

nonpareille n.f. "hundreds and thousands".

note n.f. note; bank-note; notice; bill, account.

noté adj. noted.

noter v.tr. to note.

noué adj. knotted.

nouer v.tr. to knot.

nouet n.m. bag for infusions, e.g. of tea, herbs.

nougat n.m. nougat.

nouilles n.f.pl. noodles.

nouillettes n.f.pl. small noodles.

nourriture n.f. food, nourishment.

nouveau, -el (before masc. nouns beginning with a vowel or an un-aspirated h) **-elle**, pl. **-eaux**, **-elles**, adj. new; new, fresh (e.g. new season's vegetables); fresh, further, additional (e.g. supplies).

nouveauté n.f. newness; novelty, innovation.

novembre n.m. November.

noyau, -aux n.m. nut; kernel.

numéro n.m. (cardinal) number.

nutritif, -ive adj. nutritive, nourishing.

nymphe n.f. (fanciful name for) edible frog.

O

obtenir v.tr. to obtain, to get.
obtenu adj. obtained, got.
obturé adj. sealed, stopped (aperture).
obturer v.tr. to seal, to stop (aperture).
occupé adj. occupied, taken up (space); busy, engaged (person).
occuper v.tr. to occupy, to take up (space); to engage, to busy (person).
  s'occuper de to busy oneself with, to take care of.
octobre n.m. October.
odeur n.f. smell, odour; scent.
odorat n.m. sense of smell.
œdicnème n.m. great plover.
œil, pl. **yeux** n.m. eye.
œillette n.f. oil-poppy.
  huile d'œillette n.f. poppy-seed oil.
œuf n.m. egg.
  œuf à coque soft-boiled egg.
  œuf à la neige snow egg.
  œuf à la poêle English fried egg.
  œuf de poule hen's egg, chicken's egg.
  œuf du jour new-laid egg.
  œuf dur hard-boiled egg.
  œuf en cocotte moulded egg baked in a fire-proof dish.
  œuf frais new-laid egg.
  œuf frit egg fried on both sides.
  œuf frit (à la) française egg fried in oil.
  œuf mollet fairly soft-boiled egg.
  œufe moulé moulded egg.
  œuf poché poached egg.
  œuf poêlé English fried egg.
  œuf sur le plat egg baked in the oven in an eared dish.
  œufs brouillés scrambled eggs.
  œufs de poisson hard roe of fish.
  œufs en poudre dehydrated egg(s).
  œufs filés beaten eggs poured in a thin trickle through a *chinois* (q.v.) into boiling liquid (e.g. *consommé*, q.v.).
œufrier n.m. egg-holder (usually made of wire) for boiling eggs.
œuvé adj. hard-roed (fish); berried (lobster).

office n.f. still-room.
  papier d'office n.m. dish-paper.
offre n.f. offer.
  offre d'emploi offer of employment.
  "offres d'emploi" "situations vacant".
offrir v.tr. to offer.
ognon n.m. (alternative spelling of *oignon*, q.v.
ognonnade n.f. (variety of) onion stew.
oie n.f. goose.
  oie sauvage wild goose.
oignon n.m. onion.
  oignon d'Espagne Spanish onion.
oignonade n.f. (variety of) onion stew.
oiseau, -eaux n.m. bird.
oisillon n.m. fledgling.
oison n.m. gosling.
okra n.m. okra, gombo.
oléomargarine n.f. oleomargarine, margarine.
olive n.f. olive.
  olive dénoyautée stoned olive.
  olive noire black olive.
  olive picholine large green olive.
  olive verte green olive.
  en olive (shaped) like an olive.
  tourner en olive v.tr. to shape like an olive.
omble n.m. char.
  omble chevalier char.
ombre n.m. grayling, umber.
  ombre chevalier (incorrect spelling of) *omble chevalier*, q.v.
  ombre commun grayling, umber.
  ombre de mer umbrina.
  ombre de rivière grayling, umber.
ombrine n.f. umbrina.
omelette n.f. omelette, omelet.
  omelette au naturel plain omelette.
  omelette au sucre sweet omelette.
  omelette baveuse moist omelette.
  omelette d'entremets sweet omelette.
  omelette fourrée filled omelette.
  omelette garnie garnished omelette.
  omelette nature plain omelette.
  omelette ovale oval omelette.
  omelette plate flat omelette.
omettre v.tr. to omit, to leave out.

ongle n.m. nail (of finger, paw, trotter).
  ongle de pied de porc nail of pig's trotter.
opacité n.f. opacity.
opaque adj. opaque.
opération n.f. operation.
ophidie n.f. ophidium.
or conj. now.
  n.m. gold.
orange n.f. orange.
  orange navel navel-orange.
  orange sanguine blood orange.
orangeat n.m. candied orange-peel.
ordinaire adj. ordinary; customary, usual.
ordonner v.tr. to set in order (establishment).
  v.i. to order, to command.
  ordonner à quelqu'un de faire quelque chose to order someone to do something.
ordre n.m. order, command; order, sequence; (good) order, discipline.
oreille n.f. ear.
  oreille de veau calf's ear.
orge n.f.occ.m. barley.
  grain d'orge n.m. barleycorn.
  orge mondé n.m. hulled barley.
  orge perlé n.m. pearl-barley.
orgeat n.m. orgeat syrup.
orifice n.m. aperture, orifice.
origan n.m. wild marjoram.
origine n.f. origin, source.
ormeau, -eaux n.m. ormer, haliotis.
orné adj. decorated, embellished.
  orné de decorated with, embellished with.
orner v.tr. to decorate, to embellish.
  orner de to decorate with, to embellish with.
orphie n.f. gar, garfish.
ortie n.f. nettle.
  ortie de mer sea-anemone.
ortolan n.m. ortolan bunting.
orvale n.f. clary.
os n.m. bone.
  os à moelle marrow-bone.
  os de jambon ham-bone.
oseille n.f. sorrel.
osier n.m. osier.
  panier d'osier n.m. wicker-basket.
ôter v.tr. to take off (esp. garment); to remove.

ou conj. or.
  ou bien adv.phr. or else.
où adv. where.
  où? adv. where?
oublie n.f. (usually cornet-shaped) rolled wafer.
oublié adj. forgotten; left behind.
oublier v.tr. to forget; to leave out.
oui adv. yes.
  oui, merci yes, thank you.
ouïes n.f.pl. gills (of fish).
ours n.m. bear.
  cerise d'ours n.f. bearberry.
  raisin d'ours n.m. bearberry.
oursin n.m. sea-urchin.
outarde n.f. bustard.
  grande outarde great(er) bustard.
  petite outarde field-duck, little bustard.
outardeau, -eaux n.m. young bustard.
en outre adv.phr. besides, moreover.
ouvert adj. open; opened.
ouverture n.f. opening; aperture.
  heures d'ouverture n.f.pl. opening-hours.
ouvre-boîtes n.m.inv. in pl. tin-opener.
ouvre-bouteilles n.m.inv. in pl. bottle-opener.
ouvre-caisses n.m.inv. in pl. case-opener.
ouvre-huîtres n.m.inv. in pl. oyster-knife.
ouvrir v.tr. & i. to open.
  s'ouvrir v.refl. to open.
  faire s'ouvrir v.tr. to (cause to) open (e.g. bivalve molluscs, esp. by boiling).
ovale adj. & n.m. oval.
ovoïde adj. ovoid, egg-shaped.
oxalide n.f. wood-sorrel.
oxalis n.f. wood-sorrel.

p

pacane n.f. pecan, pecan-nut.
page n.f. page (of book).
pagel n.m. sea-bream.
pagelle n.f. sea-bream.
pagure n.f. hermit-crab.
paille n.f. straw.
  paille au parmesan cheese straw.
paillette n.f. straw; small straw.

paillette d'or cheese straw.
paillette dorée cheese straw.
paillon n.m. straw case (esp. of Chianti bottle).
pain n.m. bread; loaf.
  pain bis brown bread.
  pain blanc white bread.
  pain boulot round loaf.
  pain complet wholemeal loaf.
  pain d'épices gingerbread.
  pain d'épinards spinach loaf.
  pain de flûte bread from a long thin loaf.
  pain de froment wheaten bread.
  pain de ménage household bread.
  pain de sarrasin buckwheat bread.
  pain de savon cake of soap.
  pain de seigle rye bread.
  pain de son brown bread.
  pain échaudé canary bread.
  pain frais fresh bread.
  pain grillé toast.
  pain noir black bread.
  pain perdu sweet, flavoured, made-up preparation based on left-overs of stale bread.
  pain rassis stale bread.
  pain rond round loaf.
  petit pain bread roll.
  mie de pain n.f. breadcrumb(s).
  mie de pain rassis stale bread-crumbs, crumbs from stale bread.
paire n.f. pair; brace (esp. of birds).
  une paire de faisans a brace of pheasants.
palais n.m. palate.
  palais de bœuf ox-cheek.
  palais fin delicate palate.
pâle adj. pale.
paleron n.m. chuck, chuck steak.
  paleron de bœuf chuck of beef.
palet n.m. quoit, quoit-shape.
  palets de dames (variety of) small quoit-shaped *petits fours*, q.v.
palette n.f. palette.
palmier n.m. palm-tree.
  beurre de palmier n.m. palm-butter.
  huile de palmier n.f. palm-oil.
palmiste n.m. palm-cabbage.
palombe n.f. ring-dove, ring-pigeon, wood-pigeon.
palourde n.f. (any) one of a group of small bivalve mulluscs, e.g. cockle, venus, clam.

pamplemousse n.m. or f. grape-fruit; pompelmoose, shaddock.
panache n.m. variegation (of colour).
panaché adj. variegated; mixed.
  bière panachée n.f. shandy.
  glace panachée n.f. mixed ice (-cream).
  panaché n.m. shandy.
  salade panachée n.f. mixed salad.
panachée n.f. mixture variegated in colour.
panacher v.tr. to variegate; to mix.
panade n.f. panada.
  panade pâtissière pastry panada.
panais n.m. parsnip.
pancréas n.m. pancreas.
pancréatique adj. pancreatic.
pané adj. breadcrumbed.
paner v.tr. to breadcrumb.
panic n.m. panic-grass.
  panic d'Italie Italian millet.
panier n.m. basket.
  panier à friture frying-basket.
  panier à salade wire salad-washer.
  panier d'osier wicker-basket.
  panier en pommes de terre potato basket.
  panier en sucre tiré pulled sugar basket.
panne n.f. lard.
panse n.f. belly (of beef); first stomach (of ruminant).
pantalon n.m. (pair of) trousers.
panure n.f. coating of bread-crumbs.
papaye n.f. papaw, pawpaw.
papier n.m. paper.
  papier beurre greaseproof paper.
  papier beurré buttered paper.
  papier dentelle lace paper.
  papier d'étain tin-foil.
  papier d'office dish-paper.
  papier huilé greased paper.
  papier imperméable à la graisse greaseproof paper.
  papier parcheminé greaseproof paper.
  papier sulfurisé butter paper.
papillotage n.m. (operation of) coating *en papillote*, q.v.
papillote n.f. buttered paper (in which meat or fish is cooked); pre-paration so cooked; cutlet-frill or similar decoration.

en papillote (cooked) in buttered paper.

paprika n.m. Hungarian pepper, paprika.

Pâques n.m. Easter.

paraffine n.f. paraffin.

parcelle n.f. small piece, small portion.

  parcelle de beurre small piece of butter.

paré adj. dressed, trimmed; pared; adorned, embellished.

pareil, -eille adj. like, similar.

parer v.tr. to dress, to trim; to pare; to adorn, to embellish.

parfait adj. perfect. n.m. flavoured ice-cream preparation.

parfum n.m. perfume; fragrance; bouquet (of wine); flavour (of ice-cream).

parfumé adj. perfumed; flavoured.

parler v.i. to speak, to talk.

parmesan n.m. Parmesan cheese.

parmi prep. among, amid.

paroi n.f. wall (e.g. of stomach).

parole n.f. word; remark; pledge, promise.

parr n.m. parr, young salmon before the smolt stage.

parsemé adj. sprinkled.

  parsemé de sprinkled with.

parsement n.m. sprinkling.

parsemer v.tr. to sprinkle.

  parsemer de to sprinkle with.

part n.f. part, share.

  à part apart, separately.

  servir à part v.tr. to serve apart, separately.

partagé adj. shared, shared out.

partager v.tr. to share, to share out.

partie n.f. part; section; "corner" (of kitchen).

  chef de partie head of a section in the kitchen.

  parties égales equal parts.

  en parties égales in equal parts; into equal parts.

partir v.i. to leave, to depart.

  faire partir v.tr. to start off (cooking); to bring to the boil.

partout adv. everywhere.

parures n.f.pl. scrapings, parings, trimmings.

  parures de champignons mushroom trimmings.

passé adj. passed, strained.

passe-bouillon n.m.inv. in pl. soup-strainer.

passe-lait n.m.inv. in pl. milk-strainer.

passe-purée n.m.inv. in pl. potato-masher.

passer v.tr. to pass, to strain.

  passer à la pression to pass with pressure.

  passer à la serviette to pass through a cloth.

  passer à l'étamine to pass through a cloth strainer.

  passer avec pression to pass with pressure.

  passer en foulant to pass with downward pressure.

  passer en pressant to pass with pressure.

passiflore n.f. passion-flower.

passoire n.f. sieve, strainer; colander.

  passoire à gros trous coarse sieve, coarse strainer.

  passoire à légumes colander.

  passoire à sucre sugar-sifter.

  passoire fine fine sieve, fine strainer.

pastèque n.f. water-melon.

pasteurisation n.f. pasteurization.

pasteurisé adj. pasteurized, sterilized.

pasteuriser v.tr. to pasteurize, to sterilize.

pastille n.f. pastille.

patate n.f. sweet potato; (familiar name for) potato.

  patate douce sweet potato.

pâte n.f. paste.

  pâte à beignets fritter-paste.

  pâte à brioche paste for making *brioches*, q.v.

  pâte à chou cream-bun paste.

  pâte à crêpes pancake-paste.

  pâte à foncer lining-paste.

  pâte à frire batter.

  pâte à l'eau water-paste.

  pâte alimentaire (any) pasta preparation, e.g. ravioli, spaghetti.

  pâte à l'œuf egg-wash.

  pâte à nouilles noodle-paste.

  pâte à pain dough.

  pâte à pâté pie-paste.

  pâte brisée short paste.

  pâte de guimauve marshmallow paste.

  pâte demi-feuilletée half-puff-paste.

pâte feuilletée puff-paste.

pâte homogène smooth paste, uniform paste.

pâte levée raised paste.

pâté lisse batter.

pâte non sucré unsweetened paste.

pâtes d'Italie Italian pasta preparations.

pâte sucrée sweet paste.

pâté n.m. pie.

pâté chaud hot pie.

pâté chaud de gibier hot game-pie.

pâté d'anguille eel-pie.

pâté d'entremets fruit pie.

pâté de foie gras (potted) paste made from the livers of fattened geese.

pâté froid cold pie.

patelle n.f. patella, (any) one of a group of univalve molluscs including barnacles and limpets.

pâtisserie n.f. pastry; pastry-work; pastry department.

pâtissier n.m. pastry-cook.

pâtisson n.m. squash-melon.

patron, -onne n. employer; proprietor, proprietress; boss.

patronnet n.m. young apprentice pastry-cook.

patte n.f. leg (of animal, esp. small game); leg of game bird.

patte de derrière hind leg.

patte de devant foreleg.

paupiette n.f. rolled fillet of fish, esp. of sole; rolled, stuffed slice of meat in the shape of a large cork; (any) preparation so shaped.

pavé n.m. (literally) paving-stone, (any) *chaudfroid* (q.v.), *entremets* (q.v.), &c., which is square or rectangular in finished form.

pavé d'entremets sweetmeat in the shape of a *pavé*, q.v.

pavie n.f. (variety of) clingstone peach.

pavot n.m. poppy.

huile de pavot n.f. poppy-oil.

payer v.tr. & i. to pay; to pay for.

peau n.f. skin.

peau à saucisse(s) sausage-skin.

peau de tête de veau skin of calf's head.

pec adj. found only in the phrase *hareng pec* n.m. freshly salted and barrelled unsmoked herring.

pêche n.f. peach.

pectine n.f. pectin.

pédoncule n.m. stalk, stem.

peigne n.m. pecten.

peigne commun scollop; scollop-shell.

pelé adj. peeled.

pelé à vif peeled raw.

pèle-fruits n.m.inv. in pl. fruit-knife.

peler v.tr. to peel.

peler à vif to peel raw.

pelle n.f. shovel; scoop; spatula-shaped spoon.

pelle à fromage cheese-scoop.

pelle à moutarde spatula-shaped mustard-spoon.

pelle à sel spatula-shaped salt-spoon.

pellicule n.f. skin (e.g. of grape, or on boiled milk).

pellicule rouge (des pistaches) red skin (of pistachioes).

peluches n.f.pl. leaves (e.g. of chervil, parsley).

pelure n.f. peel, skin.

pelures pl. peelings.

pelure d'oignon onion-skin.

pendant prep. during.

pendant la cuisson during (the) cooking.

pendant que conj. while.

pendre v.tr. & i. to hang.

pendu adj. hung; (game) well hung.

pendule n.f. clock.

peptique adj. peptic.

percé adj. pierced, holed.

percé de vers worm-eaten.

percer v.tr. to pierce.

perche n.f. perch.

perche commune bass.

perche de mer sea-perch, Norway haddock, bergylt.

perche de rivière bass.

perche goujonnière ruff.

perche noire bass.

perche soleil sun-fish.

perche-truite n.f. bass.

percolateur n.m. percolator.

perdreau, -eaux n.m. young partridge; (on menu) partridge.

perdrix n.f. partridge.

perdrix de neige ptarmigan.

perle n.f. pearl.

perles du Japon "pearls" made from manioc-paste.

perle noire black truffle.

perlé adj. beaded; pearl-like.
  orge perlé n.m. pearl barley.
perlot n.m. (variety of) small oyster.
persicot n.m. persico(t), liqueur made with brandy, peach kernels, sugar, etc.
persil n.m. parsley.
  persil en branches leaf parsley, picked parsley.
persillade n.f. (any) sauce preparation containing a large quantity of parsley.
persillé adj. sprinkled with chopped parsley; marbled (meat).
persiller v.tr. to sprinkle with chopped parsley.
personne n.f. person.
  n.m.inv. anyone, anybody.
  ne . . . personne (used conjunctively) nobody, no one.
  personne (used disjunctively) nobody, no one.
personnel n.m. personnel, staff.
pèse-acide pl. **pèse-acides** n.m. acidimeter.
pèse-alcool, pl. **pèse-alcools** n.m. alcoholometer.
pèse-lait n.m.inv. in pl. lactometer.
pèse-moût n.m.inv. in pl. (brewer's) saccharometer.
pèse-sirop n.m.inv. in pl. saccharometer.
pèse-vin n.m.inv. in pl. œnometer, alcoholometer.
pétale n.f. petal.
pétillant adj. semi-sparkling (wine); fizzy.
pétiller v.i. to fizz; to sparkle; to crackle (fire).
petit adj. small; little; unimportant
  petit à petit adv.phr. gradually, little by little.
  petits pois n.m.pl. peas.
petit-lait, pl. **petits-laits** n.m. whey.
pétoncle n.m. (variety of) scollop; scollop-shell.
pétri adj. kneaded (dough).
pétrir v.tr. to knead (dough).
pétrisseuse n.f. kneading-machine.
peu n.m. & adv. little.
  peu à peu adv.phr. gradually, little by little.
  un peu (de) a little.
  un peu de sel a little salt.
peut-être adv. perhaps, maybe.

phacochère n.m. wart-hog.
picholine n.f. large green olive.
pièce n.f. piece; bit, fragment.
  pièce de bœuf point of the rump of beef.
  pièce de monnaie coin.
  pièce de résistance main course, most substantial course of meal.
  pièce montée built-up preparation, esp. of pastry and sugar.
pied n.m. foot (of animal); foot (unit of length).
  pied de champignon mushroom-stalk.
  pied de cochon pig's trotter.
  pied de fenouil head of fennel.
  pied de raifort head of horseradish.
  pied de veau calf's foot.
pied-de-bouc, pl. **pieds-de-bouc** n.m. burnet saxifrage.
pied-de-chèvre, pl. **pieds-de-chèvre** n.m. burnet saxifrage.
pied-de-veau pl. **pieds-de-veau,** n.m. wild arum, "lords and ladies".
pie-grièche, pl. **pies-grièches** n.f. shrike.
pierre n.f. stone.
  pierre à aiguiser sharpening-stone, whetstone.
  pierre d'amertume gall-bladder (of fish).
pieuvre n.f. octopus.
pigeon n.m. pigeon.
  pigeon ramier ring-dove, ring-pigeon, wood-pigeon.
pigeonneau, -eaux n.m. young pigeon, squab.
pigment n.m. pigment.
pignon n.m. pine-seed.
pigrièche n.f. shrike.
pilaf n.m. pilaff.
pilaff n.m. pilaff.
pilau n.m. pilaff.
pilaw n.m. pilaff.
pilchard n.m. pilchard; (commercially) sardine.
pilé adj. ground; pounded.
piler v.tr. to grind; to pound.
  piler au mortier to pound in the mortar.
pilet n.m. pintail.
pilon n.m. pestle; drumstick (of chicken).
  pilon en bois wooden pestle.
piment n.m. pimento, capsicum.
  piment doux sweet pimento.

piment enragé (variety of) pimento from which Cayenne pepper is derived.

piment rouge red pimento.

piment vert green pimento.

pimentade n.f. (any) sauce preparation containing a large quantity of pimento.

pimprenelle n.f. burnet.

pince n.f. (pair of) tongs; claw (e.g. of crab).

pince à glace ice-tongs.

pince à pâte pastry-tongs.

pince à pâtisserie pastry-tongs.

pince de homard lobster-claw.

pinceau, -eaux n.m. brush.

pinceau à dorure pastry-brush.

pincée n.f. pinch (e.g. of salt).

pincer v.tr. to shrink (by cooking).

pinson n.m. finch.

pinson des Ardennes brambling, mountain finch.

pintade n.f. guinea-fowl.

pintadeau, -eaux n.m. young guinea-fowl.

pinte n.f. (originally) French pint (equal to nearly two English pints); pint.

pipe n.f. pipe, large cask.

piquage n.m. (the operation of) larding (meat).

piquant adj. piquant.

sauce piquante n.f. piquant sauce.

pique n.f. pick.

pique à glace ice-pick.

piqué adj. larded (meat); stuck (e.g. with cloves, garlic).

piqué d'ail stuck with garlic.

piqué de clous stuck with cloves.

piqué de lard larded with bacon.

pique-feu n.m.inv. in pl. poker.

piquer v.tr. to lard; to stick.

piquer d'ail to stick with garlic.

piquer de clous to stick with cloves.

piquer de lard to lard (with bacon).

pissaladière n.f. (variety of) tart, made in Provence, filled with onions, anchovy fillets and black olives.

pissenlit n.m. dandelion.

pistache n.f. pistachio.

pistache de terre ground-nut, monkey-nut, peanut.

pistaches en coques pl. peanuts in shell.

placard n.m. wall-cupboard.

place n.f. position (in room); place, spot; room, available accommodation.

Il n'y a pas de place There is no room.

mise en place n.f. mise en place, (ensemble of) advance preparations for cooking.

placé adj. placed, set in place.

placer v.tr. to place, to set in place.

plafond n.m. ceiling.

plainte n.f. complaint.

porter plainte contre quelqu'un to complain about somebody.

plaire v.ind.tr. to please.

plaire à quelqu'un to please someone.

s'il vous plaît if you please; please.

plaisir n.m. pleasure; cornet-shaped wafer.

planche n.f. board; plank; shelf.

planche à découper chopping-board.

planche à fromage(s) cheese-board.

planche à pâte pastry-board.

planche à pâtisserie pastry-board.

plancher n.m. floor.

planchette n.f. small board.

plante n.f. plant.

plaque n.f. sheet (of metal).

plaque à pâtisserie baking-sheet for pastry.

plaque à rôtir roasting-tray.

plaque à soufflé soufflé-tray.

plaque chauffante hot-plate.

plaque de pâtisserie baking-sheet for pastry.

plaque d'office tray with shallow lip.

plaque en tôle metal sheet.

plaquemine n.f. persimmon, American date-plum.

plastron n.m. ventral part of shell (esp. of turtle).

plat adj. flat.

n.m. dish (from which food is served onto plate); dish (of food, i.e. the food itself); dish, course, stage (of meal).

un déjeuner de quatre plats a four-course lunch(eon).

plat à entrés entrée-dish.

plat à gratin fire-proof dish for gratination.

plat allant au feu fire-proof dish.

plat allant au four oven-proof dish.

plat à œuf eared egg-dish.

plat à poisson eared fish-dish.

plat à rôtir roasting-dish.

plat à rôtir ovale oval roasting-dish.

plat à sauter pan in which to *sauter,* q.v.

plat creux deep dish.

plat de service service-dish.

plat de service allant au feu fire-proof service-dish.

plat long long service-dish.

sur le plat (of food, served) on the dish in, on, which it was cooked.

plateau, -eaux n.m. tray.

plateau d'argent (silver) salver.

plate-côte n.f. flat rib.

platine n.m. platinum.

plein adj. full.

un plein verre a glassful.

un verre plein a full glass.

pli n.m. fold.

plie n.f. plaice.

plié adj. folded.

plier v.tr. to fold.

plomb n.m. lead (metal).

plonge n.f. scullery; scullery-work; washing-up.

plongeur n.m. sculleryman; washer-up.

plongeuse n.f. washer-up.

pluches n.f.pl. leaves (e.g. of chervil, parsley).

plume n.f. feather.

à plume(s) feathered (game).

plus adv. more.

au plus at (the) most.

en plus extra, in addition.

plus grand larger, bigger.

plus de (followed by numeral) more than.

plus de vingt more than twenty.

plus que prep. & conj. more than.

plus que nous more than us.

plus facile que cela easier than that.

ne . . . plus (used conjunctively) no more, no longer.

plus (used disjunctively) no more, no longer.

pluvier n.m. plover.

œufs de pluvier plovers' eggs.

pluvier à collier ringed plover.

pluvier doré golden plover.

pochage n.m. (the operation of) poaching.

poche n.f. pocket; ladle; piping-bag; crop (of bird); gall-bladder (of fish).

poche à douille piping-bag.

poche de fiel (de poisson) gall-bladder (of fish).

poche de gravier crop (of bird).

poche pierreuse gall-bladder (of fish).

poché adj. poached.

un œuf poché a poached egg.

pocher v.tr. to poach.

pocheuse n.f. egg-poacher.

poêle n.m. stove. n.f. frying-pan.

poêlé adj. lightly braised.

poêlée n.f. (frying-)panful.

poêler v.tr. to braise lightly.

poêler à blanc to braise white.

poêler vert-cuit to braise (very) lightly.

poêlon n.m. untinned copper pan.

poids n.m. weight; metal weight (to weigh down saucepan-lid).

poids brut gross weight.

poids net net weight.

poil n.m. fur; "fur".

gibier à poil n.m. furry game; "fur".

poinçon à glace n.m. ice-pick.

point n.m. point (in space); point, detail, item; full stop (punctuation mark); point, stage.

à ce point adv.phr. at this point.

ne . . . point (used conjunctively) not at all.

point (used disjunctively) not at all.

pointe n.f. point, tip, end.

la pointe du couteau the tip of the knife.

pointe d'ail touch of garlic.

pointe d'asperge, pl. **pointes d'asperges** asparagus-tip.

pointe de cayenne point, touch, of Cayenne pepper (i.e. enough to cover the tip of a knife).

pointe de couteau knife-tip.

pointe de culotte point of the rump of beef.

pointe de muscade point, touch, of grated nutmeg (i.e. enough to cover the tip of a knife).

poire n.f. pear.

poiré n.m. perry.

poireau, -eaux n.m. leek.
poirée n.f. white beet.
 poirée à carde chard.
pois n.m. pea.
 petit pois, pl. **petits pois** garden
 pea.
 pois carré marrowfat pea.
 pois cassé split pea.
 pois chiche chick pea.
 pois chinois soya bean.
 pois frais fresh peas.
 pois secs dried peas.
poisson n.m. fish.
 poisson d'eau douce fresh-water
 fish.
 poisson de lac lake fish.
 poisson de mer sea-fish.
 poisson de rivière river fish.
 poisson de roche rock fish.
poisson-chat, pl. **poissons-chats**
 n.m. catfish.
poisson-grenouille pl. **poissons-**
 grenouilles n.m. angler.
poisson-lune, pl. **poissons-lunes**
 n.m. moon-fish; sun-fish.
poisson-soleil, pl. **poissons-soleils**
 n.m. sun-fish.
poissonnier n.m. fish-cook.
 chef poissonnier head fish-cook.
poissonnière n.f. fish-kettle.
poitrine n.f. breast.
 poitrine de bœuf brisket.
 poitrine de porc belly of pork.
poivrade n.f. (any) sauce preparation highly condimented with pepper.
 poivrade claire clear *poivrade,*
 q.v.
poivre n.m. pepper.
 poivre blanc white pepper.
 poivre de Cayenne Cayenne
 pepper (the pulverized fruit of the
 piment enragé, q.v.).
 poivre de Guinée grains of
 paradise, malaguetta pepper.
 poivre de Jamaïque allspice.
 Jamaica pepper.
 poivre indien grains of paradise,
 malaguetta pepper.
 poivre long long pepper.
 poivre moulu ground pepper.
 poivre noir black pepper.
poivré adj. peppered, condimented
 with pepper.
poivrer v.tr. to pepper, to condiment with pepper.
poivrette n.f. nigella, fennel-
 flower.

poivrière n.f. pepper-pot.
poivron n.m. allspice, Jamaica
 pepper.
 poivron doux mild allspice.
 poivron rouge hot allspice.
poli adj. polite; polished, bright;
 polished, elegant.
polir v.tr. to polish.
politesse n.f. politeness; courtesy,
 civility.
pommade n.f.
 beurre en pommade n.m.
 softened butter.
pomme n.f. apple; (occ., esp. on
 menu) potato.
 pomme aigrelette, pl. **pommes**
 aigrelettes sharp(-tasting)
 apple.
 pommes allumettes match
 potatoes.
 pomme d'api, pl. **pommes d'api**
 lady-apple.
 pomme de terre, pl. **pommes de**
 terre potato.
 pomme noisette, pl. **pommes**
 noisettes potato(es) cut into the
 shape and size of hazel-nuts.
 pomme reinette, pl. **pommes**
 reinettes pippin.
 pomme sauvage, pl. **pommes**
 sauvages crab-apple.
pommé adj. round, full-headed.
 chou pommé n.m. whiteheart
 cabbage.
 laitue pommée n.f. cabbage
 lettuce.
ponce n.f. pumice-stone.
porc n.m. pig; pork.
porcelaine n.f. porcelain, china.
 porcelaine à feu fire-proof porcelain.
porcelet n.m. piglet.
porte n.f. door.
 porte d'entrée entrance door;
 street door.
porte-raviers n.m.inv. in pl. hors
 d'œuvre(s) tray.
porter v.tr. to carry; to wear.
porteur n.m. porter.
porto n.m. port (wine).
portugaise n.f. Portuguese oyster.
posé adj. placed, laid, put.
poser v.tr. to place, to lay, to put.
pot n.m. pot; jug.
 pot en grès stoneware jug.
potage n.m. soup (in general).
 potage crème cream soup.
 potage lié bound soup.

potage purée *purée*, q.v.

potage velouté *velouté*, q.v.

pot-au-feu n.m. *bouillon* (q.v.) with garnish of meat and vegetables.

potée n.f. potful (e.g. of soup).

potiron n.m. pumpkin.

pouding n.m. pudding.

poudre n.f. powder.

poudre à lever baking-powder.

poudre de baies de gingembre ground ginger.

poudre de gingembre ground ginger.

poudre levain baking-powder.

en poudre adj.phr. pulverized.

sucre en poudre n.m. castor sugar.

pouillard n.m. young partridge; young pheasant.

poularde n.f. fattened young fowl, weighing up to 6 lb.

poule n.f. hen.

poule d'eau moor-hen.

poule de Bantam bantam-hen.

poule de Guinée guinea-hen.

poule d'Inde turkey-hen.

poule faisane hen-pheasant.

poule lagopède d'Écosse moor-hen, female moor-fowl, female red grouse.

poule-au-pot n.f. clear, unclarified chicken soup, containing chicken and turned or shaped vegetables.

poulet n.m. chicken.

poulet à la crapaudine spatch-cocked chicken.

poulet de grain corn-fed chicken.

poulet reine young spring chicken.

poulette n.f. pullet, young hen.

pouliot n.m. pennyroyal.

poulpe n.f. octopus.

poumon n.m. lung.

poupart n.m. common edible crab.

pour prep. for; (followed by infinitive) so as to, in order to.

pourboire n.m. tip, gratuity.

pourpier n.m. purslane.

pourquoi adv. & conj. why.

pourquoi? why?

pourtour n.m. circumference, periphery.

pousse n.f. shoot (of plant).

pousse de bambou bamboo-shoot.

pousse de salsifis oyster-plant shoot.

pousser v.tr. to push.

pousser à la poche to pipe (through piping-bag).

pousser au cornet to pipe (through piping-bag).

poussière n.f. dust.

poussin n.m. spring chicken.

poussoir n.m. sauasage-filler.

pouvoir v.tr. & i. to be able (to). n.m. power, powers; authority.

pralin n.m. almond-toffee (which can be pounded for use in confections).

praline n.f. sugar-almond.

praliné adj. decorated or flavoured with *pralin*, q.v. n.m. (variety of) cake decorated with almond-flavoured buttercream.

praliner v.tr. to decorate or flavour with *pralin*, q.v.

pratique adj. practical. n.f. practice; experience.

pratiquer v.tr. & i. to practise. v.tr. to make, to fashion (e.g. hole, notch).

au préalable adv.phr. beforehand, to begin with.

préalablement adv. previously.

précédemment adv. previously, before.

comme précédemment adv.phr. as previously, as before.

précédent adj. preceding, previous.

préféré adj. favourite; preferred.

préférence n.f. preference.

préférer v.tr. to prefer.

prélevé adj. removed, taken (esp. fillet from fish).

prélevé sur . . . removed from, taken from.

prélever v.tr. to remove, to take (esp. fillet from fish).

prélever sur . . . to remove, to take (esp. fillet) from (fish).

préliminaire adj. preliminary.

préliminaires n.f.pl. preliminaries.

premier, -ière adj. first.

prendre v.tr. to take. v.i. to take, to set.

faire prendre v.tr. to cause to set.

prendre feu to catch fire.

prendre le déjeuner to have lunch.

préparatifs n.m.pl. preparations (e.g. for the future).

préparation n.f. preparation, act of preparing.

préparé adj. prepared.

préparer v.tr. to prepare.

pré-salé pl. **prés-salés** n.m. salt-meadow lamb.

présent adj. present (opp. of absent).

présentation n.f. presentation; introduction; presentation (of dish, for approval).

présenter v.tr. to present; to introduce.

presque adv. almost, nearly.

presse n.f. press.
  presse à canard duck-press.
  presse légère light press.
  sous presse under a press.

pressé adj. squeezed, pressed; pressed, crowded; hurried, in a hurry.

presse-citrons n.m.inv. in pl. lemon-squeezer.

presse-purée n.m.inv. in pl. soup-machine.

presser v.tr. to squeeze, to press; to hurry, to hurry up.
  presser le pas to speed up, to "get a move on".
  presser dans un linge to squeeze in a cloth.
  se presser v.refl. to hurry (oneself) up.

pression n.f. pressure.
  forte pression strong pressure; high pressure.
  marmite sous pression n.f. pressure cooker.

pressoir n.m. fruit-press.

présure n.f. rennet.
  présure animale animal rennet.
  présure végétale vegetable rennet.

prêt adj. ready.
  n.m. loan.

prêter v.tr. to lend.

prévenir v.tr. (archaic synonym of) *empêcher*, q.v.

prier v.tr. & i. to ask, to request.
  Je vous en prie! Don't mention it! You're welcome!

prière n.f. request, entreaty.
  "Prière de ne pas fumer." "Please do not smoke." "Kindly refrain from smoking."

primer v.i. to predominate (flavour).

primeur n.f. early vegetable; early fruit; forced vegetable; forced fruit.
  primeurs pl. (garnish of) early or forced vegetables.

principal, -aux adj. principal, chief, most important.

principe n.m. principle; basis; rule.
  en principe adv.phr. in theory.

printanier, -ière adj. of the spring, spring-like.
  printanier n.m. (ensemble of) vegetables, spoon-cut or diced, used as garnish.

printemps n.m. spring.
  au printemps adv.phr. in (the) spring.
  chou de printemps n.m. spring cabbage.

pris adj. taken; taken, set.

prise n.f. pinch (e.g. of condiment).
  prise de poivre pinch of pepper.

prix n.m. price; prize.
  prix de rétail retail price.
  prix de gros wholesale price.

procédé n.m. process.

procéder v.i. to proceed.
  "Procéder comme pour . . ." "Proceed as for . . ."

prochain adj. next.
  l'année prochaine n.phr. & adv. phr. next year.

produire v.tr. to produce.

produit adj. produced.
  n.m. product.

profiter v.i. to profit; to benefit.
  profiter de quelque chose to profit from something; to make the most out of something.

profiterol(l)e n.f. *pâte à chou* (q.v.) preparation in large or small round cases.

profond adj. deep.
  peu profond shallow.

proportion n.f. proportion, ratio.
  à proportion de in proportion to.
  en proportion de in proportion to.
  à, en, proportion directe de in direct proportion, ratio, to.
  à, en, proportion inverse de in inverse proportion, ratio, to.

propre adj. own; clean.

propreté n.f. cleanliness; neatness, tidiness.

propriétaire n.m. or f. owner; proprietor, proprietress.

propriété n.f. property.

protéine n.f. protein.

prudemment adv. carefully, prudently.

prudence n.f. care, prudence.

prudent adj. careful, prudent.

prune n.f. plum.
  prune de Damas damson.
  prune de Reine-Claude greengage.

pruneau, -eaux n.m. prune.

prunelle n.f. sloe.

ptarmigan n.m. ptarmigan.

puits n.m. well.
  puits d'amour (variety of) *petit four*, q.v.

pulpe n.f. pulp; pith.

pulpeux, -euse adj. pulpy; pithy.

pulvérisateur n.m. pulverizer.

pulvérisé adj. pulverized, powdered.

pulvériser v.tr. to pulverize, to powder.

pur adj. pure.

purée n.f. mash of passed flesh, vegetable or fruit; thick passed soup.

pyramide n.f. pyramid-shape.

q

quadrillé adj. checkered (pattern).

quadriller v.tr. to checker, to mark with a checkered pattern.

qualité n.f. quality.

quand conj. when.
  quand même adv.phr. all the same, nevertheless.

quantité n.f. quantity.
  par petites quantités by small quantities, a little at a time.
  quantité voulue desired, required, quantity.

quart n.m. quarter, fourth part.
  un quart de litre a quarter of a litre.

quartier n.m. quarter (of carcase); quarter (of lemon).
  quartier d'agneau quarter of lamb.
  quartier de bœuf quarter of beef.
  quartier de derrière hindquarter.
  quartier de devant forequarter.
  cinquième quartier "fifth quarter", inedible parts of carcase, removed when animal is slaughtered, such as skin, horns, hooves.

quasi n.m. chump-end of loin.

quassia n.m. quassia.

quatre adj. four.
  couper en quatre v.tr. to cut into four, into quarters.

quatre-épices n.f.inv. in pl. nigella, fennel-flower.

quatre-quarts n.m.inv. in pl. pastry preparation made of equal quantities of eggs, flour, butter and sugar.

quatre-saisons n.f.inv. in pl. (variety of) small strawberry.

quelconque adj. any; ordinary, undistinguished.
  une sauce quelconque any sauce (whatever); some sauce or other.

quelque adj. some, any.
  quelque chose something.
  quelque chose de différent something different.
  quelque part adv.phr. somewhere.

quelquefois adv. sometimes.

quelqu'un, quelqu'une, pl. **quelques-uns, quelques-unes** pron. somebody, someone; anybody, anyone.

quenelle n.f. moulded chicken or fish forcemeat.
  quenelle à la cuiller *quenelle* (q.v.) shaped with a spoon.
  quenelle en chenille "caterpillar" *quenelle* (q.v.), shaped somewhat like a caterpillar.

question n.f. question.

queue n.f. tail; queue.
  queue de bœuf oxtail.
  queue décortiquée decorticated tail (e.g. of prawn).

quignon n.m. hunk (of bread).
  quignon de pain hunk of bread.

quinquina n.m. quinquina.

quintal, -aux n.m. (variety of) cabbage.

quitter v.tr. to leave (place).
  v.i. to leave.

quoi? interr. pron. what?

r

rabes n.f.pl. salted cod-roe.

rabiole n.f. (variety of) kohl-rabi; (variety of) swede.

râble n.m. saddle (of hare, rabbit).
  râble de lièvre saddle of hare.

rabot n.m. plane, shaver.
  rabot à glace ice-shaver.

racine n.f. root; root vegetable.
  aux racines adj.phr. & adv.phr.
  (prepared, served) with root
  vegetables.
  racine de persil parsley-root.
raclé adj. scraped (e.g. carrot).
racler v.tr. to scrape (e.g. carrot).
radicelle n.f. rootlet (esp. of
tuberous plant).
radis n.m. radish.
raffermi adj. hardened; hardened
again.
raffermir v.tr. to harden; to
harden again.
raffinade n.f. refined sugar.
raffinage n.m. (process of) refining.
raffiné adj. refined.
raffiner v.tr. to refine.
rafraîchi adj. refreshed, revived;
refreshed, cooled; chilled.
rafraîchir v.tr. to refresh, to
revive; to refresh, to cool; to chill.
ragot n.m. wild boar aged between
two and three years.
ragoût n.m. stew of game or
butcher's meat.
raidi adj. seized (esp. in boiling
fat).
raidir v.tr. to seize (esp. in boiling
fat).
raie n.f. ray, skate.
  raie bouclée common ray,
  thornback.
raifort n.m. horse-radish.
rainette n.f. pippin.
rainure n.f. channel, groove.
raiponce n.f. rampion.
raisin n.m.
  du raisin grapes.
  le raisin grapes.
  un grain de raisin a grape.
  une grappe de raisin a bunch of
  grapes.
  raisin de Corinthe pl. **raisins
  de Corinthe** currant.
  raisin de Malaga, pl. **raisins de
  Malaga** Malaga raisin.
  raisin de Smyrne, pl. **raisins de
  Smyrne** sultana.
  raisin d'ours, pl. **raisins d'ours**
  bearberry.
  raisin noir, pl. **raisins noirs**
  Malaga raisin.
  raisin sec, pl. **raisins secs** raisin.
raison n.f. reason, motive; reason,
justification; ratio, proportion.

à raison de prep.phr. In the
ratio, proportion, of.
à raison de deux par personne
allowing two per person, per
cover.
avec raison adv.phr. with reason,
rightly, justifiably.
avoir raison to be right.
sans raison adv.phr. without
reason, unreasonably, unjustifi-
ably.
raiton n.m. small ray, small skate.
râle n.m. rail.
  râle d'eau water-rail.
  râle de(s) genêt(s) land-rail,
  corncrake.
ramassé adj. gathered (together);
picked up.
ramasser v.tr. to gather (together);
to pick up.
ramequin n.m. ramekin, ramequin.
ramereau, -eaux n.m. young
wood-pigeon.
ramier n.m. ring-dove, ring-
pigeon, wood-pigeon.
ramolli adj. softened.
ramollir v.tr. to soften.
ramollissement n.m. (the process
of) softening.
rang n.m. line, row (of tables, esp.
in restaurant); rank, status.
rangé adj. tidy (room); steady
(person).
rangée n.f. line, row.
ranger v.tr. to replace, to put
(something) back in (its) place; to
tidy, to arrange; to set in order.
râpe n.f. grater.
  râpe à muscade nutmeg-grater.
râpé adj. grated (e.g. cheese).
  parmesan râpé n.m. grated
  Parmesan cheese.
râper v.tr. to grate (e.g. cheese).
rapette (or **râpette**) n.f. madwort.
rapide adj. quick, rapid, swift.
rapidement adj. quickly, rapidly,
swiftly.
rappeler v.tr. to call again; to call
back, to recall.
rapport n.m. relation, connection;
relations, connections, dealings; re-
port, statement.
  en rapport avec prep.phr. in
  relation to.
râpure n.f. gratings (e.g. of cheese).
au ras de prep.phr. at the level of;
(up) to the level of.
rascasse n.f. hog-fish.

rascouenne n.f. inner rind (of pork).

rassis adj. stale (esp. bread).
  pain rassis n.m. stale bread.

ratafia n.m. ratafia liqueur.

ratatouille n.f. made-up preparation of marrow, pimento, tomato, onion and garlic, cooked in oil.

rate n.f. spleen.
  rate de bœuf ox-spleen.

rave n.f. rape.

ravier n.m. hors d'œuvre dish.

ravigote n.f. Ravigote sauce.

ravioli n.m.pl. ravioli.

rayon n.m. stripe.

recette n.f. recipe.

recevoir v.tr. to receive; to receive, to entertain (guests).

réchaud n.m. chafing-lamp; (sideboard) hot-plate.

réchauffé adj. reheated; warmed up again.

réchauffer v.tr. to reheat; to warm up again.

recherche n.f. search; research.

recherché adj. much in demand; elegant, sophisticated.
  goût recherché n.m. sophisticated taste.

réclamation n.f. complaint.

recommandé adj. recommended.

recommander v.tr. to recommend.

recommencé adj. started again, begun again.

recommencer v.tr. & i. to start again, to begin again.

recouvert adj. covered, covered over; covered again.
  recouvert de covered with, covered over with; covered again with.

recouvrir v.tr. to cover, to cover over; to cover again.
  recouvrir de to cover with, to cover over with; to cover again with.

recrépi adj. crimped.

recrépir v.tr. to crimp.

rectangle n.m. rectangle; oblong (-shape).

rectangulaire adj. rectangular, oblong.

rectifié adj. rectified, put right; adjusted, corrected (seasoning).

rectifier v.tr. to rectify, to put right; to adjust, to correct (seasoning).

rectifier l'assaisonnement to adjust, correct, (the) seasoning.

rectifier la consistance to adjust, correct, (the) consistency.

reçu adj. received.

recueil n.m. collection, miscellany (e.g. of recipes).

recuire v.tr. to cook again.

recuit adj. re-cooked.

recuite n.f. skim-milk cheese.

récuré adj. scoured, cleaned by scouring.

récurer v.tr. to scour, to clean by scouring.

réduction n.f. reduction.

réduire v.tr. to reduce.
  réduire de moitié to reduce by (a) half.
  réduire d'un quart to reduce by a quarter.
  réduire d'un tiers to reduce by a third.

refaire v.tr. to do again; to make again.

refait adj. done again; made again.

reformé adj. reformed, reshaped, reconstituted.

reformer v.tr. to reform, to reshape, to reconstitute.

réfrigérant adj. refrigerating, freezing (apparatus, substance).
  n.m. freezing-agent; refrigerator.

réfrigérateur n.m. refrigerator.

réfrigération n.f. refrigeration.

réfrigéré adj. refrigerated.

réfrigérer v.tr. to refrigerate.

regarder v.tr. to look at.

régime n.m. diet.
  être au régime to be on a diet, to be dieting.
  régime diabétique diabetic diet.
  régime végétarien vegetarian diet.

règle n.f. rule (of behaviour, etc.).

réglé adj. regulated; set in order.

règlement n.m. regulation, ordinance.

régler v.tr. to regulate; to set in order.

réglisse n.f. liquorice (plant).
  bâton de réglisse n.m. Spanish liquorice.
  jus de réglisse n.m. liquorice.

régulier, -ière adj. regular; steady, orderly.

rehaussé adj. set off, enhanced.

rehausser v.tr. to set off, to enhance.

rein n.m. kidney (in anatomical terminology, as distinct from *rognon*, q.v.).

reine-Claude, pl. **reines-Claude** n.f. greengage.

reinette n.f. pippin.

réjouissance n.f. make-weight, bones weighed in with the meat.

relâché adj. loosened.

relâcher v.tr. to loosen.

relations n.f.pl. connections, dealings.

relevé adj. spiced, seasoned.
   très relevé highly seasoned.
   relevé n.m. remove course; summary, inventory (of stock).

relever v.tr. to spice, to season.

remercier v.tr. to thank.
   Je vous remercie Thank you.

remettre v.tr. to put back (again).

remis adj. put back (again).

remise n.f. (operation of) putting again, replacing; operation of repeating an action.

remouillage n.m. (the operation of) remoistening.

remouillé adj. remoistened.

remouiller v.tr. to remoisten.

rémoulade n.f. Rémoulade sauce.

remplacé adj. replaced (with somebody else, with something else).

remplacer v.tr. to replace (with somebody else, with something else).

rempli adj. filled.

remplir v.tr. to fill.

remué adj. moved, shifted; stirred (liquid).

remuer v.tr. to move, to shift; to stir (liquid).

rendre v.tr. to make, to cause to become (smooth, soft etc.).
   rendre lisse to make smooth.

renne n.m. reindeer.
   langue de renne n.f. reindeer's tongue.

renouvelé adj. renewed, replaced (esp. water during soaking).

renouveler v.tr. to renew, to replace (esp. water during soaking).

rentrer v.i. to come in again; to go in again; to return (home).
v.tr. to bring in; to take in.

répandre v.tr. to spread, to sprinkle; to upset, to spill.

repas n.m. meal.
   repas de carême Lenten meal.
   repas de noces wedding breakfast; (in France) wedding feast

(formerly of up to three days' duration).
   repas maigre meatless meal.
   un repas de six plats a six-course meal.

repassé adj. repassed, passed again (e.g. sauce).

repasser v.tr. to repass, to pass again (e.g. sauce).

repère n.m. sealing-paste.
   fixer au repère v.tr. to seal (pie) with semi-liquid sealing-agent.

répertoire n.m. repertory (e.g. of recipes).

replacé adj. replaced, put back in (to) place (as distinct from *remplacé*, q.v.).

replacer v.tr. to replace, to put back in(to) place (as distinct from *remplacer*, q.v.).

répondre v.i. to reply, to answer.

réponse n.f. reply, answer.

réproduire v.tr. to reproduce.

réserve n.f. reserve.
   tenir en réserve v.tr. to hold in reserve.

réservé adj. reserved; set aside; held in reserve.

réserver v.tr. to reserve; to set aside; to hold in reserve.

résidu n.m. residue.

résine n.f. resin.
   goût de résine n.m. taste of resin, esp. in flesh of some game birds.

résorbé adj. reabsorbed.

résorber v.tr. to reabsorb.

restant adj. remaining, left over. n.m. remainder.

restaurant n.m. restaurant.
   restaurant cachir Kosher restaurant.

reste n.m. remainder.
   restes pl. remains, left-overs.

rester v.i. to remain; to stay.

rétamage n.m. re-tinning.

rétamé adj. re-tinned.

rétamer v.tr. to re-tin.

retenir v.tr. to retain, to keep; to keep back, to reserve; to engage (staff).

réticulé adj. reticulate.
   anone réticulée n.f. reticulate anona, muricate anona, West Indian custard-apple, sour-sop.

retirer v.tr. to take out; to withdraw, to remove.

retirer du feu to remove from the fire, from the flame.

retour n.m. return; (operation of) sending back from dining-room to kitchen.

retourner v.tr. to turn over; to turn inside out; to return, to send back.

retrouver v.tr. to find again.

réunion n.f. reunion; meeting, social gathering.

réussi adj. successful.

réussir v.i. to succeed.

réussite n.f. successful result, success.

réveillon n.m. (in France) festive supper held in the early hours of Christmas morning after midnight Mass of the Nativity; (in France) festive New Year supper.

revenir v.i. to return, to come back.

   faire revenir v.tr. to turn brown.

reverdir v.tr. to turn green again (e.g. vegetable which has become pale).

rhubarbe n.f. rhubarb.

rhum n.m. rum.

rideau, -eaux n.m. curtain.

rien pron. (disjunctively) nothing; (conjunctively) anything.

   ne . . . rien (conjunctively) nothing.

rincé adj. rinsed; rinsed out.

rince-bouteilles n.m.inv. in pl. bottle-washer, bottle-washing machine.

rince-doigts n.m.inv. in pl. finger-bowl.

rincer v.tr. to rinse; to rinse out.

ris n.m. sweetbreads.

   ris d'agneau lamb's sweetbreads.
   ris de veau calf's sweetbreads.

rissolage n.m. (operation of) colouring (food) in a pan by turning (the food) over, usually in hot shallow butter.

   léger rissolage gentle *rissolage*, q.v.

rissole n.f. rissole.

rissolé adj. (food) coloured in a pan by turning (the food) over, usually in hot shallow butter.

rissoler v.tr. to colour (food) in a pan by turning (the food) over, usually in hot shallow butter.

rissolette n.f. small rissole.

riz n.m. rice.

riz en grains separated rice.

riz glacé polished rice.

riz gonflé puffed rice.

riz sec dry rice.

en robe de chambre adj.phr. & adv.phr. (of potatoes) cooked in their jackets.

robinet n.m. (water-)tap.

rocambole n.f. rocambole, Spanish garlic.

rogner v.tr. to pare, to trim.

rognon n.m. kidney (in kitchen and restaurant terminology, as distinct from *rein*, q.v.).

   rognon d'agneau lamb's kidney.
   rognon de coq cock's kidney.
   rognon de mouton sheep's kidney.
   rognon de veau calf's kidney.

rognonnade n.f. loin of veal still containing kidney.

rognures n.f.pl. parings, trimmings.

roi n.m. king.

   galette des Rois n.f. twelfth-cake.
   roi des cailles n.m. corncrake, land-rail.

romaine n.f. cos lettuce.

   salade de romaine n.f. cos lettuce salad.

romarin n.m. rosemary.

rompre v.tr. to break.

romsteck n.m. rumpsteak.

ronce-framboise, pl. ronces-framboises n.f. loganberry .

rond adj. & n.m. round.

   rond de beurre pat of butter.
   rond de jambon round of ham.
   rond de pain slice, round, of bread.

rondelle n.f. roundel.

rosace n.f. rosette(-shape).

rosbif n.m. roast beef.

rose n.f. rose.

   adj. inv. in compounds pink.

rosé adj. pink (wine).

roser v.tr. to colour pink.

rosette n.f. red-eye, rudd.

rossette n.f. red-eye, rudd.

rossolis n.m. sundew; rosolio cordial.

rôt n.m. roast.

   le rôt the roast course.
   le gros rôt the large roast.
   le petit rôt the small roast.

rotengle n.m. red-eye, rudd.

rôti adj. roast.

   n.m. roast, roast course.

rôtie n.f. slice of toast.
rôtir v.tr. to roast.
  rôtir saignant to roast very lightly.
rôtissage n.m. roasting.
rôtisseur n.m. roast-cook.
rouelle n.f. round slice (e.g. of bread, fruit); round (of meat).
  rouelle de veau fillet of veal.
rouge adj. & n.m. red.
  rouge de rivière shoveller (bird).
  rouge végétal vegetable red (colouring).
rougeâtre adj. reddish.
rouge-grondin, pl. **rouges-grondins** n.m. red gurnard, red gurnet.
rouge-queue, pl. **rouges-queues** n.m. redstart.
rouget n.m. red mullet.
rouille n.f. rust.
rouillé adj. rusty, rusted.
rouiller v.tr. to rust, to cause to rust.
  se rouiller v.refl. to rust.
roulade n.f. rolled slice.
  roulade de saumon rolled slice of smoked salmon.
roulé adj. rolled.
rouleau, -eaux n.m. roller.
  rouleau à pâtisserie, rouleau de pâtissier rolling-pin.
rouler v.tr. to roll.
roulette n.f. wheeled pastry-cutter.
rousselet n.m. russet-pear.
roussette n.f. spotted dog-fish.
roussi adj. browned.
roussir v.tr. & i. to brown.
roux n.m. thickening.
  roux blanc white thickening.
  roux blond fawn thickening.
  roux brun brown thickening.
royal, -ale, -aux, -ales adj. royal.
royale n.f. dice of savoury egg-custard.
royan n.m. sardine.
ruban n.m. ribbon.
rubané adj. ribboned.
rubaner v.tr. to ribbon.
russe n.f. (any) saucepan of vertical side, of height at least equal to its diameter, and usually having a single, long handle.
rutabaga n.m. swede, Swedish turnip.

S

sablier n.m. egg-timer.
sabot n.m. clog.
sac n.m. bag, sack.
saccharimètre n.m. (brewer's) saccharometer.
saccharine n.f. saccharin.
sachet n.m. bag.
  sachet d'aromates bag of aromatic herbs.
safran n.m. saffron.
  saffron bâtard safflower.
  saffron des Indes curcuma, turmeric.
safrané adj. flavoured with saffron; saffron-coloured.
safraner v.tr. to flavour with saffron; to imbue with the colour of saffron.
sagou n.m. sago.
saignant adj. underdone (e.g. steak), as distinct from *pas assez cuit*, q.v. (under *cuit*).
saigner v.i. to bleed.
saigneux, -euse adj. bloody.
  bout saigneux n.m. scrag (esp. of veal, mutton).
sain adj. healthy.
saindoux n.m. hog's lard.
saint-jacques, pl. **saints-jacques** n.m. scollop; scollop-shell.
saint-pierre, pl. **saints-pierres** n.m. John Dory.
saisi adj. seized.
saisir v.tr. to seize.
saison n.f. season.
  en saison in season.
salade n.f. salad; salad vegetable, esp. lettuce.
  salade composée compound salad.
  salade de fruits fruit salad.
  salade douce sweet salad.
  salade panachée mixed salad.
  salade simple salad made from only one vegetable.
saladier n.m. salad-bowl.
salage n.m. (operation of) salting or curing (with dry salt or with a saline solution).
salaire n.m. pay, wage(s).
salaison n.f. (operation of) salting or curing (with dry salt or with a saline solution).
  salaison du jambon (operation of) salting or curing ham.

salamandre n.f. grill for gratinating.

salami n.m. salami.

salangane n.f. salangane, swallow of Far Eastern waters.

nid de salangane n.m. swallow's nest, "bird's nest."

salarié, -ée adj. wage-earning. n. wage-earner.

sale adj. dirty.

salé adi. salt, salted. n.m. salt pork.

petit salé pickled pork.

salep n.m. salep.

saler v.tr. to salt.

sali adj. dirty, dirtied, soiled.

salière n.f. salt-cellar.

salir v.tr. to dirty, to soil.

salle n.f. hall, large room; dining-room (of restaurant); "front shop" (restaurant dining-room, as distinct from restaurant kitchen).

salmis n.m. stew of feathered game or of tame pigeon.

saloir n.m. salting-tub.

salpêtre n.m. potassium nitrate, saltpetre.

salpêtre pulvérisé powdered potassium nitrate.

salsepareille n.f. sarsaparilla.

salsifis n.m. oyster-plant, (white) salsify.

salsifis d'Espagne scorzonera, black salsify.

salsifis noir scorzonera, black salsify.

samedi n.m. Saturday.

samos n.m. Samian wine.

sandre n.f. pike-perch (of Central Europe).

sandwich, pl. sandwich(e)s n.m. sandwich.

sang n.m. blood.

sang de porc pig's blood.

sang figé congealed blood.

sanglier n.m. wild boar.

sanglier d'Afrique wart-hog.

sanguine n.f. blood-orange.

sans prep. without.

sans cesse adv.phr. incessantly, without stopping.

sans sucre adj.phr. sugarless, without sugar; savoury (e.g. pancake).

sansonnet n.m. starling.

santé n.f. health.

sapide adj. savoury, full of savour.

sapidité n.f. sapidity, (degree of) savouriness.

sapotille n.f. sapodilla, sapodilla plum, naseberry.

sarcelle n.f. teal.

sarcelle d'été garganey.

sarcelle d'hiver teal.

sardine n.f. sardine; pilchard.

sargasse n.f. sargasso.

sarment n.m. vine-shoot.

sarrasin n.m. buckwheat.

sarriette n.f. savory.

sauce n.f. sauce.

sauce anglaise egg-custard sauce.

sauce blanche white sauce.

sauce chaude warm sauce.

sauce composée compound sauce, made-up sauce.

sauce demandée required sauce.

sauce douce sweet sauce.

sauce échalote shallot sauce.

sauce froide cold sauce.

sauce maigre meatless sauce, i.e. one containing no meat or meat derivatives (also known, incorrectly, as a Lenten sauce).

petite sauce small sauce.

saucé adj. sauced, covered with sauce.

saucer v.tr. to sauce, to cover with sauce.

saucier n.m. sauce-cook.

chef saucier head sauce-cook.

saucière n.f. sauce-boat.

saucisse n.f. sausage.

saucisse de Francfort Frankfurter sausage.

saucisson n.m. smoked sausage.

sauf prep. except.

sauge n.f. sage.

sauge sclarée clary.

saumon n.m. salmon.

saumon d'Écosse fumé Scotch smoked salmon.

saumoné adj. salmon-coloured.

truite saumonée n.f. salmon-trout.

saumoneau, -eaux n.m. young salmon.

saumonière n.f. salmon-kettle.

saumure n.f. brine.

saumuré adj. salted; brined.

saumurer v.tr. to salt; to brine.

saupoudré adj. sprinkled (with powder or other solid), as distinct from *arrosé*, q.v.

saupoudrer v.tr. to sprinkle (with powder or other solid), as distinct from *arroser*, q.v.

saupoudreuse n.f. dredger, sifter, sprinkler (e.g. for salt, sugar).

saur adj.

    hareng saur n.m.   red (i.e. smoked and salted) herring.

saurel n.m.   horse-mackerel; cavally, scad.

sauté adj.   jumped in a pan.

sauter v.tr.   to jump in a pan.

    sauter à cru   to jump in a pan (from the raw state).

sauteuse n.f.   shallow stew-pan.

    sauteusc à fond épais   thick-bottomed *sauteuse*, q.v.

sautoir n.m.   deep *plat à sauter*, q.v.

saveur n.f.   flavour, savour.

    saveur résineuse   resinous flavour.

savoir v.tr.   to know.

savon n.m.   soap.

    pain de savon n.m.   cake of soap.

savonneux, -euse adj.   soapy.

    eau savonneuse n.f.   soapy water.

saxifrage n.f.   saxifrage.

scampi n.m.pl.   scampi.

scare n.m.   parrot-fish.

scarole n.f.   Batavian endive.

sceau (pl. **sceaux**) **de Notre-Dame** n.m.   black bryony.

scie n.f.   saw.

scier v.tr.   to saw.

scorsonère n.f.   scorzonera, black salsify.

seau, -eaux n.m.   bucket.

    seau à incendie   fire-bucket.

sébaste n.m.   Norway haddock, bergylt.

sébile n.f.   wooden bowl (esp. one in which eggs are beaten).

sec, sèche adj.   dry.

    à sec   in the dry state; until dry.

sèche n.f.   cuttle-fish.

séché adj.   dried.

sécher v.tr.   to dry.

second adj.   second.

seconde n.f.   second (of time).

secoué adj.   shaken, shaken up.

secouer v.tr.   to shake, to shake up.

section n.f.   section.

    section carrée   cross-section (dimension).

sectionné adj.   cut into sections.

sectionner v.tr.   to cut into sections.

segment n.m.   segment.

seiche n.f.   cuttle-fish.

seigle n.m.   rye.

    pain de seigle n.m.   rye bread.

sel n.m.   salt.

    sel blanc   table salt.

    sel d'ail   garlic salt.

    sel de céleri   celery salt.

    sel gris   kitchen salt.

    sel marin   kitchen salt.

    gros sel   kitchen salt.

selle n.f.   saddle (of large animal, as distinct from *râble*, q.v.).

    selle d'agneau   saddle of lamb.

    selle de mouton   saddle of mutton.

selon prep.   according to.

seltz n.m.   soda-water.

semaine n.f.   week.

semé adj.   sprinkled.

    semé de   sprinkled with.

semence n.f.   seed.

semer v.tr.   to sprinkle.

    semer de   to sprinkle with.

semoule n.f.   semolina.

sens n.m.   sense (e.g. of touch); sense; judgment; sense, meaning; direction (in space).

    sens hauteur   the vertical plane; in the vertical plane.

    sens longueur   lengthwise, longitudinally; down its, their, length.

sentir v.tr.   to feel; to be conscious of.

    v.i.   to smell of; to taste of.

    sentir le graillon   to smell of burnt fat; to taste greasy.

séparation n.f.   separation.

séparé adj.   separated.

séparer v.tr.   to separate.

sépia n.f.   cuttle-fish.

septembre n.m.   September.

série n.f.   series.

seringue n.f.   syringe.

serpolet n.m.   wild thyme.

serre n.f.   greenhouse.

    serre chaude   hothouse.

serré adj.   squeezed; tightened (esp. consistency).

serrer v.tr.   to squeeze; to tighten (esp. consistency).

service n.m.   service; serving (of food); service (rendered); duty, shift.

serviette n.f.   cloth; serviette.

servir v.tr. & i.   to serve.

    servir à   to be useful for.

    servir à faire quelque chose   to be useful for doing something.

    servir de   to serve as.

    se servir de   to use.

seul adj.   only, sole; alone.

seulement adv. only.
siccité adj. dryness.
  jusqu'à siccité adv.phr. to (the point of) dryness.
silence n.m. silence.
silure n.f. sheath-fish, sheat-fish, silurus.
simple adj. simple.
simulé adj. simulated, imitated.
simuler v.tr. to simulate, to imitate.
sirop n.m. syrup.
  sirop de sucre golden syrup.
siropé adj. masked with syrup; soaked in syrup.
siroper v.tr. to mask with syrup; to soak in syrup.
sirupeux, -euse adj. syrupy.
situation n.f. situation, position; condition, state; situation, job.
socle n.m. base (e.g. of rice) on which to stand made-up preparation.
soda n.m. soda-water.
soie n.f. silk.
soigné adj. carefully cooked; carefully prepared.
soigner v.tr. to cook carefully; to prepare carefully.
soigneusement adv. carefully, with care.
soigneux, -euse adj. careful, painstaking.
soin n.m. care (charge, responsibility); care, carefulness.
  avec soin with care.
  avoir soin de faire quelque chose to take care to do something.
soir n.m. evening.
soirée n.f. evening (usually with the idea of duration of time).
soja n.m. soya.
sole n.f. sole.
solide adj. solid.
solidification n.f. solidification.
solidifié adj. solidified.
solidifier v.tr. to solidify.
  se solidifier v.refl. to solidify.
sommité n.f. top, tip (of foliage of vegetable or herb).
son n.m. bran.
sonner v.tr. & i. to ring.
sonnette n.f. small bell; hand-bell; door-bell.
sorbe n.f. sorb-apple.
sorbet n.m. flavoured water-ice.
sorgho n.m. sorghum.
sorgo n.m. sorghum.

sortie n.f. departure, exit, coming out, going out; exit (passage, door); trip, excursion.
  sortie de secours emergency exit.
sortir v.i. to come out, to go out. v.tr. to bring out, to take out.
sot-l'y-laisse n.m.inv. in pl. parson's nose (of chicken).
soubise n.f. Soubise sauce.
soubisé adj. flavoured with onion; garnished with onion(s).
soubiser v.tr. to flavour with onion; to garnish with onion(s).
souchet n.m. shoveller; spoonbill duck; cyperus.
  souchet comestible chufa, rush-nut.
soucoupe n.f. saucer.
soudé adj. sealed (pie).
souder v.tr. to seal (pie).
  soufflé d'entremets sweet *soufflé*, q.v.
  soufflé sans sucre savoury *soufflé*, q.v.
soulever v.tr. to lift (e.g. paste, during mixing, to let air in).
soulier n.m. shoe.
soupçon n.m. small quantity (e.g. of garlic); dash (of liquid).
soupe n.f. (any) soup containing bread or toast; soup of a regional or peasant character.
souper n.m. supper. v.i. to have supper.
soupière n.f. soup-tureen.
source n.f. source, spring; source, origin.
sourdon n.m. cockle.
sous prep. under, beneath, below.
sous- prefix sub-, under-.
  sous-chef deputy head of the kitchen.
  sous-sol n.m. basement.
souvent adv. often.
soya n.m. soya-bean.
spaghetti n.m.pl. spaghetti.
spatule n.f. spatula.
  spatule en bois wooden spatula.
  spatule en fer metal spatula.
spécial, -aux adj. special.
spécialité n.f. speciality.
  spécialité de la maison speciality of the house.
spicanard n.m. spikenard.
spiquenard n.m. spikenard.
spirale n.f. spiral(-pattern).
spiritueux, -euse adj. spirituous.

spiritueux n.m. spirituous liquor.

spondias n.m. hog-plum.

sprat n.m. sprat.

squille n.f. mantis-shrimp.

stachys n.m. Chinese artichoke.

  stachys tubéreux Chinese artichoke.

stage n.m. period of probation; supervised period of practical experience (e.g. of catering student working in industry).

stagiaire n.m. or f. probationer; student undergoing period of practical experience in industry.

stéarine n.f. stearin.

stérilisé adj. sterilized.

stériliser v.tr. to sterilize.

sterlet n.m. variety of small Russian sturgeon.

stockfisch n.m. dried but unsalted cod.

strie n.f. scratch, scoring, striation.

  strie hélicoïdale spiral scoring, spiral striation.

stromatée n.m. stromateus, pomfret.

suc n.m. juice.

  suc d'ananas pineapple-juice.

  suc d'estragon tarragon-juice.

sucre n.m. sugar.

  sans sucre adj.phr. sugar-free; sugarless; savoury (e.g. pancake).

  sucre candi sugar candy.

  sucre cristallisé granulated sugar.

  sucre d'érable maple sugar.

  sucre en morceaux lump sugar.

  sucre en poudre castor sugar.

  sucre en tablettes lump sugar.

sucré adj. sugared; sweetened with sugar.

sucrer v.tr. to sugar; to sweeten with sugar.

sucrin n.m. sugary melon.

suer v.i. to sweat.

  faire suer v.tr. to sweat.

suffisamment adv. sufficiently.

suffisant adj. sufficient, adequate.

suif n.m. tallow.

  suif de mouton mutton fat.

suite n.f. succession, progression; sequel; something which follows another.

  de suite in succession.

  tout de suite immediately.

suivre v.tr. to follow (in space); to follow (in time).

  à suivre to follow; to be continued.

sujet n.m. subject, topic.

  au sujet de about, concerning, on the subject of.

superficie n.f. surface; area.

supérieur adj. superior; higher.

supplément n.m. supplement, addition, extra.

  en supplément adv.phr. in addition; as an extra.

supplémentaire adj. supplementary, additional, extra.

suprême n.m. most delicate fillet cuts, esp. of chicken and fish.

sur prep. on, upon.

sûr adj. sure; safe; certain.

surard n.m. elder-flower vinegar.

sureau, -eaux n.m. elder.

surelle n.f. wood-sorrel.

suret, -ette adj. sourish.

surette n.f. wood-sorrel.

sur-le-champ adv. at once, immediately.

surmulet n.m. surmullet.

surplus n.m. surplus, excess.

surprise n.f. surprise.

surtout adv. particularly, especially; above all.

surveiller v.tr. to supervise, to oversee; to watch over, to keep an eye on.

susceptible adv. susceptible.

  susceptible de . . . susceptible to . . .; liable to . . .

symétrique adj. symmetrical.

symétriquement adv. symmetrically.

système n.m. system.

t

table n.f. table.

  table d'hôte set meal, at fixed price, described on restaurant table d'hôte menu.

tableau, -eaux n.m. list, roster.

  tableau de service duty-roster.

tablette n.f. bar (esp. of chocolate).

tablier n.m. apron.

tabouret n.m. stool.

tacaud n.m. bib, whiting-pout.

tache n.f. stain, spot.

tâche n.f. task, duty.

taché adj. stained, spotted.

tacher v.tr. to stain, to spot.

tâcher v.i. to try.

  tâcher de faire quelque chose to try to do something.

tacon n.m. parr; smolt.

tadorne n.m. sheldrake.

tafia n.m. tafia rum.

  tafia de laurier bay rum.

taillé adj. cut, cut up.

taille-légumes n.m.inv. in pl, vegetable-slicer.

taille-pain n.m.inv. in pl. bread-slicer.

tailler v.tr. to cut, to cut up.

taille-racines n.m.inv. in pl. (root) vegetable-cutter.

tailloir n.m. carving-board, trencher.

talon du collier n.m. clod (of beef).

talure n.f. bruise (on fruit).

tamarin n.m. tamarind.

tamier n.m. black bryony.

taminier n.m. black bryony.

tamis n.m. sieve; strainer, tammy.

  tamis de crin hair sieve.

  tamis de fer wire sieve.

  tamis de soie silk sieve.

  tamis de toile cloth sieve.

  tamis en fer wire sieve.

  gros tamis coarse strainer.

tamisé adj. sieved.

tamiser v.tr. to sieve.

tampon n.m. base (e.g. of rice) on which to stand made-up preparation.

  tampon de riz rice *tampon*, q.v.

tanaisie n.f. tansy.

tanche n.f. tench.

tant adv. so much.

tantinet n.m. very small quantity.

tapioca n.m. tapioca.

tarif n.m. tariff, price-list.

tartelette n.f. tartlet.

tartine n.f. slice of bread and butter, bread and jam, etc.

tas n.m. pile, heap.

tasse n.f. cup.

  tasse à consommé consommé-cup.

  en tasse (consommé, served) in a consommé-cup.

tassé adj. piled up, heaped up.

tassée n.f. cupful.

tassement n.m. (operation of) piling (up).

tasser v.tr. to pile up, to heap up.

taure n.f. heifer.

taureau, -eaux n.m. bull.

teinte n.f. tint, shade.

tel, telle adj. such.

température n.f. temperature.

tempéré adj. tempered, moderated.

tempérer v.tr. to temper, to moderate.

temporaire adj. temporary.

temps n.m. time (in general, as distinct from *heure*, q.v.).

  en même temps at the same time.

  en même temps que at the same time as.

  perdre du temps to waste time.

tende n.m.

  tende de tranche topside (of beef).

tendon n.m. sinew, tendon.

tendre adj. tender.

tendron n.m. cartilage; breast (of veal), from the sternum.

tenir v.tr. to hold; to keep (e.g. warm).

  tenir au chaud to keep hot; to keep warm.

  tenir compte de to take account of, to take into account.

  tenir en réserve to hold in reserve.

tenue n.f. dress, uniform.

  tenue de cuisine kitchen dress, cook's uniform.

terme n.m. term, expression.

  termes de cuisine kitchen terms.

terminer v.tr. to end, to finish; to complete (e.g. process of cooking).

terrapène n.m. terrapin.

terre n.f. earth; earthenware.

  terre vernissée glazed earthenware.

terre-noix n.m.inv. in pl. earthnut, pig-nut.

terrine n.f. earthenware dish for cooking or service.

tête n.f. head; upper end (e.g. of cut of meat).

  tête d'aloyau head of the loin.

  tête de bœuf ox-head.

  tête de mouton sheep's head.

  tête de veau calf's head.

tétine n.f. dug, udder.

tétragone n.f. tetragonia.

  tétragone étalée New Zealand spinach.

tétras n.m. (any) bird of the family which includes blackgame and hazel-grouse.

  grand tétras blackgame.

  petit tétras blackcock.

  tétras lyre blackcock.

thé n.m. tea.

  thé de bœuf beef tea.

thé de viande beef tea.
thé vert green tea.
thon n.m. tunny(-fish).
thon blanc white tunny.
thorax n.m. thorax.
thym n.m. thyme.
thymus n.m. thymus(-gland).
tiède adj. tepid; lukewarm.
tiédi adj. made tepid; made lukewarm.
tiédir v.tr. to make tepid; to
make lukewarm.
   v.i. to become tepid; to become
lukewarm.
tiers n.m. third, third part.
tige n.f. stalk, stem.
tilleul n.m. lime-tree.
   infusion de tilleul n.f. lime-tea.
timbale n.f. silverware double container, the lower part having two
loop handles and containing liquid or
ice, and the upper part containing
food to be served.
tinamou n.m. tinamou.
tinet n.m. gambrel.
tirant n.m. sinew, tendon (in
butcher's meat).
tire-bouchon, pl. **tire-bouchons**
n.m. corkscrew.
tire-braise n.m.inv. in pl. oven
rake.
tire-moelle n.m.inv. in pl. marrow-
scoop.
tirette n.f. broad, flat tendon.
tisane n.f. infusion; tea.
tisonnier n.m. poker.
toast n.m. toasted bread, toast;
toast, after-dinner speech.
tocan n.m. very young salmon.
toile n.f. cloth.
toilette n.f. caul; crow (of pig).
   toilette de porc crow of pig,
pig's crow.
tokai n.m. Tokay.
tokay n.m. Tokay.
tomate n.f. tomato.
   tomates de conserve tinned
tomatoes.
tomaté adj. flavoured with
tomato.
tomater v.tr. to flavour with
tomato.
tomber v.i. to fall.
   faire tomber à glace v.tr. to
reduce to a glaze.
   faire tomber au beurre v.tr.
to glaze in butter.
tonneau, -eaux n.m. cask, barrel.

tonnelet n.m. small cask, small
barrel, keg.
topinambour n.m. Jerusalem
artichoke.
toque n.f. cook's high hat.
torchon n.m. duster.
tordre v.tr. to twist.
torpille n.f. cramp-fish, cramp-ray,
numb-fish, torpedo.
torréfié adj. roasted (almonds,
coffee-beans).
torréfier v.tr. to roast (almonds,
coffee-beans).
tortue n.f. (strictly) tortoise;
turtle.
   tortue de mer turtle.
   tortue verte green turtle.
   tortue claire clear turtle soup.
   fausse tortue "mock turtle";
mock turtle soup.
   vraie tortue real turtle; real
turtle soup.
   herbes à tortue n.f.pl. turtle
herbs.
   en tortue (prepared) with turtle
herbs.
tôt adv. soon.
totane n.m. sandpiper.
toujours adv. always; still.
tour n.m. turn.
   tour de feuilletage turn of puff-
pastry.
   tour de moulin turn of (the)
pepper-mill.
   à tour de rôle adv.phr. (each) in
turn.
tourier n.m. puff-pastry cook.
touristique adj. touristic, appertaining to tourists or tourist travel.
tourné adj. turned; turned, shaped
(vegetables).
tournebroche n.m. roasting-jack.
tournedos n.m. round piece of
steak, cut from the long fillet, and
weighing about 4 oz.
tourner v.tr. to turn; to turn, to
shape (vegetables).
   tourner en baril to turn barrel-
shaped.
   tourner en olive to turn olive-
shaped.
tournoyer v.tr. to stir slowly.
tourte n.f. tart.
tourteau, -eaux n.m. edible crab;
round loaf of bread.
tourtelette n.f. small tart.
tourterelle n.f. turtle-dove.
tourtière n.f. baking-tin; pie-dish.

tout, toute, pl. **tous, toutes** adj. & adv. all, every; (the) whole; all.
   tout le monde everybody.
   tout pron. everything.
   le tout n.m. the lot, everything.
   tout adv. quite, completely, entirely.
   tout prêt quite ready.
   tout de suite immediately.
   tout autour adv.phr. all round.
toxique adj. toxic.
tradition n.f. tradition.
traditionnel, -elle adj. traditional.
traitement n.m. treatment.
traité adj. treated.
traiter v.tr. to treat.
tranche n.f. slice.
   tranche de rôti cut off the joint.
   tranche épaisse thick slice.
   tranche grasse fat slice.
   tranche mince thin slice.
   tranches régulières slices of equal thickness.
tranché adj. carved; sliced.
tranchelard n.m. carving-knife.
tranche-pain n.m.inv. in pl. bread-cutter, bread-slicer.
trancher v.tr. to carve; to slice.
trancheur n.m. carver, one who carves.
tranchoir n.m. chopping-board, cutting-board, trencher.
translucide adj. translucid.
transparent adj. transparent.
transversal, -aux adj. transversal.
transversalement adv. transversally.
travail, -aux n.m. work.
travaillé adj. worked; worked, kneaded (dough).
travailler v.i. to work.
   v.tr. to work, to knead (dough); to shape, to fashion.
   travailler la pâte to knead the dough.
travers n.m. bias.
   sur le travers on the bias.
trèfle n.m. clover, trefoil.
treillage n.m. trellis, trellis-pattern.
trempage n.m. (operation of) dipping, soaking.
trempé adj. dipped, soaked.
tremper v.tr. to dip, to soak.
trépied n.m. trivet.
très adv. very; much, very much.
triage n.m. (the operation of) sorting, sorting-out.

triangle n.m. triangle.
triangulaire adj. triangular.
trié adj. sorted, sorted out.
trier v.tr. to sort, to sort out.
trigle n.m. gurnard, gurnet.
tringa n.m. sandpiper.
tripe(s) n.f.(pl.) tripe.
tripière n.f. tripe-kettle.
trique-madame n.f. white stone-crop.
triturateur n.m. triturator.
trituration n.f. trituration.
trituré adj. triturated.
triturer v.tr. to triturate.
trognon n.m. core (e.g. of apple); stump (e.g. of cabbage).
tronc n.m. collecting-box for tips; the contents of the collecting-box.
tronçon n.m. thick slice (of fish), including the central bone, and thicker than a *darne*, q.v.
tronçonné adj. cut into *tronçons*, q.v.
tronçonner v.tr. to cut into *tronçons*, q.v.
trop adv. too; too much.
   trop cuit overcooked, overdone.
tropical, -aux adj. tropical (e.g. fruit).
tropique n.m. tropic; hottest part of the oven.
trou n.m. hole.
trousse n.f. canvas roll (for knives, etc.).
troussé adj. trussed.
trousser v.tr. to truss.
trouver v.tr. to find.
truelle n.f. trowel.
   truelle à poisson fish-slice.
truffage n.m. (the operation of) garnishing with truffles.
truffe n.f. truffle.
   truffe blanche white truffle.
   truffe d'eau water caltrop(s).
   truffe noire black truffle.
truffé adj. garnished with truffles.
truffer v.tr. to garnish with truffles.
truie n.f. sow; hog-fish.
   truie de mer hog-fish.
truite n.f. trout.
   truite de lac lake trout.
   truite de rivière river trout.
   truite saumonée salmon-trout.
truitière n.f. trout-kettle.
trumeau, -eaux n.m. leg (esp. upper part of shin) of beef.
tube n.m. tube, duct; tube, pipe.
tubercule n.m. tuber.

tuer v.tr. to kill.
turban n.m. turban, turban-shape.
  turban rouge acorn-shell.
turbot n.m. turbot.
turbotière n.f. turbot-kettle.
turbotin n.m. young turbot.
tuyau, -aux n.m. pipe (e.g. for gas, water).
  tuyau d'eau water-pipe.
  tuyau de gaz gas-pipe.
type n.m. type; (slang) type, character, chap.

U

usage n.m. usage; custom, practice.
usé adj. used up; worn out.
user v.tr. to use up; to wear out.
usité adj. used, in use.
ustensile n.m. utensil.
  ustensile allant au feu fire-proof utensil.
  ustensile allant au four oven-proof utensil.
  ustensile de cuisine kitchen utensil.
  ustensile spécial special utensil.
utile adj. useful.
utilisable adj. usable, utilizable.
utilisé adj. used, utilized.
utiliser v.tr. to use, to utilize.
utilité n.f. usefulness.

V

vacances n.f.pl. holidays, vacation.
  en vacances on holiday, on vacation.
vairon n.m. minnow.
vaisselle n.f. crockery; plates, dishes, etc.; washing-up.
  faire la vaisselle to do the washing-up.
  vaisselle de porcelaine china.
  vaisselle de terre earthenware.
valable adj. valid, good; valid, cogent.
valence n.f. (name given in Paris to the) Valencia orange.
valeur n.f. value.
  de valeur adj.phr. of value, valuable.
vandoise n.f. vendace.
vanille n.f. vanilla.
vanillé adj. flavoured with vanilla.

vaniller v.tr. to flavour with vanilla.
vanneau, -eaux n.m. lapwing, peewit, green plover.
  œufs de vanneau n.m.pl. plovers' eggs.
vapeur n.f. vapour; water-vapour, steam.
  vapeur d'eau water-vapour, steam.
vaporisé adj. vaporized.
vaporiser v.tr. to vaporize.
variante n.f. variant, variation (e.g. in recipe, method).
varié adj. varied, various, miscellaneous.
varier v.tr. to vary.
veau, -eaux n.m. calf; veal.
  veau de lait sucking-calf.
végétarien, -enne adj. & n. vegetarian.
veille n.f. day before, previous day.
  la veille adv.phr. (on) the day before, (on) the previous day.
veine n.f. vein.
velours n.m. velvet.
  adj. velvety.
velouté n.m. soup thickened with egg-yolk or double cream; fundamental sauce, of chicken, veal or fish, thickened with *roux blond*, q.v.
venaison n.f. venison.
  basse venaison small venison (e.g. hares and wild rabbits).
  grosse venaison large venison.
vendre v.tr. to sell.
vendredi n.m. Friday.
  le vendredi saint Good Friday.
vénéneux, -euse adj. poisonous (e.g. mushroom).
venir v.i. to come.
ventral, -aux adj. ventral.
ventre n.m. belly.
vénus n.f. venus, (variety of) bivalve mollusc.
ver n.m. worm.
  ver de viande maggot.
verdâtre adj. greenish.
verjus n.m. verjuice.
vermeil, -eille adj. mellow (fruit).
vermicelle n.m. vermicelli.
vermicelli n.m.pl. vermicelli.
vermout(h) n.m. vermouth.
véron n.m. minnow.
verre n.m. glass.
  verre à liqueur liqueur glass.
  verre à vin wine glass.
  un plein verre a glassful.

un verre plein a full glass.
verrerie n.f. glassware.
vers prep. toward(s); (in time) towards, about.
verser v.tr. to pour.
vert adj. & n.m. green.
verveine n.f. verbena.
vesou n.m. cane-juice.
vessie n.f. bladder.
  vessie natatoire swimming-bladder (of fish).
vestiaire n.m. cloakroom.
veston n.m. jacket.
vêtements n.m.pl. clothes, clothing.
viande n.f. meat.
  viande de boucherie butcher's meat.
  viande blanche white meat.
  viande blonde white meat.
  viande noire dark meat, brown meat.
  viande rouge red meat.
  viande(s) conservée(s) preserved meat.
  viandes froides cold buffet.
vide adj. empty.
  n.m. space, empty space.
  à moitié vide adj.phr. half empty.
vide-bouteille(s) n.m.inv. in pl. siphon.
vide-citron, pl. **vide-citrons** n.m. lemon-squeezer.
videlle n.f. corer; wheeled cutter.
vide-pomme, pl. **vide-pommes** n.m. apple-corer.
vider v.tr. to empty.
  vider à moitié to half empty.
vieille n.f. wrasse.
  vieille de mer wrasse.
vieux, vieille adj. old.
vigne n.f. vine.
  feuille de vigne n.f. vine-leaf.
vigneau, -eaux n.m. periwinkle, winkle.
vignot n.m. periwinkle, winkle.
vin n.m. wine.
  vin blanc white wine.
  vin rosé pink wine.
  vin rouge red wine.
  vin chambré wine at room-temperature.
  vin mousseux sparkling wine.
  vin pétillant semi-sparkling wine.
  vin viné fortified wine.
  vin rouge de Bordeaux claret.

  vin blanc du Rhin hock.
  vin de Malvoisie Malmsey (wine).
  vin de table table wine.
vinaigre n.m. vinegar.
  vinaigre d'estragon tarragon vinegar.
  vinaigre de vin wine vinegar.
vinaigré adj. flavoured with vinegar.
vinaigrer v.tr. to flavour with vinegar.
vinaigrette n.f. oil and vinegar dressing.
violet, -ette adj. violet (colour).
  violet n.m. violet (colour).
  violette n.f. violet (flower).
viscéral, -aux adj. visceral.
viscères n.m.pl. viscera.
visite n.f. visit.
visiter v.tr. to visit.
vitamine n.f. vitamin.
vite adv. quickly, rapidly, fast.
vivant adj. live, alive.
  poisson(s) vivant(s) n.m. live fish(es).
  truite vivante n.f. live trout.
vive n.f. weever.
vivement adv. briskly.
vivier n.m. live fish tank.
vodka n.f. vodka.
voici dem.prep. here is; here are.
voilà dem.prep. there is; there are.
voir v.tr. & i. to see.
voiture n.f. trolley.
  voiture à entremets sweet-trolley, cold trolley.
  voiture à hors d'œuvre hors d'œuvre(s) trolley.
  voiture à trancher carving-trolley.
  voiture chaude hot trolley.
vol n.m. theft.
  petits vols pl. petty theft(s), pilfering.
volaille n.f. poultry.
volailleur n.m. poulterer.
vol-au-vent n.m.inv. in pl. made-up preparation consisting of a round or oval puff-pastry case containing a designated filling.
  vol-au-vent de volaille chicken *vol-au-vent*, q.v.
volonté n.f. desire, wish.
  à volonté adv.phr. as desired.
vomer n.m. moon-fish.
vouloir v.tr. & i. to wish; to wish to; to want.

voulu adj. wanted, desired, required.
    la consistance voulue n.f. the desired, required, consistency.
vrai adj. real; true.

W

whisky n.m. whisky.

X

xérès n.m. sherry.

Y

yeux n.m. (plural of) *œil*, q.v.

Z

zandre n.f. pike-perch.
zeste n.m. outer peel (of orange, lemon).
    zeste confit candied peel.
ziste n.m. white layer immediately underneath the outer peel (of orange, lemon).

APPENDIX TO

FRENCH - ENGLISH

Appendix to
French – English

a

âcre adj. acrid.
africain adj. African.
agréablement adv. pleasantly.
aiguillette de bœuf f. point of the rump of beef.
algérien, -enne adj. Algerian.
aliment n.m. aliment, food.
allemand adj. German.
alsacien, -enne adj. Alsatian.
américain adj. American.
andalou, -ouse adj. Andalusian.
ange de mer n.m. angel-fish.
anglais adj. English.
angoumois adj. of Angoulême.
anguille de mer f. conger eel.
annonceur n.m. announcer, "barker" (in kitchen).
antibois adj. of Antibes.
anversois adj. of Antwerp.
arachide n.f. peanut, ground-nut, monkey-nut.
arbrisseau, -eaux n.m. shrub.
arbuste n.m. shrub.
ardennais adj. of the Ardennes.
arlésien, -enne adj. Arlesian, of Arles.
arrêter v.tr. to stop.
aubergiste n.m. or f. innkeeper.
auvergnat adj. of Auvergne.
aveyronnais adj. of Aveyron.

b

badois adj. of Baden.
barbarine n.f. (variety of) squash-melon.
béarnais adj. of Béarn.
bernois adj. of Berne.
berrichon, -onne adj. of Berry.
bête n.f. animal, beast.
biarrot adj. of Biarritz.
biscaïen, -enne adj. Biscayan, of Biscay.
bohémien, -enne adj. Bohemian.
bolonais adj. of Bologna.

bondelle n.f. (variety of) small silver trout, found in Swiss lakes.
bordelais adj. of Bordeaux.
bosniaque adj. Bosnian.
bosnien, -enne adj. Bosnian.
brésilien, -enne adj. Brazilian.
bressan adj. of Bresse.
breton, -onne adj. Breton.
brosse à farine f. flour-brush.
brunois adj. of Brunoy.
bruxellois adj. of Brussels.
buccin n.m. whelk.
bureau de contrôle m. control office.
byzantin adj. Byzantine.

c

calaisien, -enne adj. of Calais.
cancalais adj. of Cancale.
cardamome n.m. cardamom.
châtaigne n.f. sweet Spanish chestnut.
chayot(t)e n.f. chow-chow.
coulibiac n.m. (variety of) Russian layered pie, containing salmon, eggs, *vésiga* (q.v.), etc.
crochet n.m. butcher's hook.

d

danois adj. Danish.
dartois n.m. made-up pastry preparation, with savoury filling, and with puff-pastry covering marked with diagonal striations.
dauphinois adj. of Dauphiné.
deauvillais adj. of Deauville.
délice n.m. fillet of sole folded over on itself so that the wide end covers the narrow one.
dieppois adj. of Dieppe.
dijonnais adj. of Dijon.
dorure anglaise f. egg-wash.
dunois adj. of Dunois.

e

écossais adj. Scottish, Scots.
égyptien, -enne adj. Egyptian.
épice composée f. compound
  spice.

f

fade adj. insipid.
farine de maïs f. corn-flour.
  farine de riz rice-flour.
fécampois adj. of Fécamp.
fibreux, -euse adj. fibrous.
flamand adj. Flemish.
florentin adj. Florentine.
fogas n.m. Danubian pike-perch
  (also found in Lake Balaton).
foie de veau m. calf's liver.
français adj. French.

g

gascon, -onne adj. Gascon.
gaulois adj. Gaulish.
genevois adj. of Geneva.
génois adj. Genoese.
gnocchi n.m.pl. gnocchi.
goujon n.m. small piece of fillet
  (esp. of sole) shaped like a small fish
  and usually fried.
grec, grecque adj. Greek.
grenoblois adj. of Grenoble.

h

haut-parleur n.m. loudspeaker.
havanais adj. Havanese, of Havana.
havrais adj. of (Le) Havre.
hollandais adj. Dutch.
hongrois adj. Hungarian.
hyérois adj. of Hyères.

i

indien, -enne adj. Indian.
infra-rouge adj. infra-red.
insipide adj. tasteless.
irlandais adj. Irish.
islandais adj. Icelandic.
italien, -enne adj. Italian.

j

japonais adj. Japanese.
jardinière n.f. garnish of an ensemble of fresh carrots, turnips and
  French beans, suitably turned or
  shaped, and of kidney beans, peas
  and cauliflower-tops.
javanais adj. Javanese.
jurassien, -enne adj. of the Jura.

l

languedocien, -enne adj. of
  Languedoc.
liégeois adj. of Liège.
ligurien, -enne adj. Ligurian.
limousin adj. of Limoges.
livonien, -enne adj. Livonian.
livournais adj. of Leghorn.
lompe n.f. lump, lump-fish, lump-
  sucker.
lorrain adj. Lorrainese, of Lorraine.
loup marin m. wolf-fish, cat-fish.
lucernois adj. of Lucerne.
lyonnais adj. of Lyon.

m

mâconnais adj. of Mâcon.
madrilène adj. of Madrid.
maltais adj. Maltese.
marguerite n.f. daisy; (stylized)
  daisy-shape (esp. of white of hard-
  boiled egg).
marmiton n.m. scullion.
marocain adj. Moroccan.
mentonnais adj. of Menton(e).
mexicain adj. Mexican.
milanais adj. Milanese.
mollusque n.m. mollusc.
monégasque adj. Monesgasque, of
  Monaco.
moscovite adj. Muscovite, of
  Moscow.
mostèle n.f. rockling.
mostelle n.f. rockling.
mustèle n.f. rockling.

n

napolitain adj. Neapolitan, of
  Naples.
narbonnais adj. of Narbonne.

navarrais adj. Navarrese, of Navarre.
niçois adj. of Nice.
nîmois adj. of Nîmes.
nivernais adj. of Nevers.
normand adj. Norman, of Normandy.
norvégien, -enne adj. Norwegian.

O

oranais adj. of Oran.
orléanais adj. of Orleans.
ostendais adj. of Ostend.

p

palermitain adj. of Palermo.
palois adj. of Pau.
parisien, -enne adj. Parisian.
parmesan adj. Parmesan.
pastillage n.m. gum-paste.
patte natatoire f. swimmeret (e.g. of lobster).
percheron, -onne adj. of Perche.
périgourdin adj. of Périgord.
persan adj. Persian.
phocéen, -enne adj. Phocaean.
piémontais adj. Piedmontese.
pisan adj. Pisan.
poêle à omelettes f. omelette-pan.
polonais adj. Polish.
portugais adj. Portuguese.
poulardine n.f. (variety of) young table-fowl.
prix de revient m. cost price.
  prix de vente sale price.
provençal adj. Provençal.

r

régimier n.m. diet-cook.
rillauds n.m.pl. pork-butchery preparation of pork lean and fat, finely chopped, seasoned and cooked.
rillettes n.f.pl. *rillauds* (q.v.) pounded after cooking.
rillons n.m.pl. (another name for) *rillauds*, q.v.
risotto n.m. rizotto.
riz à entremets m. sweetened rice.
  riz Caroline, riz caroline Carolina rice.
  riz créole (variety of) savoury rice preparation.

riz pilaf, riz pilaff, riz pilau, riz pilaw braised rice.
rochelois adj. of La Rochelle.
romain adj. Roman.
rondeau, -eaux n.m. large, fairly shallow, round stew-pan with a loop handle on each side.
rondelle n.f. smaller version of the *rondeau*, q.v.
rôtisserie n.f. steak-house; cooking unit used for roasting on the spit.
rôtissoire n.f. Dutch oven.
rouennais adj. of Rouen.
roumain adj. Rumanian.
royan n.m. sardine.
rubrique n.f. heading, title.
russe adj. Russian.

S

sabayon n.m. zabaione; (preparation of) yolks of eggs beaten to incorporate air, and used as a basic thickening.
sablé n.m. (variety of) shortbread biscuit.
saillant adj. bulging, prominent (esp. eye of freshly-caught fish).
salicoque n.f. variety of shrimp.
salmigondis n.m. salmagundi, variety of stew made of one or several kinds of reheated meat.
salpicon n.m. basic preparation, esp. of meat or fish, bound with a sauce.
sanglé adj. (substance in a container) packed round with ice (to freeze the substance).
sangler v.tr. to pack round (substance in a container) with ice (to freeze the substance).
sanglier de mer m. boar-fish.
sarladais adj. of Sarlat.
savarin n.m. made-up sweet preparation, of raised paste, in the shape of an annulus, soaked in syrup and flavoured (e.g.) with rum.
savoyard adj. Savoyard, of Savoy.
sébaste n.m. sea-perch, Norway haddock, bergylt.
séchage n.m. (operation of) drying (esp. of fish).
sel gemme m. rock salt.
sibérien, -enne adj. Siberian.
sicilien, -enne adj. Sicilian.
singé adj. dusted with flour (which is then cooked on).

singer v.tr. to dust (meat) with flour and then to cook the flour on.
soissonnais adj. of Soissonnais.
sorbetière n.f. machine for making *sorbet*, q.v.
soufflé n.m. soufflé.
premier sous-chef m. first deputy head of the kitchen.
sous-noix n.f. piece of meat cut from under the *noix*, q.v.
strasbourgeois adj. of Strasbourg.
suédois adj. Swedish.
suisse adj. Swiss.
surlonge n.f. cut (of beef) between the *paleron* (q.v.) and the *talon du collier*, q.v.

t

tarte n.f. enclosed tart.
tirer v.tr. to draw.
touffe n.f. tuft; bunch.
toulonnais adj. of Toulon.
toulousain adj. of Toulouse.
trouvillois adj. of Trouville.
truite arc-en-ciel f. rainbow trout.
truite de mer salmon-trout.
turc, turque adj. Turkish.
tyrolien, -enne adj. Tyrolean, Tyrolese.

V

vacherin n.m. (variety of) *gâteau* (q.v.) based on meringue.

vanné adj. (sauce) stirred.
vanner v.tr. to stir (sauce).
varsovien, -enne adj. of Warsaw.
vauclusien, -enne adj. of Vaucluse.
vénitien, -enne adj. Venetian.
véronais adj. Veronese, of Verona.
verrat n.m. boar.
vert-cuit adj. (meat) cooked just enough to seal it, but so that it is still *saignant*, q.v.
vésiga n.f. spinal marrow of the sturgeon.
vichyssois adj. of Vichy.
viennois adj. Viennese.
vif, vive adj. live; brisk (flame); raw.
    feu vif n.m. brisk flame, quick fire.
    peler à vif v.tr. to peel raw.
visqueux, -euse adj. viscous.
vivarais adj. of Vivarais; of Viviers.
voile n.m. thin coating.
voilé adj. thinly coated.
voiler v.tr. to coat thinly.

W

westphalien, -enne adj. Westphalian.

Z

zesté adj. (orange, lemon) having had the *zeste* (q.v.) removed.
zester v.tr. to remove the *zeste* (q.v.) from (orange, lemon).

VOCABULARY
ENGLISH – FRENCH

English – French

a

abdomen n. abdomen, m.
abdominal adj. abdominal.
ability n. habileté, f.
to be able to v.tr. & i. pouvoir.
above prep. & adv. dessus.
absence n. absence, f.; (of materials) défaut, m.
  in the absence of prep.phr. à défaut de.
absinth(e) n. absinthe, f.
to absorb v.tr. absorber.
absorbed adj. absorbé.
to accept v.tr. accepter.
accompanied adj. accompagné.
accompaniment n. accompagnement, m.
to accompany v.tr. accompagner.
according to prep.phr. selon.
acid adj. acide, acidulé.
  n. acide, m.
  acetic acid acide acétique.
  salicylic acid acide salicylique.
acidimeter n. pèse-acide, m.
acidity n. acidité, f.
to acidulate v.tr. aciduler.
acidulated adj. acidulé.
acorn n. gland, m.
acorn-shell n. balane, f., gland (m.) de mer, turban (m.) rouge.
acquaintance n. connaissance, f.
to be acquainted with v.tr. connaître.
to add v.tr. ajouter.
  to add up v.tr. additionner.
adderwort n. bistorte, f.
addition n. addition, f.; (supplement) supplément, m.
  in addition en plus, en supplément.
additional adj. supplémentaire.
adept adj. habile.
adequate adj. suffisant.
adequately adv. suffisamment.
to adhere v.i. adhérer.
to adjust v.tr. mettre à point, mettre au point; (seasoning) rectifier.

to adjust for consistency mettre à point de consistance.
adjusted adj. mis à point, mis au point; (seasoning) rectifié.
adjustment n. mise (f.) à point, mise au point.
  adjustment of consistency mise à point de consistance, mise au point de consistance.
in advance adv.phr. à l'avance.
to aerate v.tr. aérer, gazéifier.
aerated adj. aéré, gazéifié.
after prep. après.
afternoon n. après-midi, m. or f.
afterwards adv. après, ensuite.
against prep. contre.
agar-agar n. gélose, f.
agaric n. agaric, m.
agreement n. accord.
albumen n. albumen, m.
albumin n. albumine, f.
alcohol n. alcool, m.
alcoholic adj. alcoolique.
alcoholometer n. pèse-alcool, m.
ale n. bière, f.
  brown ale bière brune.
  dark ale bière noire.
  pale ale bière blonde.
alexanders n. maceron (m.) potager.
alkaloid adj. alcaloïde.
  n. alcaloïde, m.
all adj. & pron. tout.
  above all surtout.
alliaceous adj. alliacé.
allice-shad n. grande alose, f.
to allow v.tr. laisser, permettre.
  to allow to glaze laisser tomber à glace.
  to allow to harden laisser prendre.
  to allow to rise laisser lever.
  to allow to set laisser prendre.
allspice n. poivron, m., poivre (m.) de Jamaïque, quatre épices, f.pl.
almond n. amande, f.
  bitter almond amande amère.
  sweet almond amande douce.
almost adv. presque.
already adv. déjà.

also adv. aussi; également.
alternate adj. alterné.
  to alternate v.tr. alterner.
always adv. toujours.
to amalgamate v.tr. amalgamer.
amalagamated adj. amalgamé.
amid prep. parmi.
amomum n. amome, m.
among prep. parmi.
amphibian n. amphibie, m.
amphibious adj. amphibie.
amygdalic adj. amygdalin.
amygdalin n. amygdaline, f.
analogous adj. analogue.
anchovy n. anchois.
  anchovy fillet filet (m.) d'anchois.
anethum n. anet(h), m.
angel-fish n. angelot, m., ange (m.)
  de mer.
angelica n. angélique, f.
angler(-fish) n. baudroie, f.,
  boudreuil, m., crapaud (m.), de mer,
  diable (m.), de mer, lotte (f.) de
  mer, poisson-grenouille, m.
animal n. animal, m., bête, f.
  black game animal (e.g. boar)
  gibier (m.) noir.
  farmyard animal animal de
  basse-cour.
anise n. anis, m.
  star anise anis étoilé, badian,
  m., badiane, f.
aniseed n. anis, m.; graine (f.)
  d'anis.
anisette-cordial n. anisette, f.
annulus n. collerette, f.; (of
  mushroom) bague, f.
annulus-shape n. collerette, f.
anona n. anone, f.
  muricate anona anone muriquée.
  reticulate anona anone réticulée.
answer n. réponse, f.
to answer v.i. répondre.
antenna n. antenne, f.
anthyllis n. anthyllide, f.
apart adv. à part.
aperture n. ouverture, f., orifice,
  m.
aponeurosis n. aponévrose, f.
appellation n. appellation, f.,
  dénomination, f.
appetite n. appétit, m.
apple n. pomme, f.
  queening apple calville, f.
apple-corer n. vide-pomme, m.
apprentice n. apprenti, m.;
  apprentie, f.

apprenticeship n. apprentissage,
  m.
appropriate adj. approprié, convenable.
to appropriate v.tr. approprier.
appropriately adv. convenablement.
apricot n. abricot, m.
  clingstone apricot alberge, f.
April n. avril, m.
apron n. tablier, m.
arbutus n. arbousier, m.
arbutus-berry n. arbouse, f.
argentina n. argentine, f.
aroma n. aroma, m.
aromatic adj. aromatique.
  n. aromate, m.
to aromatize v.tr. aromatiser.
aromatized adj. aromatisé.
to arrange v.tr. arranger,
  aménager, disposer.
arrow-root n. arrow-root, m.
artichoke n.
  Chinese artichoke crosne, m.,
  crosne du Japon, stachys, m.,
  stachys tubéreux.
  globe artichoke artichaut, m.
  Jerusalem artichoke topinambour, m., artichaut (m.) d'hiver.
artichoke-base n. fond (m.)
  d'artichaut.
article n. article, m.
wild arum n. gouet, m., pied-de-
  veau, m.
ash n. cendre, f.
to ask v.tr. demander.
  to ask for demander.
asparagus n. asperge, f.
asparagus-tip n. pointe (f.)
  d'asperge.
asperula n. aspérule, f.
aspic n. aspic, m.
to assist v.tr. aider.
assistant n. commis, m.
astringent adj. astringent.
  n. astringent, m.
atherine n. athérine, f.
to attach v.tr. attacher.
attached adj. attaché.
attention n. attention, f.
  to pay attention to faire attention
  à; avoir soin de.
to attenuate v.tr. atténuer.
attenuated adj. atténué.
to augment v.tr. augmenter.
  to augment with additionner de.
August n. août, m.
autumn n. automne, m.

average adj. moyen.
  n. moyenne, f.
avocet n. avocette, f.
to avoid v.tr. éviter.
  to avoid doing something éviter de faire quelque chose.
away from prep.phr. hors de, en dehors de.
  away from the flame hors du feu.

b

baba-mould n. moule (m.) à baba.
back n. dos, m.
backbone n. (of fish) arête (f.) médiane, grande arête.
bacon n. lard, m.
  flitch of bacon flèche (f.) de lard.
  larding bacon lard à piquer.
  streaky bacon lard maigre.
bacon-rind n. couenne, f.
bacteria n.pl. bactéries, f.pl.
bacterium n. bactérie, f.
bad adj. mauvais.
badly adv. mal.
bag n. sac, m.
  small bag sachet, m.
to bake v.tr. (faire) cuire au four.
baker n. boulanger, m.
bakery n. boulangerie, f.
baking n. cuisson (au four), f.
baking-powder n. levure (f.) artificielle, poudre (f.) à lever, poudre levain.
baking-sheet for pastry n. plaque (f.) à pâtisserie, plaque de pâtisserie.
baking-tin n. tourtière, f.
balance n. équilibre, m.
to balance v.tr. équilibrer.
balanced adj. équilibré.
ball n. boule, f.
  small ball boulette, f.
ball-shape n. boule, f.
  small ball-shape boulette, f.
balm n. mélisse, f.
bamboo n. bambou, m.
bamboo-shoot n. pousse (f.) de bambou.
banana n. banane, f.
band n. bande, f.
banquet n. banquet, m., festin, m.
bantam-cock n. coq (m.) de Bantam.
bantam-hen n. poule (f.) de Bantam.

bar n. (of chocolate) tablette, f.
barbel n. (fish) barbeau, m., barbillon, m.; (of fish) barbe, f., barbillon, m.
barberry n. épine-vignette, f.
to bark v.i. aboyer.
barker n. aboyeur, m.
barley n. orge, usually f. but occ. m.
  hulled barley orge (m.) mondé.
  pearl barley orge (m.) perlé.
barleycorn n. grain (m.) d'orge.
barm n. levain (m.) de bière, levure (f.) de bière.
barnacle n. bernache, f., bernacle, f.
barrel n. tonneau, m., baril, m., fût, m.
  small barrel tonnelet, m.
to barrel v.tr. entonner.
barrelled adj. entonné.
base n. fond, m., base, f.
  base of artichoke fond d'artichaut.
  base of vegetables (for braising) matignon, f.
basella n. baselle, f.
basement n. sous-sol, m.
basil n. basilic, m.
basin n. bassin, m.
basis n. base, f.; principe, m.
basket n. panier, m.
  open basket corbeille, f.
  potato basket panier en pommes de terre.
  pulled sugar basket panier en sucre tiré.
bass n. perche (f.) commune, perche noire, perche de rivière, perche-truite, f.
  black bass bar (m.) noir.
  striped bass bar rayé.
to baste v.tr. arroser.
basted adj. arrosé.
basting n. arrosage, m.
bat n. (for beating) batte, f.
batch n. (of loaves) fournée, f.
bath n. bain, m.
batrachian n. batracien, m.
batter n. pâte (f.) à frire, pâte lisse.
bay n. (leaf) laurier, m.; (in mixing pastry ingredients) fontaine, f.
bayleaf n. feuille (f.) de laurier.
to be v.i. être.
  to be hungry avoir faim.
  to be thirsty avoir soif.
beaded adj. perlé.
bean n. fève, f.; haricot, m.

broad bean fève de(s) marais.
French bean haricot vert.
haricot bean haricot blanc.
kidney bean fève de haricot.
green kidney bean fève verte, chevrier, m.
small kidney bean flageolet, m.
French nigger bean haricot noir.
runner bean haricot d'Espagne.
Soissons bean haricot de Soissons.
soya bean pois chinois.
bean-pod n. cosse (f.) de haricot.
  bean-pods cosses de haricots.
bean-shuck n. cosse (f.) de haricot.
  bean-shucks cosses de haricots.
bear n. ours, m.
bearberry n. cerise (f.) d'ours, raisin (m.) d'ours.
beard n. barbe, f.
  Jupiter's beard joubarbe, f., artichaut (m.) des toits.
to beard v.tr. (oyster) ébarber.
bearded adj. (oyster) ébarbé.
to beat v.tr. battre.
  to beat a point battre à pointe.
  to beat stiffly to a fluffy consistency battre en neige.
beaten adj. battu.
beater n. battoir, m.
  wooden beater battoir en bois.
beautiful adj. beau.
because conj. parce que.
to become v.i. devenir.
  to become frozen geler.
  to become ropy (wine) graisser.
bed n. lit, m.
  bed of vegetables (usually for braising) matignon, f.
  watercress bed cressonnière, f.
beechnut n. faine, f., faîne, f., fêne, f.
beef n. bœuf, n.
  roast beef rosbif, m.
beefsteak n. bifteck, m.
beer n. bière, f.
  dark beer bière noire.
  light beer bière blonde.
beet n. bette, f.
  white beet poirée, f.
beetroot n. betterave, f.
before prep. avant.
  adv. avant, auparavant.
  conj. avant que.
beforehand adv. auparavant, au préalable, préalablement.
to begin v.tr. & i. commencer.
  to begin again recommencer.

belly n. ventre, m.; (of beef) panse, f.; (of pork) poitrine, f.
  belly of pork poitrine de porc.
below prep. sous.
beneath prep. sous.
to benefit v.i. profiter.
bergamot n. bergamot(t)e, f.
berried adj. (lobster) œuvé.
berry n. baie, f.
beside prep. à côté de.
besides adv. en outre.
best adj. le meilleur; de première qualité.
  adv. le mieux.
better adj. meilleur.
  adv. mieux.
between prep. entre.
beverage n. breuvage, m., boisson, f.
bias n. travers, m.
  on the bias sur le travers.
bib n. bavette, f.; (fish) tacaud, m.
big adj. grand; (bulky) gros.
bilberry n. airelle (f.) myrtille, myrtille, f.
bill n. note, f.; (in restaurant) addition, f.
  bill of fare carte, f.
to bind v.tr. lier.
  to bind lightly (sauce) lier légèrement.
binding n. (of sauce) liaison, f.
bird n. oiseau, m.
  wading bird échassier, m.
biscuit n. biscuit, m.
  ship's biscuit biscuit de mer.
  wafer biscuit gaufrette, f.
bistort n. bistorte, f.
bit n. morceau, m.
bitter adj. amer.
  bitter(s) n. amer, m.
black adj. noir.
blackberry n. mûre (f.) de ronce, mûre sauvage.
blackbird n. merle, m.
blackcock n. petit coq (m.) de bruyère, coq (m.) des bouleaux, petit tétras, m., tétras lyre.
black-currant n. groseille (f.) noire, cassis, m.
to blacken v.tr. noircir.
  blackened adj. noirci.
blackgame n. grand tétras, m.
blackish adj. noirâtre.
bladder n. vessie, f.
blade n. (of knife) lame, f.
to blanch v.tr. blanchir; (almonds) dérober.

blanched adj. blanchi; (almonds) dérobé.

blancmange n. blanc-manger, m.

blank n. blanc, m.

blaze n. flambée, f.

bleak n. ablette, f.

to bleed v.i. saigner.

blend n. mélange, m.

to blend v.tr. mélanger.

blended adj. mélangé.

block n. bloc, m.

blood n. sang, m.
  congealed blood sang figé.
  pig's blood sang de porc.

blood-orange n. sanguine, f.

bloody adj. saigneux.

blossom n. fleurs, f.pl.

blow n. coup, m.

to blow v.i. souffler.

blue adj. bleu.
  n. bleu, m.
  dark blue bleu foncé.
  light blue bleu clair.

bluish adj. bleuâtre.

boar n. verrat, m.
  wild boar sanglier, m.
  young wild boar marcassin, m.

board n. planche, f.
  small board planchette, f.

to boil v.i. bouillir.
  v.tr. faire bouillir, bouillir.
  to boil away v.i. ébouillir, bouillir à bouilli perdu.
  to boil away v.tr. (faire) bouillir à bouilli perdu.
  to boil down v.i. se consommer, v.refl.
  to boil over v.i. déborder.

boiled adj. bouilli.
  boiled away ébouilli.

boiling n. ébullition, f.; bouillon, m.
  gentle boiling petite ébullition.

bone n. os, m.

to bone v.tr. désosser; (fish) désarêter.

boned adj. désossé; (fish) désarêté.

bone-marrow n. moelle, f.

boning n. désossage, m.

boning-knife n. couteau (m.) à désosser.

bonito n. bonite, f.

book n. livre, m.

borage m. bourrache, f.

border n. bord, m., bordure, f.

to border v.tr. border.

bordered adj. bordé.

borecole n. chou (m.) frisé.

boss n. patron, m.; patronne, f.

bottle n. bouteille, f.

to bottle v.tr. (wine) mettre en bouteilles; (fruit) mettre en bocal.

bottle-opener n. ouvre-bouteilles, m.
  crown cork bottle-opener décapsulateur, m.

bottle-washer n. rince-bouteilles, m.

bound adj. lié.
  lightly bound (sauce) légèrement lié.

bouquet n. (of wine) bouquet, m., parfum, m., fumet, m.

bowl n. bassin, m., bol, m.; (of spoon) cuilleron, m.

box n. boîte, f.

boy n. garçon, m.

brace n. (of birds) paire, f.
  a brace of pheasants une paire de faisans.

brain(s) n. cervelle, f.
  calves' brains cervelle(s) de veau.

to braise v.tr. braiser.
  to braise lightly poêler.

braised adj. braisé.
  lightly braised poêlé.

braising n. braisage, m.
  brown braising braisage à brun.
  white braising braisage à blanc.

braising-fire n. feu (m.) de braise, braise, f.

braising-pan n. braisière, f.

braising-stock n. fonds (m.) de braisage.

brambling n. pinson (m.) des Ardennes.

bran n. son, m.

branch n. branche, f.
  small branch branchette, f.
  very small branch branchillon, m.

brand n. marque, f.
  a good brand une bonne marque.

brandy n. eau-de-vie, f.

brawn n. fromage.
  pork brawn fromage de porc.

bread n. pain, m.
  black bread pain noir.
  brown bread pain bis, pain de son.
  buckwheat bread pain de sarrasin.
  canary bread pain échaudé, echaudé, m.
  fresh bread pain frais.
  household bread pain de ménage.

hunk of bread   quignon (m.) de pain.

rye bread   pain de seigle.

stale bread   pain rassis.

wheaten bread   pain de froment.

finest wheaten bread   mousseau, m., moussot, m.

white bread   pain blanc.

breadcrumb(s)   n.   mie (f.) de pain; (for frying) chapelure, f.

     stale breadcrumbs   mie de pain rassis.

to breadcrumb   v.tr.   paner.

breadcrumbed   adj.   pané.

bread-cutter   n.   tranche-pain, m.

bread-fruit   n.   fruit (m.) à pain.

bread-knife   n.   couteau (m.) à pain.

bread-slicer   n.   taille-pain, m., tranche-pain, m.

breadth   n.   largeur, f.

bread-toaster   n.   grille-pain, m.

to break   v.tr.   casser; rompre.

     to break an egg   casser un œuf.

breakage(s)   n.   casse, f.

breakfast   n.   petit déjeuner, m.

     wedding breakfast   repas (m.) de noces.

to breakfast   v.i.   déjeuner, prendre le petit déjeuner.

bream   n.   brème, f.

breast   n.   poitrine, f.

breast-bone   n.   (esp. of chicken) bréchet, m.

brigade   n.   brigade, f.

to brighten   v.tr.   (appearance, colour) aviver.

brill   n.   barbue, f.

brilliant   adj.   brillant.

brim   n.   bord, m.

to bring   v.tr.   apporter; (person) amener.

     to bring in   rentrer.

     to bring near   approcher.

     to bring out   sortir.

     to bring to the boil   amener à ébullition, faire partir.

     to bring up (from below) monter.

brioche-mould   n.   moule (m.) à brioche.

brisk   adj.   vif.

brisket   n.   poitrine (f.) de bœuf.

briskly   adv.   vivement.

brittle   adj.   cassant, croquant.

broad   adj.   large.

broken   adj.   cassé.

broom   n.   balai, m.

     butcher's broom   fragon (m.) épineux.

brought   adj.   apporté; (person) amené.

     brought in   rentré.

     brought near   approché.

     brought out   sorti.

     brought to the boil   amené à ébullition.

     brought up (from below) monté.

brown   adj.   brun.

   n.   brun, m.

     dark brown   brun foncé.

     light brown   brun clair.

to brown   v.tr. & i.   roussir.

   v.tr.   (butter) faire revenir.

browned   adj.   roussi; (butter) revenu.

brownish   adj.   brunâtre.

bruise   n.   meurtrissure, f.; (on fruit) talure, f.

brush   n.   brosse, f.

to brush   v.tr.   brosser.

brushed   adj.   brossé.

Brussels sprout   n.   chou (m.) de Bruxelles.

     Brussels sprouts   choux de Bruxelles.

black bryony   n.   tamier, m., taminier, m., sceau (m.) de Notre-Dame.

bubble   n.   bulle, f.; (in liquid) bouillon, m.

buck   n.   daim, m.

bucket   n.   seau, m.

buckwheat   n.   sarrasin, m., blé (m.) noir.

bud   n.   bourgeon, m.

buffet   n.   buffet, m.

     cold buffet   buffet froid, viandes (f.) froides.

bugloss   n.   buglosse, f.

bulb   n.   bulbe, f.

     electric light bulb   ampoule, f.

to bulge   v.i.   bomber.

bulging   adj.   bombé.

bulk   n.   gros, m.

     in bulk   en gros.

bull   n.   taureau, m.

bulrush   n.   massette, f.

bunch   n.   bouquet, m., botte, f.; (of grapes) grappe, f.

     a bunch of grapes   une grappe de raisin.

bundle   n.   botte, f.

bung   n.   bonde, f.

bung-hole   n.   bonde, f.

ortolan bunting   n.   ortolan, m.

burbot   n.   lotte, f., lotte de rivière.

burdock   n.   bardane, f.

burn n. brûlure, f.
to burn v.tr. & i. brûler.
burned adj. brûlé.
burnet n. pimprenelle, f.
   burnet saxifrage pied-de-bouc, m., pied-de-chèvre, m.
burning adj. brûlant.
bush n. buisson, m.
business n. commerce, m., maison, f.
bustard n. outarde, f.
   great(er) bustard grande outarde.
   little bustard petite outarde, canepetière, f.
   young bustard outardeau, m.
busy adj. occupé.
to busy v.tr. occuper.
   to busy oneself with s'occuper de.
but conj. mais.
butcher n. boucher, m.
butchery n. boucherie, f.
butter n. beurre, m.
   anchovy butter beurre d'anchois.
   basil butter beurre de basilic.
   black butter beurre noir.
   clarified butter beurre clarifié.
   compound butter beurre composé.
   crayfish butter beurre d'écrevisse(s).
   dairy butter beurre de laiterie.
   hazel-nut butter beurre de noisette.
   melted butter beurre fondu.
   mustard butter beurre moutardé.
   nut-brown butter beurre noisette.
   parsley butter beurre de persil.
   pistachio butter beurre de pistaches.
   snail butter beurre d'escargot(s).
   softened butter beurre en pommade.
   tarragon butter beurre d'estragon.
to butter v.tr. beurrer.
buttered adj. beurré.
butter-machine n. machine (f.) à beurre.
buttermilk n. lait (m.) de beurre, babeurre, m.
butter-shaper n. frise-beurre, m.
buttery adj. butyreux.
button n. bouton, m.

C

cabbage n. chou, m.
   red cabbage chou rouge.
   Savoy cabbage chou de Milan, chou de Savoie.
   spring cabbage chou de printemps.
   turnip cabbage chou-rave, m.
   pickled white cabbage choucroute, f.
   whiteheart cabbage chou pommé.
cabbage-heart n. cœur (m.) de chou.
café n. café, m.
caffeine n. caféine, f.
cake n. gâteau, m.
   cake of soap pain (m.) de savon.
calamary n. calmar, m.
calendar n. calendrier, m.
   gastronomic calendar calendrier gastronomique.
calf n. veau, m.
   sucking calf veau de lait.
to call v.tr. appeler.
   to call again v.tr. rappeler.
   to call back v.tr. rappeler.
called adj. appelé.
calorie n. calorie, f.
   large calorie grande calorie.
   small calorie petite calorie.
water caltrop(s) n. écharbot, m., macle, f., macre, f., truffe (f.) d'eau.
calyx n. calice, m.
camomile n. camomille, f.
campanula n. campanule, f.
(tin) can n. boîte (f.) en fer blanc.
candied adj. candi.
   sugar candy n. sucre (m.) candi.
to candy v.tr. candir.
cane-juice n. vesou, m.
canned adj. de conserve, adj.phr.
capelin n. capelan, m.
caper n. câpre, f.
caplin n. capelan, m.
capon n. chapon, m.
capsicum n. piment, m.
caramel n. caramel, m.
to caramelize v.tr. caraméliser.
caramelized adj. caramélisé.
carapace n. carapace, f.
caraway n. carvi, m., cumin (m.) des prés.
carbohydrate n. hydrate (m.) de carbone.

carcase n. carcasse, f.
carcass n. carcasse, f.
card n. carte, f.
cardoon n. cardon, m.
care n. prudence, f.; soin, m.
  with care avec soin.
careful adj. prudent; soigneux, minutieux.
carefully adv. prudemment; soigneusement.
carefulness n. soin, m.
carmine n. carmin, m.
carp n. carpe, f.
  leather carp carpe cuir.
  mirror carp carpe (à) miroir(s).
  young carp carpeau, m.
  very small carp carpillon, m.
carrot n. carotte, f.
to carry v.tr. porter.
  to carry away emporter, enlever.
cartilage n. cartilage, m., tendron, m.
cartilaginous adj. cartilagineux.
to carve v.tr. découper, trancher.
carved adj. découpé, tranché.
carver n. (person) trancheur, m.
carving n. découpage, m.
carving-board n. tailloir, m., tranchoir, m.
carving-fork n. bident, m., four-chette (f.) à découper.
carving-knife n. tranchelard, m., couteau (m.) à découper.
carving-trolley n. voiture (f.) chaude, voiture (f.) à trancher.
case n. caisse, f.
casein n. caséine, f.
case-opener n. ouvre-caisses, m.
cashew-nut n. noix (f.) d'acajou.
cask n. tonneau, m., baril, m., fût, m.
  large cask pipe, f.
  small cask tonnelet, m.
to cask v.tr. entonner.
casked adj. entonné.
cassava n. cassava, f., manioc, m.
cassia n. cannelle (f.) de Chine.
to castrate v.tr. châtrer.
castrated adj. châtré.
to catch v.tr. attraper.
  to catch fire v.i. prendre feu.
catfish n. poisson-chat, m., loup (m.) marin.
caul n. coiffe, f., crépine, f., toilette, f.
cauldron n. chaudron, m.
cauliflower n. chou-fleur, m.
cauliflower-top n. boule (f.) de chou-fleur.

cavally n. saurel, m.
caviar(e) n. caviar, m.
  grey caviar caviar gris.
cavity n. cavité, f.
to cease v.tr. & i. cesser.
ceiling n. plafond, m.
(lesser) celandine n. ficaire, f.
celebration n. fête, f.
celeriac n. céleri-rave, m.
celery n. céleri, m.
  stick of celery morceau (m.) de céleri.
  stringy celery céleri cordé.
cell n. cellule, f.; (of honeycomb) alvéole, m. or f.
cellar n. cave, f.
centaury n. centaurée, f.
  great(er) centaury grande cen-taurée.
  lesser centaury petite centaurée.
centilitre n. centilitre, m.
centimetre n. centimètre, m.
  cubic centimetre centimètre cube.
central adj. central.
centre n. centre, m.
cephalopod n. céphalopode, m.
cereal adj. céréale, f.
  n. céréale, f.
certain adj. sûr.
chafing-lamp n. réchaud, m.
chain n. chaîne, f.
champagne n. champagne, m.
  sparkling champagne cham-pagne mousseux.
  still champagne champagne non mousseux.
channelling-knife n. couteau (m.) à canneler, couteau à décorer les citrons.
chaps n. bajoue, f.
char n. omble (m.) chevalier, omble.
chard n. bette, f., blette, f., carde, f., poirée (f.) à carde.
charlotte-mould n. moule (m.) à charlotte.
cheap adj. à bon marché, adj.phr.
check n. bon, m.
  order check bon de commande.
to checker v.tr. chiqueter, quad-riller.
checkered adj. (pattern) chiqueté, quadrillé.
checking n. contrôle, m.
cheek n. joue, f.
  calf's cheek joue de veau.
cheeks n. bajoue, f.

cheese n. fromage, m.
  cow's milk cheese fromage de vache.
  ewe's milk cheese fromage de brebis.
  goat's milk cheese fromage de chèvre.
  Gruyère cheese gruyère, m.
  Parmesan cheese parmesan, m.
  round (of) cheese meule (f.) de fromage.
  skim-milk cheese fromage maigre, recuite, f.
cheese-board n. planche (f.) à fromage(s).
cheese-scoop n. pelle (f.) à fromage.
cheese-tub n. moule (m.) à fromage.
chelone n. chélonée, f.
cherry n. cerise, f.
  bitter cherry griotte, f.
  pickled cherry bigarreau (m.) confit.
  white-heart cherry bigarreau, m.
  wild cherry merise, f.
  winter cherry alkékenge, f., cerise d'hiver, coquerelle, f., coqueret, m.
cherry-tree n. cerisier, m.
chervil n. cerfeuil, m.
  bulbous chervil, tuberous chervil cerfeuil bulbeux.
chestnut n. marron, m.; châtaigne, f.
  chestnut preserved in sugar marron glacé.
chicken n. poulet, m.
  corn-fed chicken poulet de grain.
  spatch-cocked chicken poulet à la crapaudine.
  spring chicken poussin, m.
  young spring chicken poulet reine.
chicory n. endive, f.; chicorée, f.
  wild chicory barbe-de-capucin, f.
chief adj. principal.
  n. chef, m.
to chill v.tr. frapper, rafraîchir.
chilled adj. frappé, rafraîchi.
chimney n. cheminée, f.
china n. faïence (f.) fine, vaisselle (f.) de porcelaine, porcelaine, f.
chine n. échine, f.
  chine of pork échinée, f.
(game) chips n. croustilles, f.pl.
chit n. bon, m.

chitterlings n.pl. andouille, f.
(small) chitterling-sausage n. andouillette, f.
chive n. ciboulette, f., cive, f., civette, f.
chlorophyll n. chlorophylle, f.
chocolate n. chocolat, m.
choice n. choix, m.
  choice adj. de choix.
choke n. (of artichoke) foin, m.
  choke of artichoke foin d'artichaut.
to choose v.tr. choisir.
chop n. côtelette, f.
  chump chop côtelette de gigot.
  loin chop côtelette de filet, côte (f.) première.
  pork chop côtelette de porc.
to chop v.tr. hacher.
  to chop up hacher.
  to chop (up) coarsely hacher grossièrement.
  to chop (up) finely hacher menu.
chopped adj. haché.
  chopped up haché.
  coarsely chopped grossièrement haché.
  finely chopped finement haché.
chopper n. hachoir, m.
chopping n. hachage, m.
  chopping up hachage, m.
chopping-block n. hachoir, m.
chopping-board n. hachoir, m., planche (f.) à découper, tranchoir, m.
chopping-knife n. hachoir, m.
chops n. bajoue, f.
chow-chow n. brionne, f., chayot(t)e, f.
Christmas n. Noël, m.
chrysanthemum n. chrysanthème, m.
chrysophrys n. daurade, f.
chub n. chevesne, m., chevaine, m., meunier, m.
chuck n. paleron, m.
chufa n. souchet (m.) comestible.
chump-end n. (of loin) quasi, m.
cicatricule n. (of egg) germe, m.
cider n. cidre, m.
cinders n.pl. cendre, f.
cinnamon n. cannelle, f.
  Ceylon cinnamon cannelle de Ceylan.
  China cinnamon cannelle de Chine.
circle n. cercle, m.
to circle v.tr. cercler.
circled adj. cerclé.

circumference n. pourtour, m.

citron n. cédrat, m.

citronella n. citronnelle, f.

claret n. vin (m.) rouge de Bordeaux.

clarification n. clarification, f.

clarified adj. clarifié.

  clarified soup consommé, m.

to clarify v.tr. clarifier.

clary n. sauge (f.) sclarée, orvale, f.

class n. classe, f.

classical adj. classique.

clavaria n. clavaire, f., barbe-de-chèvre, f.

claw n. (of crab) pince, f.

clean adj. propre, net.

to clean v.tr. nettoyer.

  to dry clean nettoyer à sec.

cleaned adj. nettoyé.

  dry cleaned nettoyé à sec.

cleaning n. nettoyage, m.

  dry cleaning nettoyage à sec.

cleanliness n. propreté, f.

to cleanse v.tr. épurer.

cleansed adj. épuré.

clear adj. clair.

to clear v.tr. débarrasser.

cleaver n. couperet, m., feuille (f.) à fendre.

clerk n. commis, m.

clinker n. escarbilles, f.pl.

cloakroom n. vestiaire, m.

clock n. pendule, f.

clod n. (of beef) talon (m.) du collier.

clog n. sabot, m.

to clog v.tr. (pipe) boucher.

to close v.tr. fermer.

closed adj. fermé.

closing n. fermeture, f.

clot n. (e.g. in curdled milk) caillot, m.

to clot v.tr. & i. cailler.

cloth n. linge, m., serviette, f.

  kitchen cloth linge de cuisine.

clothes n.pl. vêtements, m.pl.

clothing n. vêtements, m.pl.

clotted adj. caillé.

clove n. clou (m.) de girofle, girofle, m.; (of garlic) gousse, f.

  a clove un clou de girofle.

  a clove of garlic une gousse d'ail.

clover n. trèfle, m.

clumsy adj. gauche, maladroit.

to coagulate v.tr. lier.

coagulated adj. lié.

coal n. charbon, m.

coal-box n. boîte (f.) à charbon.

coal-fish n. colin, m.

coarse adj. gros, grossier.

coarsely adv. grossièrement.

  coarsely chopped grossièrement haché.

  coarsely shredded ciselé.

  to shred coarsely ciseler.

to coat v.tr. enrober, masquer, napper.

  to coat a spoon masquer une cuiller.

  to coat with enrober de, masquer de, napper de.

  to coat with aspic aspiquer.

  to coat with breadcrumb(s) paner.

  to coat with flour fariner.

coated adj. enrobé, masqué, nappé.

  coated with enrobé de, masqué de, nappé de.

  coated with aspic aspiqué.

  coated with breadcrumb(s) pané.

  coated with flour fariné.

coating n. nappe, f., enduit, m.

  coating of breadcrumb(s) panure, f.

cob n. (of bread) miche, f.

cob-nut n. aveline, f., noisette, f.

cochineal n. cochenille, f.

cockerel n. coq, m.

cockle n. bucarde, f., clovisse, f., coque, f., sourdon, m.

cock-pheasant n. faisan, m.

cockscomb n. crête (f.) de coq.

cocoa n. cacao, m.

coco-nut n. noix (f.) de coco, coco, m.

coco-plum n. icaque, f.

cod n. morue, f.; cabillaud, m.

  dried cod merluche, f., merlus, m.

  fresh cod cabillaud, morue fraîche, morue franche.

  salt cod morue, morue verte (salée).

cod-roe n. (salted) rabes, f.pl.

coffee n. café, m.

coffee-bean n. grain (m.) de café.

coffee-mill n. moulin (m.) à café.

coffee-spoon n. cuiller (f.) à café.

coffeespoonful n. cuillerée (f.) à café.

coin n. pièce (f.) de monnaie.

cola n. kola, m.

colander n. passoire, f., passoire à légumes.

cola-nut n. noix (f.) de kola.

cold adj. froid.
  n. froid, m.
  to be cold (person) avoir froid.
colour n. couleur, f.
  predominating colour couleur dominante.
to colour v.tr. colorer.
  v.i. se colorer, v.refl.
  to colour golden dorer.
  to colour lightly blondir.
  to colour pink roser.
  to take colour se colorer, v.refl.
coloured adj. coloré.
  lightly coloured blondi.
colouring adj. colorant.
  n. colorant, m.
  golden colouring dorure, f.
colourless adj. incolore.
column n. colonne, f.
column-mould n. moule (m.) à colonne.
column-shape n. colonne, f.
to come v.i. venir.
  to come back revenir.
  to come in entrer.
  to come in again rentrer.
  to come out sortir.
command n. ordre, m.
commodity n. denrée, f.
compact adj. compacte.
to complain v.i. se plaindre, porter plainte.
  to complain about somebody porter plainte contre quelqu'un.
complaint n. réclamation, f., plainte, f.
complement n. complément, m.
complementary adj. complémentaire.
complete adj. complet, entier.
to complete v.tr. compléter.
completely adv. entièrement; (when followed by adjective or adverb) tout.
compote n. compote, f.; marmelade, f.
compote-dish n. compotier, m.
to compress v.tr. comprimer.
compressed adj. comprimé.
to comprise v.tr. comprendre.
to concentrate v.tr. concentrer.
concentrated adj. concentré.
condiment n. condiment, m.
to condiment v.tr. condimenter.
  to condiment with pepper poivrer.
condimented adj. condimenté.

condimented with pepper poivré.
condimenting n. condimentation, f.
cone n. cône, m.
  truncated cone cône tronqué.
cone-shape n. cône, m.
confectioner n. confiseur, m.; confiseuse, f.
confectionery n. confiserie, f.
to congeal v.tr. congeler, figer.
congealed adj. congelé, figé.
congelation n. congélation, f.
conger n. congre, m.
  black conger murène, f.
conium n. ciguë, f.
connoisseur n. connaisseur, m.; connaisseuse, f.
conserves n.pl. conserves, f.pl.
consistency n. consistance, f.
  desired consistency, required consistency consistance voulue.
  soft consistency consistance moelleuse.
  syrupy consistency consistance sirupeuse.
consommé-cup n. tasse (f.) à consommé.
constituent n. ingrédient, m.
to constitute v.tr. constituer.
to consume v.tr. consommer.
to contain v.tr. contenir.
container n. contenant, m.
content n. contenu, m.
  fat(ty) content matières (f.) grasses.
  contents contenu.
contrast n. contraste, m.
control n. contrôle, m.
convenient adj. commode.
convex adj. bombé.
cook n. cuisinier, m.
  assistant cook commis (m.) de cuisine.
  cook in charge of a "corner" of the kitchen chef (m.) de partie.
  cook who prepares hors d'œuvre(s) hors d'œuvrier, m.
  apprentice cook apprenti cuisinier.
  female apprentice cook apprentie cuisinière.
  female cook cuisinière, f.
  puff-pastry cook tourier, m.
to cook v.tr. cuire, faire cuire, cuisiner.
  v.i. cuire.
  to cook again recuire.

cooked adj. cuit, cuisiné.
  well cooked bien cuit.
cooker n. cuisinière, f.
  electric cooker cuisinière à électricité.
  gas cooker cuisinière à gaz.
  pressure cooker marmite (f.) sous pression, cuiseur (m.) à pression, autoclave, m.
cookery n. cuisine, f.
  high-class cookery haute cuisine.
  Kosher cookery cuisine cachir.
  Lenten cookery cuisine de carême.
  meatless cookery cuisine maigre.
cooking n. cuisine, f.; (operation) cuisson, f.
cooking-fat n. graisse, f.
cooking-liquor n. jus (m.) de cuisson, cuisson, f.
  short cooking-liquor court-bouillon, m.
cooking-stock n. fonds, m.
cooking-time n. temps (m.) de cuisson, cuisson, f.
cool adj. frais.
to cool v.tr. rafraîchir.
cooled adj. rafraîchi.
coot n. foulque, f.
  bald coot foulque noire.
copied adj. copié.
copper n. cuivre, m.
  tinned copper cuivre étamé.
copy n. (of book) exemplaire, m.; (from original) copie, f.
to copy v.tr. copier.
coral n. (of lobster) corail, m.
cordial n. cordial, m.
  blackcurrant cordial cassis, m.
core n. (e.g. of apple) trognon, m.
corer n. videlle, f.
coriander n. coriandre, m.
cork n. (of bottle) bouchon, m.; (substance) liège, m.
to cork v.tr. boucher.
corked adj. bouché.
corkscrew n. tire-bouchon, m.
corn n. blé, m.; grain, m.
  Indian corn maïs, m.
corncrake n. râle (m.) de(s) genêt(s), roi (m.) des cailles.
corner n. coin, m.; (of kitchen) partie, f.
cornet n. cornet, m.
cornet-shape n. cornet, m.
corn-flakes n.pl. flocons (m.) d'avoine.
cornflour n. farine (f.) de maïs.

corn-salad n. mâche, f., bourcette, f., doucette, f., doucette de Paris.
to correct v.tr. corriger; (seasoning) rectifier.
corrected adj. corrigé; (seasoning) rectifié.
to count v.tr. compter.
course n. (of meal), plat, m.; (of study) cours, m.
  remove course relevé, m.
  roast course rôti, m.; rôt, m.
  of course adv.phr. bien entendu.
cover n. (lid) couvercle, m.; (fork and spoon) couvert, m.; (place at table) couvert, m.
to cover v.tr. couvrir.
  to cover again recouvrir.
  to cover with a crust croûter.
  to cover with gum gommer.
  to cover with sauce saucer.
covered adj. couvert, recouvert.
  covered again recouvert.
  covered over recouvert.
  covered with a crust croûté.
  covered with gum gommé.
  covered with sauce saucé.
covering n. couverture, f.
cowslip n. coucou, m.
crab n. crabe, m.
crab-apple n. pomme (f.) sauvage.
crack n. fente, f.
to crack v.tr. (nut) casser; (lobster) fendre.
cracked adj. cassé; fendu.
to crackle v.i. (fire) pétiller.
crackling n. (of roast pork), couenne, f.
  cracklings n.pl. fritons, m.pl.
cradle n. berceau, m.
cradle-shape n. berceau, m.
craft n. métier, m.
craftsman n. artisan, m.
craftsmanship n. métier, m.
cramp-fish n. torpille, f.
cramp-ray n. torpille, f.
cranberry n. airelle (f.) rouge.
crane n. grue, f.
  young crane gruau, m.
cranium n. crâne, m.
crawfish n. langouste, f.
crayfish n. écrevisse, f.
  gutted crayfish écrevisse châtrée.
cream n. crème, f.
  Bavarian cream bavarois, m.
  fresh cream crème fraîche.
  pastry cream crème pâtissière.
  sour cream crème aigre.

soured cream crème aigrie.
thick cream crème épaisse.
whipped cream crème fouettée.
to cream v.tr. crémer; (milk) écrémer.
creamed adj. crémé; (milk) écrémé.
creamer n. écrémeuse, f.
creaming n. écrémage, m.
creamy adj. crémeux.
cress n. cresson, m.
garden cress cresson alénois, cresson de jardin.
crest n. crête, f.; (of bird) huppe, f.
crested adj. (bird) huppé.
crest-shape n. crête, f.
to crimp v.tr. recrépir.
crimped adj. recrépi.
crisp adj. cassant, croustillant.
crisp n. croustille, f.
crockery n. vaisselle, f.
crop n. (of bird) jabot, m., gave, f., poche, f.
cross n. croix, f.
cross-pattern n. croix, f.
cross-section n. (dimension) section (f.) carrée.
cross-shape n. croix, f.
crow n. (bird) corbeau, m.; (of calf) fraise, f.; (of pig) toilette, f.
calf's crow fraise de veau.
pig's crow toilette de porc.
crowded adj. pressé.
crown n. couronne, f.
crown-shape n. couronne, f.
cruet n. ménagère, f.
oil-and-vinegar cruet huilier, m.
cruet-set n. ménagère, f.
crumb n. mie, f.; (of crumbed bread) miette, f.
crumbs from stale bread mie de pain rassis.
to crumb v.tr. chapelurer.
crumbed adj. chapeluré.
to crumble v.tr. émietter.
crumbled adj. émietté.
crunchy adj. croquant, croustillant.
to crush v.tr. broyer, écraser, piler.
crushed adj. broyé, écrasé, pilé.
crust n. croûte, f.
piece of crust croûton, m.
small crust croûtelette, f.
crustacean n. crustacé, m.
crusty adj. croustillant.
crystal n. cristal, m.
to crystallize v.tr. cristalliser; (fruit) candir.

crystallized adj. cristallisé; (fruit) candi.
cube n. cube, m.
cubic adj. cube.
cubic centimetre centimètre (m.) cube.
cucumber n. concombre, m.
ridged cucumber concombre brodé.
culinary adj. culinaire.
cumin n. cumin, m.
cup n. tasse, f.
cupful n. tassée, f.
curaçao n. curaçao, m.
curcuma n. curcuma, m., saffron (m.) des Indes.
curd n. grumeau, m.
curd(s) caillé, m.
curds grumeaux, pl.
to curdle v.tr. cailler.
v.i. cailler, former des grumeaux, se mettre en grumeaux.
curdled adj. caillé.
to cure v.tr. saler; fumer; (herrings) saurer.
cured adj. salé; fumé; (herrings) sauré.
curlew n. courlieu, m., courlis, m.
curly adj. frisé.
currant n. raisin (m.) de Corinthe.
curry n. kari, m.
curtain n. rideau, m.
egg-yolk custard crème (f.) anglaise.
custard-apple n. corossol, m.
West Indian custard-apple anone (f.) muriquée, anone réticulée.
custom n. habitude, f., usage, m.
customary adj. ordinaire.
cut adj. coupé, haché, taillé.
cut into pieces dépecé.
cut into sections sectionné.
cut on the bias escalopé.
cut up débité, découpé, dépecé, détaillé, haché, taillé.
cut off the joint n. tranche (f.) de rôti.
to cut v.tr. couper, hacher, tailler.
to cut into pieces dépecer.
to cut into sections sectionner.
to cut on the bias escaloper.
to cut up débiter, découper, dépecer, détailler, hacher, tailler.
cutlery n. coutellerie, f.
cutlet n. côtelette, f.
chicken cutlet côtelette de volaille.
lamb cutlet côtelette d'agneau.

uncovered cutlet côte (f.) découverte, basse côte, basse-côte, f.

veal cutlet côtelette de veau.

cutlet-bat n. abatte, f., batte (f.) à boucherie.

cutlet-frill n. manchette, f.

cutter n. (four-bladed) couteau (m.) à quatre lames; (mandolin) mandoline, f.; (wheeled) videlle, f.

cutting n. détail, m.; (operation) hachage, m.

    cutting up découpage, m., hachage.

cutting-board n. tranchoir, m.

cuttle-fish n. seiche, f., sèche, f., sépia, f.

cylinder n. cylindre, m.

cylinder-shape n. cylindre, m.

cyperus n. souchet, m.

d

dab n. carrelet, m., limande, f.

dabchick n. petit grèbe, m.

dace n. dard, m.

dagger n. dague, f.

daily adj. journalier, quotidien.

to damp v.tr. humecter.

damped adj. humecté.

damson n. prune (f.) de Damas.

dandelion n. pissenlit, m.

dariole-mould n. moule (m.) à dariole.

dark adj. (colour) foncé.

date n. (day) date, f.; (fruit) datte, f.

American date-plum n. plaquemine, f.

day n. jour, m.; journée, f.

    day before veille, f.

    on the day before adv.phr. la veille.

    next day lendemain, m.

    on the next day adv.phr. le lendemain.

    previous day veille, f.

    on the previous day adv.phr. la veille.

day-book n. livre (m.) journalier, journal, m.

dead adj. mort.

dealer n. négociant, m.; négociante, f.

dealing n. marché, m.

dear adj. cher.

death n. mort, f.

to decant v.tr. (liquid) décanter; (solid) dépoter.

decanted adj. (liquid) décanté; (solid) dépoté.

decanter n. carafe (f.) à décanter.

decanting n. (liquid) décantation, f.; (solid) dépotage, m.

December n. décembre, m.

decigram n. décigramme, m.

decilitre n. décilitre, m.

to decorate v.tr. décorer, garnir, orner.

    to decorate with meringue meringuer.

decorated adj. décoré, garni, orné.

    decorated with meringue meringué.

decoration n. décor, m., garniture, f., ornement, m.

    decoration with meringue meringuage, m.

decorative adj. décoratif.

to decorticate v.tr. décortiquer.

decorticated adj. décortiqué.

deep adj. profond.

fallow deer n. daim, m.

defect n. défaut, m.

deficiency n. insuffisance, f.

to deform v.tr. déformer.

defreezing n. dégivrage, m.

defreezing-compartment n. (of refrigerator) bac (m.) à dégivrage.

to defrost v.tr. décongeler.

defrosted adj. décongelé.

defrosting n. décongélation, f.

to deglaze v.tr. déglacer.

deglazed adj. déglacé.

deglazing n. déglaçage, m.

deglazing-stock n. fonds (m.) de déglaçage.

delicate adj. délicat; mignon.

delicately adv. délicatement.

delicious adj. délicieux.

delightful adj. délicieux.

demijohn n. dame-jeanne, f.

denomination n. appellation, f., dénomination, f.

density n. densité, f.

to depart v.i. partir.

department n. département, m.

    pastry department pâtisserie, f.

departure n. départ, m.

deposit n. dépôt, m.

depot n. dépôt, m.

description n. description, f.

to deserve v.tr. mériter.

to desiccate v.tr. dessécher.

desiccated adj. desséché.

desiccation n. dessiccation, f.

to designate v.tr. dénommer, nommer.

designated adj. dénommé, nommé.

designation n. appellation, f., dénomination, f.

to desire v.tr. vouloir.

desired adj. voulu.
　the desired consistency la consistance voulue.

dessert n. dessert, m.

dessert-knife n. couteau (m.) à dessert.

dessert-spoon n. cuiller (f.) à dessert, cuiller à entremets.

to detach v.tr. détacher.

detached adj. détaché.

detail n. détail, m.

to detail v.tr. détailler.

detailed adj. détaillé.

to deteriorate v.i. se corrompre, v.refl.

to develop v.tr. développer.

developed adj. développé.

devil n. diable, m.

to devil v.tr. diabler.

devilled adj. diablé.

dextrin n. dextrine, f.

dextrose n. dextrose, m. or f.

diameter n. diamètre, m.

diametrical adj. diamétral.

dice n.pl. dés, m.pl.
　dice of savoury egg-custard royale, f.

die n. dé, m.

to die v.i. mourir.

diet n. régime, m.
　diabetic diet régime diabétique.
　vegetarian diet régime végétarien.
　to be on a diet être au régime.

difference n. différence, f.

different adj. différent.

differently adv. autrement.

to digest v.tr. digérer.

digested adj. digéré.

digestion n. digestion, f.

dill n. anet(h) (m.) odorant.

to dilute v.tr. diluer, mouiller.

diluted adj. dilué, mouillé.

dilution n. dilution, f., mouillage, m.

to dine v.i. dîner.

dinner n. dîner, m.
　to have dinner dîner, prendre le dîner.

to dip v.tr. tremper.

dipped adj. trempé.

dipping n. trempage, m.

direction n. (management) direction, f.; (in space) sens, m.

dirk n. dague, f.
　dirk of honour dague d'honneur.

dirtied adj. sali.

dirty adj. sale.

to dirty v.tr. salir.

to discover v.tr. découvrir.

discovered adj. découvert.

to disguise v.tr. déguiser.

disguised adj. déguisé.

dish n. plat, m.
　deep dish plat creux.
　fire-proof dish plat allant au feu.
　fire-proof dish for gratination plat à gratin.
　hors d'œuvre(s) dish ravier, m.
　oven-proof dish plat allant au four.
　special dish (i.e. preparation) mets (m.) spécial.

dish-cloth n. lavette, f.

dish-mop n. lavette, f.

dish-paper n. papier (m.) d'office.

dish-water n. eau (f.) de vaisselle, eau grasse.

to dismantle v.tr. défaire.

dismantled adj. défait.

to display v.tr. étaler, montrer.

displayed adj. étalé, montré.

to dissolve v.tr. dissoudre; fondre.
　to dissolve v.i. se dissoudre.

dissolved adj. dissous.

to divide v.tr. diviser.
　to divide into four diviser en quatre.

divided adj. divisé.
　divided into four divisé en quatre.

to do v.tr. faire.
　to do again refaire.

doe n. biche, f.
　doe of tame rabbit lapine, f.

doe-hare n. hase, f.

dogberry n. cornouille, f.

dogfish n. chien (m.) de mer, aiguillat, m., milandre, m.
　spotted dogfish gatangier, m.; roussette, f.

dome n. dôme, m.

dome-mould n. moule (m.) à dôme.

dome-shape n. dôme, m.

dominant adj. dominant.

done adj. fait.
　done again refait.

door n.   porte, f.
  entrance door   porte d'entrée.
dotterel n.   guignard, m.
double adj.   double.
dough n.   pâte (f.) à pain.
down n.   duvet, m.
dozen n.   douzaine, f.
draff n.   drèche, f., drêche, f.
to drain v.tr.   égoutter.
drained adj.   égoutté.
draining n.   égouttage, m.
draining-board n.   égouttoir, m.
draining-rack n.   égouttoir, m.
wicker draining-tray n.   clayon, m.
drake n.   canard, m.
dregs n.pl.   lie, f.
dress n.   (uniform) tenue, f.
  kitchen dress   tenue de cuisine.
to dress v.tr.   garnir, apprêter, parer.
  to dress with oil   huiler.
dressed adj.   garni, apprêté, paré.
  dressed with oil   huilé.
dressing n.   (oil and vinegar) vinaigrette, f.
dried adj.   séché, desséché.
  dried (leguminous) vegetables   légumes (m.) secs.
  dried thoroughly   desséché.
drink n.   boisson, f., breuvage, m.
to drink v.tr. & i.   boire.
dripping n.   graisse (f.) de rôti, lèchefrite, f.
  beef dripping   graisse de bœuf.
drop n.   goutte, f.
to drop v.tr.   laisser tomber.
droplet n.   gouttelette, f.
drumstick n.   (of chicken) pilon, m.
dry adj.   sec.
to dry v.tr.   sécher, dessécher.
  to dry thoroughly   dessécher.
drying n.   dessiccation, f.; (of fish) séchage, m.
pastry drying-rack n.   clayon, m.
dryness n.   siccité, f.
  to (the point of) dryness   adv. phr.   jusqu'à siccité.
duck n.   canard, m.
  Barbary duck   canard de Barbarie.
  female duck   cane, f.
  spoonbill duck   souchet, m.
  tufted duck   morillon, m.
  wild duck   canard sauvage.
duckling n.   caneton, m., canardeau, m.
duck-press n.   presse (f.) à canard.

duct n.   tube, m.
dug n.   tétine, f.
duration n.   durée, f.
during prep.   pendant.
  during (the) cooking   pendant la cuisson.
dust n.   poussière, f.
to dust v.tr.   (e.g. with sugar) saupoudrer.
duty n.   (stint of work) service, m.
  on relief duty   adv.phr.   en garde.
duty-roster n.   contrôle (m.) de service, tableau (m.) de service.

e

each adj.   chaque.
ear n.   oreille, f.
  calf's ear   oreille de veau.
to earn v.tr.   gagner.
earth n.   terre, f.
earthenware n.   faïence, f., vaisselle (f.) de terre, terre, f.,
  glazed earthenware   terre vernissée.
earth-nut n.   gland (m.) de terre, noix (f.) de terre, terre-noix, m.
easily adv.   facilement.
Easter n.   Pâques, m.
Easter-ledges n.   bistorte, f.
easy adj.   facile.
to eat v.tr.   manger.
economical adj.   économe; économique.
economy n.   économie, f.
edge n.   bord, m.
to edge v.tr.   border.
edged adj.   bordé.
edging n.   bordure, f.
to edulcorate v.tr.   édulcorer.
edulcorated adj.   édulcoré.
eel n.   anguille, f.
  conger eel   congre, m.
  black conger eel   murène, f.
  fresh-water eel, river eel   anguille de rivière.
eel-pie n.   pâté (m.) d'anguille.
egg n.   œuf, m.
  chicken's egg   œuf de poule.
  dehydrated egg(s)   œufs en poudre.
  hen's egg   œuf de poule.
  new-laid egg   œuf du jour, œuf frais.
  egg fried in oil   œuf frit (à la) française.

egg fried on both sides œuf frit.
English fried egg œuf à la poêle, œuf poêlé.
hard-boiled egg œuf dur.
moulded egg œuf moulé.
plovers' eggs œufs de vanneau.
poached egg œuf poché.
scrambled eggs œufs brouillés.
snow egg œuf à la neige.
soft-boiled egg œuf à la coque.
fairly soft-boiled egg œuf mollet.
egg-boiler n. coquetière, f.
egg-cup n. coquetier, m.
egg-holder n. (of wire, for holding eggs) œufrier, m.
egg-plant n. aubergine, f., melon-gène, f.
egg-poacher n. pocheuse, f.
egg-shaped adj. ovoïde.
egg-spoon n. cuiller (f.) à œufs.
egg-timer n. sablier, m.
egg-wash n. pâte (f.) à l'œuf.
egg-white n. blanc (m.) d'œuf.
egg-yolk n. jaune (m.) d'œuf.
an egg-yolk un jaune d'œuf.
elder n. sureau, m.
elecampane n. aunée (f.) hélène.
electric n. électrique.
electricity n. électricité, f.
element n. élément, m.
nutritive element élément nutritif.
elementary adj. élémentaire.
to eliminate v.tr. éliminer.
elixir n. élixir, m.
elliptical adj. elliptique.
to embellish v.tr. orner, parer.
embellished adj. orné, paré.
embossing-block n. (for pastry) gaufreuse, f.
to employ v.tr. employer; (equipment) utiliser.
employed adj. employé; (equipment) utilisé.
employee n. employé, n.; employée, f.
employer n. patron, m.; patronne, f.
employment n. emploi, m.
empty adj. vide.
half empty à moitié vide.
to empty v.tr. vider.
to half empty vider à moitié.
emulsion n. émulsion, f.
enamel n. émail, m.
to enamel v.tr. émailler.
enamelled adj. émaillé.

to enhance, v.tr. rehausser.
enhanced adj. rehaussé.
to enclose v.tr. enfermer.
enclosed adj. enfermé.
to encrust v.tr. incruster.
encrusted adj. incrusté.
end n. (in time) fin, f.; (in space) bout, m.
best end of lamb carré (m.) d'agneau.
endive n. chicorée, f.; endive, f.
Batavian endive scarole, f., escarole, f.
to engage v.tr. (staff) retenir.
engaged adj. (staff) retenu.
to enjoy v.tr. goûter, savourer.
enjoyed adj. goûté, savouré.
enough adv. assez, suffisamment.
ensemble n. ensemble, m.
to enter v.i. entrer.
v.tr. (a room) entrer dans.
entire adj. entier.
entirely adv. entièrement; (followed by adjective or adverb) tout.
entrance n. entrée, f.
entree-dish n. plat (m.) à entrées.
to enumerate v.tr. détailler, énumérer.
epidermis n. épiderme, m.
equal adj. égal.
n. égal, m.
to equal v.tr. égaler.
equalled adj. égalé.
equally adv. également.
equilibrium n. équilibre, m.
equipment n. matériel, m.
kitchen equipment matériel de cuisine.
equivalent adj. équivalent.
n. équivalent, m.
error n. erreur, f.
erythraea n. petite centaurée, f.
especially adv. surtout.
essence n. essence, f.
essential adj. essentiel; indispensable.
to establish v.tr. établir.
establishment n. établissement, m.
etiquette n. étiquette, f., protocole, m.
to evaporate v.tr. évaporer.
v.i. s'évaporer, v.refl.
evaporated adj. évaporé.
evaporation n. évaporation, f.
even adj. (number) pair.
adv. même.
evening n. soir, m.; (with the idea of duration) soirée, f.

ever adv. jamais, q.v.
every adj. tout.
everybody pron. tout le monde.
everyday adj. journalier, quotidien, de tous les jours; ordinaire.
everything pron. tout.
everywhere adv. partout.
ewe n. brebis, f.
to exceed v.tr. dépasser.
excellence n. excellence, f.
excellent adj. excellent.
except prep. sauf.
excess n. excès, m., surplus, m.
exit n. sortie, f.
  emergency exit sortie de secours.
exotic adj. exotique.
expense(s) n. frais, m.pl.
  at my expense à mes frais.
expensive adj. cher.
experience n. expérience, f., pratique, f.
expert n. connaisseur, m.; connaisseuse, f.
to express v.tr. exprimer.
expressed adj. exprimé.
to extend v.tr. (sauce) allonger.
  to extend with allonger de.
extended adj. (sauce) allongé.
  extended with allongé de.
external adj. externe.
to extinguish v.tr. éteindre.
extinguished adj. éteint.
extra adj. supplémentaire.
  adv. en plus, en supplément.
  n. supplément, m.
extract n. extrait, m.
to extract v.tr. extraire.
extracted adj. extrait.
extremity n. (in space) bout, m.
eye n. œil, m.; (of potato) germe, m.
  eyes yeux, m.pl.

f

to fail v.i. manquer.
fairly adv. assez.
to fall v.i. tomber.
false adj. faux.
family n. famille, f.
famous adj. célèbre.
fardel n. (of ruminant) feuillet, m.
farinaceous adj. farinacé, farineux.
farm n. ferme, f.
farmyard n. basse-cour, f.
fascia n. aponévrose, f.
fashion n. (manner) façon, f.; (style, taste) goût, m.

to fashion v.tr. façonner; (e.g. hole, notch) pratiquer.
fashioned adj. façonné; (e.g. hole, notch) pratiqué.
fast adj. rapide.
  adv. rapidement, vite.
  n. jeûne, m.
  Lenten fast jeûne du carême, carême, m.
fat adj. gras.
  n. graisse, f.
  fat (of meat) gras, m.
  beef fat graisse de bœuf.
  deep fat (for frying) grande friture, f.
  green fat (of the turtle) graisse verte (de la tortue de mer).
  hog's fat graisse de porc, axonge, f.
  mutton fat suif (m.) de mouton.
  smoking fat graisse fumante.
  gently smoking fat graisse légèrement fumante.
  strongly smoking fat graisse franchement fumante.
  fats n.pl. matières (f.) grasses.
fatless adj. (meat) maigre.
to fatten v.tr. engraisser.
  to fatten up engraisser.
fattened adj. gras, engraissé.
  fattened liver foie gras.
fattening adj. engraissant.
  n. engraissement, m.
  fattening up engraissement, m.
fatty adj. gras.
fault n. défaut, m.
favourite adj. préféré.
fawn adj. (stock) blond.
  n. (young deer) faon, m.
feast n. fête, f.
feather n. plume, f.
  "feather" gibier (m.) à plume(s).
feathered adj. (game) à plume(s).
February n. février, m.
to feel v.tr. sentir.
fennel n. fenouil, m.; anet(h) (m.) doux.
  bulbous fennel, tuberous fennel fenouil tubéreux.
fennel-apple n. fenouillet, m., fenouillette, f.
fennel-flower n. nigelle, f., poivrette, f. quatre-épices, f.
fennel-liqueur n. fenouillette, f.
fenugreek n. fenugrec, m.
ferment n. ferment, m.
to ferment v.tr. fermenter.
fermentation n. fermentation, f.
fermented adj. fermenté.

fibre n. fibre, f.

field-duck n. petite outarde, f., canepetière, f.

fieldfare n. litorne, f.

fifth adj. cinquième.
n. cinquième, m.

fig n. figue, f.

filament n. filament, m.

filbert n. aveline, f., noisette, f.

to fill v.tr. remplir, emplir; (omelette) fourrer; (sausage) entonner.

filled adj. rempli, empli; (omelette) fourré; (sausage) entonné.
filled omelette omelette (f.) fourrée.

fillet n. filet, m.

to fillet v.tr. (fish) lever en filets, lever les filets de, enlever les filets de, désarêter.
to fillet a fish (en)lever les filets d'un poisson.

filleted adj. (fish) désarêté.

filter n. filtre, m.

to filter v.tr. filtrer.

filtered adj. filtré.

fin n. (of fish) nageoire, f.

finch n. pinson, m.
mountain finch pinson des Ardennes.
snow finch niverolle, f.

to find v.tr. trouver.
to find again retrouver.

fine adj. beau; fin.

finely adv. finement.

finger n doigt, m.
lady's fingers anthyllide (f.) vulnéraire.

finger-biscuit n. biscuit (m.) à cuiller.

finger-bowl n. rince-doigts, m.

finger-stall n. doigtier, m.

to finish v.tr. finir, terminer; apprêter, garnir.
v.i. finir.
to finish doing something finir de faire quelque chose.

finishing n. finissage, m.
finishing off finissage.

fire n. feu, m.; (conflagration) incendie, m.
on fire brûlant.
slow fire feu doux.
brisk fire feu vif.
to catch fire prendre feu.

fire-bucket n. seau (m.) à incendie.

fire-extinguisher n. extincteur (m.) d'incendie.

fire-proof adj. allant au feu.

fire-proof dish plat (m.) allant au feu.

firing n. coup (m) de feu.

firm adj. ferme.
firm to the touch ferme sous le doigt.
n. commerce, m., maison, f.

firmness n. fermeté, f.

first adj. premier.
first adv. d'abord.
at first d'abord.
first of all tout d'abord, en premier lieu.

fish n. poisson, m.
fresh-water fish poisson d'eau douce.
lake fish poisson de lac.
live fish poisson vivant.
river fish poisson de rivière.
rock fish poisson de roche.
sea(-water) fish poisson de mer.
fresh sea-water fish (in general) marée, f.

fish-bone n. arête, f.

fish-cook n. poissonnier, m.
head fish-cook chef poissonnier.

fish-kettle n. poissonnière, f.

fish-knife n. couteau (m.) à poisson.

fish-slice n. truelle (f.) à poisson.

to fix v.tr. fixer.

fixed adj. fixé.

fixtures n.pl. aménagements, m.pl.

to fizz v.i. pétiller.

fizzy adj. pétillant.

flag n. drapeau, m., pavillon, m.
sweet flag acore, m.

flake n. flocon, m.
corn flakes flocons d'avoine.

flame n. flamme, f.; feu, m.
brisk flame feu vif.
gentle flame feu doux.
low flame feu doux.
quick flame feu vif.

to flame v.tr. flamber.

flamed adj. flambé.

flan n. flan, m.
milk flan flan au lait.
savoury milk flan flan au lait sans sucre.
savoury flan flan sans sucre.

flan-crust n. croûte (f.) à flan.

flank n. (of beef) flanchet, m.
thin flank (of beef) grasset, m., hampe, f.

flan-ring n. cercle (m.) à flan.

flat adj. plat.

to flatten v.tr. aplatir.
flattened adj. aplati.
flavour n. saveur, f.; parfum, m.
to flavour v.tr. parfumer.
  to flavour with lemon citronner.
  to flavour with mustard moutarder.
  to flavour with onion soubiser.
  to flavour with saffron safraner.
  to flavour with tomato tomater.
  to flavour with vanilla vaniller.
  to flavour with vinegar vinaigrer.
flavoured adj. parfumé.
  flavoured with lemon citronné.
  flavoured with mustard moutardé.
  flavoured with onion soubisé.
  flavoured with saffron safrané.
  flavoured with tomato tomaté.
  flavoured with vanilla vanillé.
  flavoured with vinegar vinaigré.
flax n. lin, m.
to flay v.tr. (ox) écorcher.
flayed adj. (ox) écorché.
fledgling n. oisillon, m.
flesh n. chair, f.
  cooked flesh chair cuite.
  raw flesh chair crue.
fleshy adj. charnu.
flipper n. (of turtle) nageoire, f.
flitch n. flèche, f.
  flitch of bacon flèche de lard.
floor n. plancher, m.
flounder n. flet, m.
flour n. farine, f.
  buckwheat flour farine (f.) de sarrasin, gruau (m.) de sarrasin.
  manioc flour moussache, f.
  sieved flour farine tamisée.
  fine wheat flour gruau, m.
  pure wheaten flour fleur (f.) de farine.
to flour v.tr. fariner.
flour-bin n. farinière, f.
floured adj. fariné.
floury adj. farineux.
†to flow v.i. couler.
flower n. fleur, f.
  small flower fleurette, f.
floweret n. fleurette, f.
flower-shape n. fleur, f.
fluid adj. fluide.
  n. fluide, m.
flute n. (loaf) flûte, f.
flute-shape n. flûte, f.
fluting-knife n. couteau (m.) à canneler, couteau à décorer les citrons.

flying-fish n. exocet, m.
foam n. mousse, f.
to foam v.i. mousser.
foamy adj. mousseux.
fold n. pli, m.
to fold v.tr. plier.
folded adj. plié.
to follow v.tr. suivre.
following adj. suivant.
fondant fondant, m.
food n. nourriture, f., manger, m.
  farinaceous food farinage, m.
  fried food (in general) friture, f.
  preserved food conserve(s), f.
foodstuff n. denrée, f.
foot n. pied, m.
  calf's foot pied de veau.
for conj. car.
  prep. pour.
forcemeat n. farce, f.
  kidney-suet forcemeat godiveau, m.
foreign adj. étranger.
foreleg n. patte (f.) de devant.
forequarter n. quartier (m.) de devant.
to forget v.tr. oublier.
forgotten adj. oublié.
fork n. fourchette, f.
form n. forme, f.
to form v.tr. former.
formed adj. formé.
former adj. ancien.
formerly adv. anciennement.
four adj. quatre.
fourth adj. quatrième.
  n. quatrième, m.
fragile adj. cassant, fragile.
fragment n. fragment, m., morceau, m.
fragrance n. parfum, m.
franc n. franc, m.
  the new French franc le nouveau franc français.
francolin n. francolin, m.
frangipane n. frangipane, f.
free adj. (unrestricted) libre; (costing nothing) gratuit.
  free of charge adv.phr. gratis.
to freeze v.tr. & i. geler, congeler.
freezing n. congélation, f.
freezing-agent n. réfrigérant, m.
frequent adj. fréquent.
frequently adv. fréquemment.
fresh adj. frais; (as replacement) nouveau.
Friday n. vendredi, m.
  Good Friday le vendredi saint.

fried adj. frit.
  fried in (deep) fat   frit à la (grande) friture.
fritter n. beignet, m.
  corn fritter   beignet de maïs.
fritter-paste n. pâte (f.) à beignets.
frog n. grenouille, f.
  frog's leg   cuisse (f.) de grenouille.
  frogs' legs   cuisses de grenouille.
from prep. de.
froth n. mousse, f.
frothy adj. mousseux.
frozen adj. gelé, congelé.
frugal adj. frugal.
fruit n. fruit, m.
  crystallized fruit   fruits (pl.) candis.
  (any) early fruit   primeur, f.
  (any) forced fruit   primeur, f.
  fresh fruit   fruits (pl.) frais.
  passion-flower fruit   barbadine, f.
fruit-dish n. compotier, m.
fruiterer n. fruitier, m.
fruit-knife n. pèle-fruits, m.
fruit-press n. pressoir, m.
fry n. (lamb's) animelles, f.pl.; (pig's) fressure, f.; (fried food) friture, f.
to fry v.tr. frire, faire frire.
  v.i. frire.
frying n. friture, f.
frying-basket n. panier (m.) à friture.
frying-fat n. friture, f.; graisse (f.) à friture.
frying-pan n. poêle, f.
full adj. plein.
  full glass   verre (m.) plein.
full-headed adj. (cabbage) pommé.
fumes n.pl. fumée, f.
to function v.i. fonctionner; (machine) marcher.
funnel n. entonnoir, m.
fur n. poil, m.
  "fur"   gibier (m.) à poil, poil, m.
furnace n. fourneau, m.
to furnish v.tr. (room) meubler; (commodity) fournir.
furnished adj. (room) meublé; (commodity) fourni.

g

galingale n. galanga, m.
gall n. fiel, m.
gall-bladder n. (of fish) poche (f.)

de fiel, poche, poche **pierreuse**, pierre (f.) d'amertume.
  gall-bladder of fish   poche de fiel de poisson.
gambrel n. tinet, m.
game n. (wild) gibier, m.
  black game   coq (m.) de bruyère.
  feathered game   gibier à plume(s).
  furred game   gibier à poil.
game-pie n. pâté (m.) de gibier.
  hot game-pie   pâté chaud de gibier.
gander n. jars, m.
gar n. orphie, f.
garden n. jardin, m.
  kitchen garden   jardin potager.
garfish n. orphie, f.
garganey n. sarcelle (f.) d'été.
garlic n. ail, m.
  Spanish garlic   rocambole, f.
  clove of garlic   gousse (f.) d'ail.
  touch of garlic   pointe (f.) d'ail.
garnish n. garniture, f.
to garnish v.tr. garnir.
  to garnish with sippets   croûtonner.
  to garnish with truffles   truffer.
garnished adj. garni.
  garnished with sippets   croûtonné.
  garnished with truffles   truffé.
garrot n. garrot, m.
gas n. gaz, m.
gas-pipe n. tuyau (m.) de gaz.
gast(e)ropod n. gastéropode, m.
gast(e)ropodous adj. gastéropode.
gastric adj. gastrique.
gastronome(r) n. gastronome, m.
gastronomic adj. gastronomique.
gastronomy n. gastronomie, f.
to gather v.tr. ramasser.
  to gather together   ramasser.
gathered adj. ramassé.
  gathered together   ramassé
gazelle n. gazelle, f.
gelatin(e) n. gélatine, f.
  sheet of gelatin(e)   feuille (f.) de gélatine.
gelatinous adj. gélatineux.
to geld v.tr. châtrer.
gelded adj. châtré.
general adj. général.
generally adv. généralement.
gentian n. gentiane, f.
gentian-bitters n. gentiane, f.
gentleman n. monsieur.
germ n. germe, m.
to get v.tr. obtenir.

to get high v.i. (meat, esp. game) se faisander, v. refl.
gherkin n. cornichon, m.
giblets n.pl. abat(t)is, m.pl.
gill n. (of fish) branchie, f.
   gills (of fish) ouïes, f.pl.; (of oyster) barbe, f.
gillyflower n. giroflée, f.
gin n. genièvre, m., gin, m.
ginger n. gingembre, m.
   ground ginger poudre (f.) de (baies de) gingembre.
   preserved ginger gingembre confit.
gingerbread n. pain (m.) d'épices.
to give v.tr. donner.
   to give a light donner du feu.
gizzard n. gésier, m.
gland n. glande, f.
glass n. verre, m.
   crystal glass cristal, m.
   full glass verre plein.
   liqueur glass verre à liqueur.
   wine glass verre à vin.
glassful n. plein verre, m.
   a glassful un plein verre.
glassware n. verrerie, f.
glaze n. glace, f.
to glaze v.tr. glacer.
   to glaze quickly glacer vivement.
glazed adj. glacé.
glazing n. glaçage, n.
glue n. colle, f.
glutton n. gourmand, m.; gourmande, f.
glycerin(e) n. glycérine, f.
glycerol n. glycérine, f.
to go v.i. aller.
   to go in entrer.
   to go out sortir.
   to go up monter.
   to go down descendre.
goat n. chèvre, f.
   young goat chevreau, m., cabri, m.
goby n. gobie, m., goujon (m.) de mer.
godwit n. barge, f.
goglet n. gargouillette, f., gargoulette, f.
gold n. or, m.
golden adj. doré; d'or.
golden-eye n. garrot, m.
gombo n. gombo, m., okra, m., ketmie (f.) comestible.
good adj. bon; (valid) valable.
goods n.pl. marchandise(s), f.
goods-lift n. monte-charge, m.
goose n. oie, f.

barnacle goose, bernacle goose bernache, f., bernacle, f.
wild goose oie sauvage.
gooseberry n. groseille (f.) verte, groseille à maquereau (verte).
   Cape gooseberry coqueret (m.) du Pérou.
   dessert gooseberry groseille tigrée.
gosling n. oison, m.
got adj. obtenu.
goulash n. goulach, m., goulache, f.
gourd n. courge, f.
gourmand n. gourmand, m.; gourmande, f.
gourmet n. gourmet, m.
gout n. goutte, f.
gradually adv. petit à petit, peu à peu.
grain n. grain, m.; (of meat) fil, m.
   Guinea grains, grains of paradise graines (f.) de paradis, malaguette, f., maniguette, f., poivre (m.) de Guinée.
gram n. (unit of weight) gramme, m.
to granulate v.tr. granuler.
granulated adj. granulé.
granulation n. granulation, f.
granule n. granule, m.
grape n. grain (m.) de raisin.
   bunch of grapes grappe (f.) de raisin.
grapefruit n. pamplemousse, m. or f.
to grate v.tr. râper.
grated adj. râpé.
grater n. râpe, f.
to gratinate v.tr. gratiner.
gratinated adj. gratiné.
gratination n. gratinage, m.
grating n. (metal) grille, f.
gratis adv. gratis.
gratuity n. pourboire, m.
gravy n. (accompanying roast) jus (m.) de rôti.
grayling n. ombre, m., ombre commun, ombre de rivière.
grease n. graisse, f.
to grease v.tr. graisser.
greased adj. graissé.
greaseproof adj. imperméable à la graisse.
greasy adj. graisseux.
great adj. grand.
greaves n.pl. fritons, m.pl.
grebe n. grèbe, m.

great(er) crested grebe (grand) grèbe huppé.
little grebe petit grèbe.
greedy adj. gourmand.
green adj. vert.
n. vert, m.
greens légumes (m.) verts.
greengage n. prune (f.) de Reine-Claude, reine-Claude, f.
greenhouse n. serre, f.
greenish adj. verdâtre.
grey adj. gris.
n. gris, m.
grid n. gril, m.
grill n. gril, m.; (grilled meat) grillade, f.
double grill gril double.
grill for gratination salamandre, f.
to grill v.tr. & i. griller.
grill-cook n. grillardin, m.
grilled adj. grillé.
grilled meat grillade, f.
grilling n. grillage, m.
grilse n. grilse, m.
to grind v.tr. moudre, piler.
grinding n. mouture, f.
griskin n. échinée, f.
grissini n.pl. gressins, m.pl.
gristle n. cartilage, m.; croquant, m.
groove n. cannelure, f., rainure, f.
grooving-knife n. couteau (m.) à canneler, couteau à décorer les citrons.
ground adj. moulu, pilé.
freshly ground fraîchement moulu.
ground-nut n. cacahouette, f., cacahuète, f., pistache (f.) de terre, arachide, f.
groundling n. loche (f.) de rivière.
group n. groupe, m.
grouse n. (red) lagopède (m.) rouge d'Écosse.
female (red) grouse poule (f.) lagopède d'Écosse.
pintailed grouse ganga, m.
gruel n. bouillie, f., gruau, m.
guard n. garde, f.
on guard en garde, de garde.
guava n. goyave, f., guyave, f.
gudgeon n. goujon, m.
guest n. invité, m.; invitée, f.
guinea-fowl n. pintade, f.
young guinea-fowl pintadeau, m.
guinea-hen n. poule (f.) de Guinée.

guinea-poult n. pintadeau, m.
gullet n. gosier, m., gorge, f.
gulp n. gorgée, f.
gum n. gomme, f.
to gum v.tr. gommer.
gum-arabic n. gomme (f.) arabique.
gummed adj. gommé.
gummy adj. gommeux.
gurnard n. grondin, m, trigle, m.
red gurnard rouge-grondin, m.
gurnet n. grondin, m., trigle, m.
red gurnet rouge-grondin, m.
gut n. boyau, m.
to gut v.tr. vider; (crayfish) châtrer.
gutted adj. vidé; (crayfish) châtré.

h

habit n. habitude, f.
haddock n. aiglefin, m., aigrefin, m.
smoked haddock haddock, m., aiglefin (m.) fumé.
hake n. colin, m., merluche, f., merlus, m.
half- adj. demi-.
half n. moitié, f.
half-bottle n. demi-bouteille, f.
half-dozen n. demi-douzaine, f.
half-glass n. demi-verre, m.
half-glaze n. demi-glace, f.
half-hour n. demi-heure, f.
half-litre n. demi-litre, m.
half-lobster n. demi-homard, m.
half-moon n. demi-lune, f.
half-saddle n. demi-selle, f.
half-shell n. (of lobster) demi-carapace, f.
half-tomato n. demi-tomate, f.
halibut n. flétan, m.
haliotis n. ormeau, m.
ham n. jambon, m.
cured ham jambon salé.
lean of ham maigre (m.) de jambon.
small ham jambonneau, m.
smoked ham jambon fumé.
unsmoked ham jambon non fumé.
ham-bone n. os (m.) de jambon.
ham-cooker n. jambonnière, f.
ham-knife n. couteau (m.) à jambon.
hammer n. marteau, m.
hand n. main, f.
helping hand coup (m.) de main.
the left hand la main gauche.

the right hand la main droite.
hand-bell n. sonnette, f.
to hang v.tr. & i. pendre.
  to hang v.tr. (game) faisander;
  (meat) mortifier.
hanging n. (of game) faisandage, m.
hard adj. dur.
hard-boiled adj. dur.
  hard-boiled egg œuf (m.) dur.
hard-roed adj. (fish) œuvé.
to harden v.tr. durcir, raffermir.
  v.i. durcir, se raffermir.
  to harden again v.tr. raffermir.
  v.i. durcir, se raffermir.
hardened adj. durci, raffermi.
  hardened again raffermi.
hare n. lièvre, m.
  jugged hare civet (m.) de lièvre.
  saddle of hare râble (m.) de
  lièvre.
  young hare levraut, m.
hat n. chapeau, m.
  cook's high hat toque, f.
hatchet n. hache, f.
haunch n. hanche, f.; (of venison)
  cuissot, m., cimier, m., gigue, f.
to have v.tr. avoir.
  to have breakfast déjeuner,
  prendre le petit déjeuner.
  to have dinner dîner.
  to have lunch déjeuner, prendre
  le déjeuner.
  to have supper souper.
hay n. foin, m.
hazel-grouse n. gelinotte, f., coq
  (m.) des marais.
hazel-hen n. gelinotte, f., coq (m.)
  des marais.
  Pyrenean hazel-hen ganga, m.
hazel-nut n. noisette, f., aveline, f.
head n. tête, f.; (of boar) hure, f.
  boar's head hure de sanglier.
  calf's head tête de veau.
  mushroom head chapeau (m.)
  de champignon.
  sheep's head tête de mouton.
  head of fennel pied (m.) de
  fenouil.
  head of horse-radish pied de
  raifort.
  head of the loin tête d'aloyau.
health n. santé, f.
healthy adj. sain.
heap n. tas, m.
to heap up v.tr. tasser, entasser.
heaped adj. tassé, entassé.
  heaped up entassé.
to hear v.tr. entendre.

heart n. cœur, m.
heart-cherry n. guigne, f.
heart-shape n. cœur, m.
heat n. chaleur, f.; calorique, m.
  gentle heat chaleur douce.
  latent heat calorique latent.
to heat v.tr. chauffer.
heated adj. chauffé.
heating adj. chauffant.
  n. chauffage, m.
  central heating chauffage central.
heavy adj. lourd.
heifer n. génisse, f., taure, f.
height n. hauteur, f.
held adj. tenu.
  held in reserve réservé, tenu en
  réserve.
to help v.tr. aider.
  v.i. venir en aide.
hemispherical   adj.   demi-
  sphérique.
hemlock n. ciguë, f.
hen n. poule, f.
  young hen poulette, f.
hen-linnet n. linotte, f.
hen-pheasant n. faisane, f., poule
  (f.) faisane.
herb n. herbe, f.
  mixed herbs fines herbes.
  pot herbs herbes potagères.
  turtle herbs herbes à tortue.
herb-bennet n. benoîte, f.
hermit-crab n. pagure, f.
hermetic adj. hermétique.
hermetically   adv.   hermétiquement.
herring n. hareng, m.
high adj. haut; (game) faisandé.
  to get high (game) se faisander.
highly adv. fortement.
  highly seasoned   fortement
  assaisonné.
hind adj. (leg) de derrière.
  n. biche, f.
hindquarter n. quartier (m.) de
  derrière.
  hindquarters pl. arrière-train, m.
hippophagy n. hippophagie, f.
hock n. (of bacon) jarret, m.;
  (wine) vin (m.) blanc du Rhin.
hog-fish n. rascasse, f., truie (f.) de
  mer, truie.
hog-plum n. spondias, m.
to hold v.tr. tenir; (contents)
  contenir.
  to hold in reserve réserver,
  tenir en réserve.

hole n. trou, m.
holed adj. troué, percé.
holiday(s) n. vacances, f.pl.
  on holiday en vacances.
hollow adj. creux.
  n. creux, m.; cavité, f.
to hollow v.tr. creuser.
  to hollow out creuser, évider.
hollowed adj. creusé.
  hollowed out creusé, évidé.
holly n. houx, m.
homogeneous adj. homogène.
honey n. miel, m.
honeycomb n. alvéole, m. or f.
honeycombed adj. alvéolé.
hoopoe n. huppe, f.
hop n. houblon, m.
  hop-shoots jets (m.) de houblon.
horn n. corne, f.
horn-shape n. corne, f.
hors d'œuvre(s) n.pl. hors d'œuvre, m.pl.
  hors d'œuvre(s) dish ravier, m.
  hors d'œuvre(s) tray porte-raviers, m.
  hors d'œuvre(s) trolley voiture (f.) à hors d'œuvre.
horse n. cheval, m.
horse-bean n. féverol(l)e, f., fèverol(l)e, f., gourgane, f.
horse-chestnut n. marron (m.) d'Inde.
horsehair n. crin, m.
horse-mackerel n. saurel, m.
horse-parsley n. maceron (m.) potager.
horse-radish n. raifort, m.
host n. hôte, m.
hostess n. hôtesse, f.
hot adj. chaud.
  fairly hot assez chaud.
  hot enough assez chaud, suffisamment chaud.
  to keep hot tenir au chaud.
hotel n. hôtel, m.
hotelier n. hôtelier, m.; hôtelière, f.
hothouse n. serre (f.) chaude.
hot-plate n. réchaud, m., plaque (f.) chauffante; (in kitchen) table (f.) chaude.
hour n. heure, f.
house n. maison, f.
houseleek n. artichaut (m.) des toits, joubarbe, f.
how adv. comment.
  how? comment?
  how many comment.

how many? comment?
how many carrots? combien de carottes?
how much combien.
how much? combien?
how much flour? combien de farine?
huckleberry n. airelle (f.) myrtille.
hung adj. pendu; (game) faisandé; (meat) mortifié.
hunger n. faim, f.
to be hungry v.i. avoir faim.
hunk n. (of bread) quignon, m.
hurdle n. claie, f.
  wicker hurdle claie en osier.
  grape-sorting hurdle clayette, f.
hurried adj. pressé.
to hurry v.tr. presser.
  v.i. se dépêcher, v.refl., presser le pas, se presser, v.refl.
  to hurry up v.tr. presser.
  v.i. se dépêcher, v.refl., presser le pas, se presser, v.refl.
hurt n. mal, m.
to hurt v.tr. faire mal à.
  to hurt oneself se faire mal.
husk n. (of fruit) coque, f.; (of fruit, nut) brou, m.; (of walnut) écale, f.
to husk v.tr. (walnut) écaler.
husked adj. (walnut) écalé.
hydrate n. hydrate, m.
hygiene n. hygiène, f.
hygienic adj. hygiénique.
hyssop n. hysope, f.

i

ibex n. bouquetin, m.
ice n. glace, f.
  broken ice glace broyée.
  dry ice neige (f.) carbonique.
  on ice sur glace.
to ice v.tr. glacer.
ice-cave n. glacière, f.
ice-cream n. crème (f.) glacée, glace, f.
  mixed ice-cream glace panachée.
ice-cube n. glaçon, m.
iced adj. glacé.
ice-pick n. pique (f.) à glace, poinçon (m.) à glace.
ice-pudding n. bombe (f.) glacée.
ice-shaver n. rabot (m.) à glace.
ice-tongs n. pince (f.) à glace.
icing n. glaçage, m.
identical adj. identique.

ill adj. malade.
illness n. maladie, f.
to imbue v.tr. imbiber.
  to imbue with imbiber de.
imbued adj. imbibé.
  imbued with imbibé de.
to imitate v.tr. imiter, simuler.
imitated adj. imité, simulé.
immediate adj. immédiat.
immediately adv. tout de suite,
sur-le-champ.
impermeable adj. imperméable.
importance n. importance, f.
important adj. important.
to impregnate v.tr. imbiber.
  to impregnate with imbiber de.
impregnated adj. imbibé.
  impregnated with imbibé de.
impressive adj. impressionnant.
to improvise v.tr. improviser.
improvised adj. improvisé.
impure adj. impur.
impurity n. impureté, f.
in prep. dans.
  adv. dedans.
inadequacy n. insuffisance, f.
inadequate adj. insuffisant.
to incise v.tr. inciser, ciseler.
incised adj. incisé, ciselé.
to include v.tr. comprendre.
included adj. compris.
incomplete adj. incomplet.
incompletely adv. incomplètement.
to incorporate v.tr. incorporer.
incorporated adj. incorporé.
increase n. (in wages, prices)
majoration, f.
to increase v.tr. augmenter.
to incrust v.tr. incruster.
incrusted adj. incrusté.
to indent v.tr. denteler.
indented adj. dentelé.
to indicate v.tr. indiqué.
indicated adj. indiqué.
indigenous adj. indigène.
industrial adj. industriel.
industriousness n. industrie, f.
industry n. industrie, f.
  the hotel and catering industry
l'industrie hôtelière.
inexpensive adj. économique.
inferior adj. inférieur.
to inflate v.tr. gonfler.
inflated adj. gonflé.
to inform v.tr. renseigner.
information n. renseignement(s),
m.

infra-red adj. infra-rouge.
to infuse v.tr. infuser.
infused adj. infusé.
infusion n. infusion, f.; thé, m.
  weak infusion infusion légère.
ingredient n. ingrédient, m.
inn n. auberge, f.
innkeeper n. aubergiste, m. or f.;
hôtelier, m.; hôtelière, f.
innovation n. nouveauté, f.
to insert v.tr. introduire.
inside prep. dans.
  adv. dedans.
  adj. intérieur.
  n. intérieur, m.
insipid adj. fade.
instant n. instant, m.
instantaneous adj. instantané.
instantaneously adv. instantanément.
insufficiency n. insuffisance, f.
insufficient adj. insuffisant.
insufficiently adv. insuffisamment.
to intercalate v.tr. intercaler.
intercalated adj. intercalé.
interesting adj. intéressant.
interior adj. intérieur.
  n. intérieur, m.
internal adj. interne.
to intersperse v.tr. intercaler.
interspersed adj. intercalé.
interstice n. interstice, m.
intestine n. intestin, m.
  large intestine gros intestin.
  small intestine intestin grêle;
petit boyau, m.
to introduce v.tr. introduire;
(persons) présenter.
inventory n. inventaire, m.
inula n. aunée, f.
iron n. fer, m.
isinglass n. colle (f.) de poisson,
ichtyocolle, f.
  book isinglass ichtyocolle en
livre.
  leaf isinglass ichtyocolle en cœur.
  lyre isinglass ichtyocolle en
lyre.
isomeric adj. isomère.
item n. article, m.
  item of furniture meuble, m.

j

jacket n. veston, m.
jack-fruit n. jaque, f.
jack-snipe n. bécassin, m.

jam n. confiture, f.
  quince jam cotignac, m.
jam-dish n. confiturier, m.
jam-pot n. confiturier, m.
January n. janvier, m.
jasmine n. jasmin, m.
jaw n. mâchoire, f.
jelly n. gelée, f.
  aspic jelly gelée d'aspic.
  calves' foot jelly gelée de pied de veau.
  guava jelly confiture (f.) de goyave, confiture de guyave.
  red-currant jelly gelée de groseille(s).
jet n. (of liquid, steam) jet, m.
job n. (task) travail, m., tâche, f.; (employment) emploi, m., situation, f.
John Dory n.phr. Jean-doré, m., saint-pierre, m.
join n. jointure, f.
to join v.tr. joindre.
joint n. jointure, f.
jowl n. (of salmon) hure, f.
  salmon's jowl hure de saumon.
Judas-tree n. gainier, m.
jug n. pot, m., carafe, f.
  small jug cruchon, m.
juice n. jus, m., suc, m.
  coloured juice jus coloré.
juicy adj. juteux.
jujube n. jujube, f.
July n. juillet, m.
June n. juin, m.
juniper-berry n. baie (f.) de genévrier, baie de genièvre, genièvre m.

k

kale n. (curly) chou (m.) frisé.
kangaroo n. kangourou, m.
to keep v.tr. garder, retenir.
  to keep back garder, retenir.
  to keep hot tenir au chaud.
kernel n. noyau, m.
ketmia n. ketmie, f.
kid n. chevreau, m., cabri, m.
kidney n. rein, m.; rognon, m.
  calf's kidney rognon de veau.
  cock's kidney rognon de coq.
  lamb's kidney rognon d'agneau.
  sheep's kidney rognon de mouton.
kidney-vetch n. anthyllide (f.) vulnéraire.

to kill v.tr. tuer.
king n. roi, m.
Kirschwasser n. kirsch, m.
kissing-crust n. (of loaf) baisure, f.
kitchen n. cuisine, f.
kitchen-knife n. couteau (m.) de cuisine.
kitchen-range n. fourneau (m.) de cuisine.
to knead v.tr. malaxer, pétrir, travailler.
  to knead the dough travailler la pâte.
kneaded adj. malaxé, pétri, travaillé.
kneading-machine n. pétrisseuse f.
knee n. genou, m.
knife n. couteau, m.
  butcher's knife couteau de boucher.
knife-blade n. lame (f.) de couteau.
knife-tip n. pointe (f.) de couteau.
knot n. nœud, m.
to knot v.tr. nouer.
knotted adj. noué.
to know v.tr. savoir; (to be acquainted with) connaître.
  to know a language savoir une langue.
knowledge n. connaissance, f.
knuckle n. crosse, f.; (of veal) jarret, m.
kohl-rabi n. chou-rave, m.
Kosher adj. cachir.
kromesky n. cromesquis, m.
Kümmel n. kummel, m.

l

label n. étiquette, f.
lack n. (insufficiency) défaut, m., manque, m.; (total absence) absence, f.
to lack v.i. manquer.
lactic adj. lactique.
lactometer n. pèse-lait, m.
ladle n. louche, f., poche, f.
lady n. dame, f.
lady-apple n. pomme (f.) d'api, api, m.
laevulose n. lévulose, f.
lager n. bière (f.) blonde allemande.
lagopus n. lagopède.
lamb n. agneau, m.
  ewe lamb agnelle, f.

milk(-fed) lamb   agneau de lait.
  Pauillac lamb   agneau de Pauillac.
  salt-meadow lamb   pré-salé, m.
  wether lamb   agneau, m.
  young lamb   agnelet, m.
lambkin   n.   agnelet, m.
laminated   adj.   feuilleté.
lamprey   n.   lamproie, f., marbrée,
  f.
  larval lamprey   ammocète, m.,
    lamprillon, m., lamproyon, m.
  river lamprey   lamproie fluviale,
    lamproie d'alose.
  sea lamprey   lamproie de mer,
    lamproie marine.
land-rail   n.   râle (m.) de(s) genêt(s),
  roi (m.) des cailles.
lapwing   n.   vanneau, m.
lard   n.   saindoux, m.
  hog's lard   axonge, f., graisse (f.)
    de porc.
  rendered lard   cretons, m.pl.
to lard   v.tr.   (to cover with strips
  of bacon) barder; (to stick with
  bacon) larder, piquer de lard.
larded   adj.   (covered with strips of
  bacon) bardé; (stuck with bacon)
  lardé, entrelardé.
  larded with   lardé de, entrelardé
    de.
  larded with bacon   piqué de lard.
larder   n.   garde-manger, m.
larder-cook   n.   garde-manger, m.
  head larder-cook   chef garde-
    manger.
larding   n.   piquage, m.
larding-needle   n.   aiguille (f.) à
  piquer, lardoire, f.
lardoon   n.   lardon, m.
large   adj.   grand; (bulky) gros.
lark   n.   alouette, f.
  lark in season   mauviette, f.
last   adj.   dernier.
  last   adv.   en dernier lieu.
  at last   enfin.
to last   v.i.   durer.
latent   adj.   latent.
lattice-pattern   n.   grillage, m.
laurel   n.   laurier, m.
lavaret   n.   lavaret, m.
law   n.   loi, f.
to lay   v.tr.   coucher, poser.
to lay out   étaler.
layer   n.   couche, f., épaisseur, f.
lead   n.   (metal) plomb, m.
leaf   n.   feuille, f.
  small leaf   feuillette, f.
  outer leaves   feuilles extérieures.

to leak   v.i.   couler.
lean   adj.   maigre.
  lean (of meat)   maigre, m.
least   adv.   moins.
  at least   adv.phr.   au moins.
leather   n.   cuir, m.
leathery   adj.   (meat) coriace.
to leave   v.tr.   laisser.
  v.i.   partir, quitter.
  to leave (place)   quitter.
  to leave out   omettre.
  to leave out (by mistake)
    oublier.
leaven   n.   levain, m.
leek   n.   poireau, m.
lees   n.pl.   lie, f.
  lees of wine   lies de vin.
left   adj.   gauche.
  n.   gauche, f.
left-overs   n.pl.   restes, m.pl.,
  débris, m.pl., desserte, f.
leg   n.   (of human being) jambe, f.;
  (of chicken) cuisse, f.; (of beef) gîte,
  m., gîte-gîte, m., trumeau, m.; (of
  game bird, of small game animal)
  patte, f.; (of lamb, of mutton) gigot,
  m.; (of pork) cuissot, m.
  chicken leg   cuisse de poulet.
  frog's legs   cuisses de grenouille.
  front leg (e.g. of hare)   patte de
    devant.
  hind leg (e.g. of hare)   patte de
    derrière.
  leg of lamb   gigot d'agneau.
legumin   n.   légumine, f.
lemon   n.   citron, m.
lemon-balm   n.   citronnelle, f.,
  mélisse (f.) officinale.
lemon-juice   n.   jus (m.) de citron.
lemon-peel   n.   écorce (f.) de
  citron.
  candied lemon-peel   citronnat,
    m.
lemon-squeezer   n.   presse-citrons,
  m., vide-citron(s), m.
to lend   v.tr.   prêter.
length   n.   (in space) longueur, f.;
  (in time) durée, f.; (of fish, from eye
  to tail) bat, m.
to lengthen   v.tr.   allonger, ral-
  longer.
Lent   n.   carême, m.
lentil   n.   lentille, f.
less   prep.   moins.
  adv.   moins.
  n.   moins, m.
  less than   moins que; (before
    numeral) moins de.

to lessen v.tr. diminuer.
lessened adj. diminué.
to let v.tr. laisser.
lettuce n. laitue, f.
  cabbage lettuce laitue pommée.
  cos lettuce laitue romaine, romaine, f.
  lamb's lettuce mâche, f., bourcette, f., doucette (f.) de Paris, doucette.
  lettuce salad salade (f.) de laitue.
lettuce-heart n. cœur (m.) de laitue.
  cos lettuce-heart cœur de romaine.
leveret n. levraut, m.
levulose n. lévulose, f.
lid n. couvercle, m.
to lift v.tr. lever.
light adj. (colour) clair; (beer) blond; (weight) léger.
  n. lumière, f.; (for lighting oven) feu, m.
to light v.tr. (fire, oven) allumer; (to illuminate) éclairer.
lighted adj. (fire, oven) allumé; (illuminated) éclairé.
lighting n. éclairage, m.
lightly adv. légèrement.
lights n. (offal) mou, m.
like adj. pareil.
  prep. comme.
limb n. membre, m.
lime n.
  sour lime limon, m.
  sweet lime lime, f.
lime-juice n. jus (m.) de limon.
lime-tea n. infusion (f.) de tilleul.
lime-tree n. tilleul, m.
line n. ligne, f.; (of tables) rang, m.
to line v.tr. (with paste) foncer.
lined adj. (with paste) foncé.
linen n. linge, m.
ling n. lingue, f.
lining-paste n. pâte (f.) à foncer.
linnet n. linot, m., linotte, f.
lip n. lèvre, f.; (rim) bord, m.
liqueur n. liqueur, f.
  blackcurrant liqueur cassis, m.
  peppermint liqueur crème (f.) de menthe.
  ratafia liqueur ratafia, m.
liquid adj. liquide.
  n. liquide, m.
liquor n. alcool, m.
  spirituous liquor spiritueux, m.
liquorice n. jus (m.) de réglisse; (plant) réglisse, f.

Spanish liquorice bâton (m.) de réglisse.
list n. liste, f.
to listen v.i. écouter.
  to listen to v.tr. écouter.
litchi n. letchi, m., litchi, m.
litre n. litre, m.
little adj. petit.
  adv. peu.
  n. peu, m.
  a little un peu.
  a little salt un peu de sel.
  little by little adv.phr. peu à peu, petit à petit.
live adj. vivant.
liver n. foie, m.
  chicken's liver foie de volaille.
loach n. loche, f.
  common loach loche franche.
loaf n. pain, m.
  round loaf pain rond, pain boulot.
  wholemeal loaf pain complet.
loan n. prêt, m.
lobster n. homard, m.
  Norway lobster langoustine, f., homard de Norvège.
  spiny lobster langouste, f.
lobster-claw n. pince (f.) de homard.
log n. bûche, f.
  yule log bûche de Noël.
loganberry n. ronce-framboise, f.
logwood n. campêche, m.
loin n. longe, f.
long adj. long.
to look v.i. regarder.
  to look after garder; s'occuper de.
  to look at regarder.
  to look for chercher.
to loosen v.tr. (consistency) relâcher, détendre; (food, from inner surfaces of cooking utensil) affranchir.
loosened adj. (consistency) relâché, détendu; (food, from inner surfaces of cooking utensil) affranchi.
loquat n. nèfle (f.) du Japon.
"lords and ladies" n.phr. gouet, m.
lot n. beaucoup, m.inv.
  a lot adv. beaucoup.
  a lot of beaucoup de.
  a lot of people beaucoup de gens.
loud adj. fort.
loudly adv. fort.
loudspeaker n. haut-parleur, m.
lovage n. livèche, f.

low adj. bas; (flame) doux, petit.
lower adj. inférieur; (flame) plus doux, plus petit.
lozenge-shape n. losange, f.
lukewarm adj. tiède.
lump n. bloc, m.; (in porridge) motton, m.; (of sugar) morceau, m.
lunch n. déjeuner, m.
to lunch v.i. déjeuner, prendre le déjeuner.
luncheon n. déjeuner, m.
lung n. poumon, m.
  lungs (offal) mou, m.
luxurious adj. luxueux, de luxe.
luxury adj. de luxe.
  n. luxe, m.

m

macaroon n. macaron, m.
mace n. macis, m., fleur (f.) de muscade.
to macerate v.tr. macérer.
  to macerate in rum macérer au rhum.
macerated adj. macéré.
  macerated in rum macéré au rhum.
maceration n. macération, f.
machine n. machine, f.
  bottle-washing machine rince-bouteilles, m.
  potato-peeling machine machine à éplucher les pommes de terre.
  washing-up machine moto-laveur, m.
mackerel n. maquereau, m., merlan (m.) bleu.
madder n. garance, f.
madder-wort n. garance, f.
made adj. fait.
  made again refait.
Madeira n. (wine) madère, m.
madeleine-mould n. moule (m.) à madeleine, moule madeleine.
  hinged madeleine-mould moule madeleine à griffe.
madwort n. rapette, f., râpette, f.
maggot n. ver (m.) di viande.
mahogany n. acajou, m.
maize n. maïs, m.
make n. marque, f.
  a good make une bonne marque.
to make v.tr. faire; (smooth, soft) rendre.
  to make again refaire.
  to make smooth rendre lisse.

make-weight n. réjouissance, f.
mallard n. canard (m.) sauvage, malard, m., malart, m.
  young (of the) mallard halbran, m.
mallow n. mauve, f.
Malmsey n. (wine) malvoisie, m.
man n. homme, m.
management n. direction, f.
manager n. gérant, m.
manageress n. gérante, f.
mango n. mangue, f.
manioc n. cassave, f., manioc, m.
manner n. (way, fashion) façon, f.
mantis-shrimp n. squille, f.
manure n. engrais, m.
maranta n. marante, f.
maraschino n. marasquin, m.
marble n. marbre, m.
to marble v.tr. marbrer.
marbled adj. marbré; (meat) persillé.
marc n. marc, m.
marc-brandy n. eau-de-vie (f.) de marc, eau-de-vie-de-marc, f.
March n. mars, m.
margarine n. margarine, f., oléomargarine, f.
marinade n. marinade, f.
  cooked marinade marinade cuite.
  raw marinade marinade crue.
to marinade v.tr. mariner.
marinaded adj. mariné.
marinading n. marinage, m.
to marinate v.tr. mariner.
marinated adj. mariné.
marinating n. marinage, m.
marjoram n. (sweet) marjolaine, f.; (wild) origan, m.
mark n. marque, f.
  trade mark marque.
  registered trade mark marque déposée.
to mark v.tr. marquer.
marked adj. marqué.
market n. marché, m.
  the Common Market le Marché commun.
marmalade n. marmelade, f.
  quince marmalade cotignac, m.
marrow n. (animal) moelle, f.; (vegetable) courgette, f.
  spinal marrow moelle épinière.
  spinal marrow (of beef or veal) amourettes, f.pl.
marrow-bone n. os (m.) à moelle.
marrow-scoop n. tire-moelle, m.

marrowy adj. moelleux.
Marsala n. (wine) marsala, m.
marsh-mallow n. (plant) guimauve, f.
marzipan n. massepain, m.
mask n. masque, m.
to mask v.tr. masquer; (to conceal) déguiser.
  to mask with masquer de.
  to mask with syrup siroper.
masked adj. masqué; (concealed) déguisé.
  masked with masqué de.
  masked with syrup siropé.
master n. maître, m.
match n. (lucifer) allumette, f.
maté n. maté, m.
material n. (equipment) matériel, m.; (subject-matter) matière, f.
  raw materials matières premières.
mature adj. mûr.
May n. mai, m.
mayonnaise n. mayonnaise, f.
meal n. repas, m.
  a four-course meal un repas de quatre plats.
  Lenten meal repas de carême.
  meatless meal repas maigre.
means n. moyen, m.
  by means of prep.phr. au moyen de.
meanwhile adv. entretemps, entre-temps.
measure n. mesure, f.
to measure v.tr. mesurer.
measured adj. mesuré.
meat n. viande, f.
  brown meat viande noire.
  butcher's meat viande de boucherie, chair (f.) de boucherie.
  cooked meat viande cuite, chair cuite.
  dark meat viande noire.
  pork-butcher's meat charcuterie f.
  preserved meat viande(s) conservée(s).
  raw meat viande crue, chair crue.
  red meat viande noire.
  white meat viande blanche, viande blonde.
meat-jelly n. glace (f.) (de viande).
meatless n. maigre.
  meatless meal repas (m.) maigre.
meat-plate n. assiette (f.) plate.
meat-safe n. garde-manger, m.
medallion n. médaillon, m.

medallion-shape n. médaillon, m.
medium adj. moyen; (steak) cuit à point.
medlar n. nèfle, f.
  Neapolitan medlar azerole, f.
medulla n. (oblongata) moelle (f.) allongée; (spinalis) moelle épinière.
meeting n. réunion, f.
melilot n. mélilot, m.
melissa n. citronnelle, f.
mellow adj. (fruit) vermeil.
melon n. melon, m.
  cantaloup melon cantaloup, m.
  sugary melon melon sucrin, sucrin, m.
melon-husk n. coque (f.) de melon.
to melt v.tr. fondre; (in liquid) dissoudre.
melted adj. fondu; (in liquid) dissous.
melting adj. fondant.
membrane n. membrane, f.
menu n. menu, m.
  "economy" menu menu touristique.
  gastronomic menu menu gastronomique.
  luxury menu menu gastronomique.
  tourist menu menu touristique.
merchant n. commerçant, m., marchand, m.
  wholesale merchant négociant, m.
merganser n. harle, m.
  hooded merganser harle huppé.
meringue n. meringue, f.
merit n. mérite, m.
to merit v.tr. mériter.
metal n. métal, m.
metallic adj. métallique.
method n. méthode, f.
microbe n. microbe, m.
midday n. midi, m.
middle n. milieu, m. adj. moyen.
mildew n. barbe, f.
milfoil n. achillée, f., millefeuille, f., mille-feuille, f.
milk n. lait, m.
  coco-nut milk lait de coco.
  skim milk lait écrémé.
milk-strainer n. passe-lait, m.
milk-weed n. lait (m.) d'âne, laiteron, m.
milky adj. laiteux.
mill n. moulin, m.
to mill v.tr. moudre.

milled adj. moulu.
  freshly milled fraîchement moulu.
milling n. mouture, f.
millstone n. meule, f.
millstone-shape n. (esp. of cheese) meule, f.
mince n. hachis, m.
to mince v.tr. hacher.
minced adj. haché.
mincer n. hachoir, m., hache-viande, m., machine (f.) à hacher.
mincing-machine n. hachoir, m., machine (f.) à hacher.
mineral adj. minéral.
  n. minéral, m.
  mineral water eau (f.) minérale.
minnow n. vairon, m., véron, m.
mint n. menthe, f.
  adj. neuf.
minus prep. moins.
minute n. minute, f.
mirror n. miroir, m., glace, f.
miscellaneous adj. varié.
missel-thrush n. draine, f., drenne, f.
mistake n. erreur, f.
to mix v.tr. mélanger; (esp. of contrasting colours) panacher.
  to mix in amalgamer.
  to mix together mélanger.
mixed adj. mélangé; (esp. of contrasting colours) panaché.
  mixed ice-cream glace (f.) panachée.
  mixed in amalgamé.
  mixed salad salade (f.) panachée.
  mixed together mélangé.
mixing n. mélange, m.
mixture n. mélange, m.
to moderate v.tr. tempérer, modérer.
moderated adj. tempéré, modéré.
modern adj. moderne.
moist adj. humide.
to moist v.tr. humecter.
to moisten v.tr. (with added liquid) mouiller.
moistened adj. humecté; (with added liquid) mouillé.
moistening n. (operation) mouillage, m.; (liquid) mouillement, m.
  short moistening court mouillement.
  (operation of) moistening with white stock mouillage à blanc.
molasses n. mélasse, f.
moment n. instant, m., moment, m.

Monday n. lundi, m.
money n. argent, m.
monkey-nut n. cacahouette, f., cacahuète, f., pistache (f.) de terre, arachide, f.
month n. mois, m.
moon-fish n. poisson-lune, m., vomer, m.
moor-cock n. lagopède (m.) rouge d'Écosse mâle.
moor-fowl n. lagopède (m.) rouge d'Écosse.
  female moor-fowl poule (f.) lagopède d'Écosse.
moor-hen n. poule (f.) lagopède d'Écosse; poule (f.) d'eau.
more adv. plus.
  pron. plus.
  n. plus, m.
  more than plus que; (followed by numeral) plus de.
  more than us plus que nous.
  more than fifty plus de cinquante.
morel n. morille, f.
morello n. griotte, f.
moreover adv. en outre, d'ailleurs.
morillon n. morillon, m.
morning n. matin, m.; (with the idea of duration) matinée, f.
mortadella n. mortadelle, f.
mortar n. mortier, m., égrugeoir, m.
mosaic n. mosaïque, f.
mosaic-pattern n. mosaïque, f.
most adv. le plus.
  at most au plus.
mould n. moule, m.
  channelled mould moule cannelé.
  grooved mould moule cannelé.
  hinged mould moule à griffe, moule à charnière.
  six-sided mould moule hexagonal.
  smooth mould moule uni.
to mould v.tr. mouler.
moulded adj. moulé.
mouth n. bouche, f.
mouthful n. bouchée, f.; (of liquid) gorgée, f.
to move v.i. bouger, se déplacer.
  v.tr. remuer.
moved adj. remué, déplacé.
much adv. & pron. beaucoup.
  n. beaucoup, m.
  as much adv. autant.
  so much adv. tant.
mucilaginous adj. mucilagineux.

mulberry n. mûre, f.

mullet n. mulle, m., muge, m.

  grey mullet mulet, m., muge capitan, muge capiton.

  red mullet rouget, m., mulle barbu.

  striped mullet mulet de mer, muge à grosse tête.

muricate adj. muriqué.

muscat n. muscat, m.

muscle n. muscle, m.

muscular adj. musculaire.

mushroom n. champignon, m.

  boletus mushroom bolet, m.

  button mushroom champignon de Paris.

  cantharellus mushroom chanterelle, f., girol(l)e, f.

  club-top mushroom barbe-dechèvre, f., clavaire, f.

  cultivated mushroom champignon de couche.

  field mushroom champignon de prairie.

  flap mushroom cèpe, m.

mushroom-stalk n. pied (m.) de champignon.

musk-pear n. muscat, m.

  winter musk-pear muscadelle, f.

mussel n. moule, f.

must n. (of grapes) moût, m.

mustard n. moutarde, f.

  English mustard moutarde anglaise.

  French mustard moutarde française; (in French recipe-books, often) moutarde ordinaire.

  German mustard moutarde allemande.

  white mustard moutarde blanche.

  mustard and cress moutarde blanche et cresson alénois.

mustard-pot n. moutardier, m.

mustard-spoon n. cuiller (f.) à moutarde; (spatula-shaped) pelle (f.) à moutarde.

mutton n. mouton, m.

muzzle n. museau, m., mufle, m.

myrtle n. myrte, m.

n

nail n. clou, m.; (of finger, paw, trotter) ongle, m.

name n. nom, m.

registered trade name nom déposé.

to name v.tr. nommer, dénommer.

named adj. nommé, dénommé.

napiform adj. napiforme.

naseberry n. sapodille, f., nèfle (f.) d'Amérique.

nasturtium n. capucine, f.

  nasturtium salad salade (f.) de capucine(s).

natatory adj. natatoire.

national adj. national.

native adj. indigène.

natural adj. naturel.

naturally adv. naturellement; (of course) bien entendu.

navel-orange n. orange (f.) navel.

nearly adv. presque.

neat adj. propre.

neatly adv. proprement.

neatness n. propreté, f.

necessary adj. nécessaire.

  absolutely necessary indispensable.

neck n. cou, m.; collet, m.; (of bottle) goulot, m.

  neck of lamb cou d'agneau.

  neck of veal collet de veau.

nectar n. nectar, m.

nectarine n. brugnon, m., nectarine, f.

need n. besoin, m.

  in case of need au besoin.

to need v.tr. avoir besoin de.

needle n. aiguille, f.

neroli n. néroli, m.

nerve n. nerf, m.

  dorsal nerve nerf dorsal.

nest n. nid, m.

  swallow's nest nid d'hirondelle, nid de salangane.

nest-shape n. nid, m.

net adj. (weight) net.

  n. filet, m.

nettle n. ortie, f.

neuter adj. neutre.

neutral adj. neutre.

never adv. jamais, q.v.

nevertheless adv. quand même.

new adj. nouveau; (mint, unused) neuf.

newness n. nouveauté, f.

newspaper n. journal, m.

next adj. (in space) prochain; (in time) prochain, suivant.

  next to à côté de.

nigella n. nigelle, f., poivrette, f., quatre-épices, f.

nitrate n. nitrate, m.
  potassium nitrate nitrate de potasse.
noodle n. nouille, f.
  small noodle nouillette, f.
noodle-paste n. pâte (f.) à nouilles.
noon n. midi, m.
nose n. nez, m.
  "parson's nose" (of chicken) croupion, m., sot-l'y-laisse, m.
notch n. entaille, f.
to notch v.tr. entailler.
notched adj. entaillé.
note n. note, f.
to note v.tr. noter, remarquer.
noted adj. noté, remarqué.
nothing pron. rien, q.v.
notice n. (on notice-board) avis, m.
to notice v.tr. remarquer, observer.
nougat n. nougat, m.
nourishing adj. nutritif.
nourishment n. alimentation, f., nourriture, f.
novelty n. nouveauté, f.
November n. novembre, m.
now adv. maintenant.
  conj. or.
number n. (cardinal) numéro, m.; (plural quantity) nombre, m.
  even number nombre pair.
  odd number nombre impair.
numb-fish n. torpille, f.
numerous adj. nombreux.
nut n. noyau, m.; noix, f.
  Brazil nut noix du Brésil.
nut-crackers n. casse-noisette(s), m.
nutmeg n. noix (f.) muscade, muscade, f.
nutmeg-grater n. râpe (f.) à muscade.
nutrition n. alimentation, f.; (as study) hygiène (f.) alimentaire.
nutritive adj. nutritif.

O

oat n. avoine, f.
  false oat faux froment, m., fromental, m.
oatmeal n. farine (f.) d'avoine, gruau (m.) d'avoine.
oats n. avoine, f.
oblong adj. rectangulaire.
  n. rectangle, m.
oblong-shape n. rectangle, m.

to obtain v.tr. obtenir.
occupation n. emploi, m., situation, f.
occupied adj. occupé.
to occupy v.tr. occuper.
October n. octobre, m.
octopus n. poulpe, f., pieuvre, f.
odour n. odeur, f.
œnometer n. pèse-vin, m.
of prep. de.
offal n. abats, m.pl.
offer n. offre, f.
  offer of employment offre d'emploi.
to offer v.tr. offrir.
office n. bureau, m.
often adv. souvent.
oil n. huile, f.
  almond oil huile d'amande.
  cooking oil huile de cuisine.
  fuel oil mazout, m.
  linseed oil huile de lin.
  olive oil huile d'olive.
  poppy-seed oil huile d'œillette.
  smoking oil huile fumante.
  walnut oil huile de noix.
to oil v.tr. graisser, huiler.
oiled adj. graissé, huilé.
oil-poppy n. œillette, f.
okra n. okra, m., gombo, m., ketmie (f.) comestible.
old adj. vieux.
oleomargarine n. oléomargarine, f.
olive n. olive, f.
  black olive olive noire.
  green olive olive verte.
  large green olive olive picholine, picholine, f.
  stoned olive olive dénoyautée.
omelet n. omelette, f.
omelette n. omelette, f.
  filled omelette omelette fourrée.
  flat omelette omelette plate.
  garnished omelette omelette garnie.
  moist omelette omelette baveuse.
  oval omelette omelette ovale.
  plain omelette omelette nature, omelette au naturel.
  sweet omelette omelette d'entremets, omelette au sucre.
omelette-pan n. poêle (f.) à omelettes.
to omit v.tr. omettre.
on prep. sur.
  adv. dessus.

once adv. une fois.
  at once (immediately) tout de suite, sur-le-champ; (simultaneously) à la fois.
onion n. oignon, m.
  Spanish onion oignon d'Espagne.
  spring onion ciboule, f.
  Welsh onion ciboule, f.
onion-skin n. prelure (f.) d'oignon.
only adj. seul.
  adv. seulement.
opacity n. opacité, f.
opaque adj. opaque.
open adj. ouvert.
to open v.tr. ouvrir; (molluscs, by heating in water) faire s'ouvrir.
  v.i. s'ouvrir.
opened adj. ouvert.
opening n. ouverture, f.
opening-hours n. heures (f.pl) d'ouverture.
operation n. opération, f.
  purifying operation épuration, f.
ophidium n. ophidie, f., donzelle, f.
optional adj. facultatif.
optionally adv. facultativement.
or conj. ou.
  or else ou bien.
orach n. arroche, f., follette, f.
orange n. orange, f.
  bitter orange bigarade, f.
  blood orange orange sanguine, sanguine, f.
  Seville orange bigarade, f.
orange-blossom n. fleur(s) (f.) d'oranger.
orange-juice n. jus (m.) d'orange.
orange-peel n. écorce (f.) d'orange.
  candied orange-peel orangeat, m.
order n. ordre, m.; (from customer to waiter) commande, f.; (sequence) suite, f.
to order v.i. ordonner.
  v.tr. (food, drink) commander.
  to order someone to do something ordonner à quelqu'un de faire quelque chose.
ordinary adj. ordinaire.
orifice n. orifice, m.
origin n. origine, f.
oriole n. loriot, m.
ormer n. ormeau, m., oreille (f.) de mer.
osier n. osier, m.
other adj. & pron. autre.
otherwise adv. autrement.
outer adj. externe.

outside prep. hors de, en dehors de.
  adv. dehors, en dehors.
oval adj. ovale.
  n. ovale m.
oven n. four, m.
  brisk oven four vif.
  electric oven four à électricité.
  field oven four de campagne.
  gas oven four à gaz.
  low oven four doux.
  medium oven four moyen.
  moderate oven four modéré.
ovenful n. fournée, f.
oven-proof adj. allant au four.
overdone adj. (cooked too much) trop cuit.
to overflow v.i. déborder.
overtime n. heures (f.pl.) hors cloche, heures supplémentaires.
ovoid adj. ovoïde.
own adj. propre.
owner n. propriétaire, m. or f.; patron, m.; patronne, f.
ox n. bœuf, m.
ox-cheek n. joue (f.) de bœuf, palais (m.) de bœuf.
ox-head n. tête (f.) de bœuf.
ox-spleen n. rate (f.) de bœuf.
oxtail n. queue (f.) de bœuf.
ox-tongue n. langue (f.) de bœuf.
oyster n. huître, f.
  oyster from Marennes (Charente-Maritime) marennes, f.
  Portuguese oyster portugaise, f., gryphée, f.
oyster-catcher n. bécasse (f.) de mer, huîtrier, m.
oyster-knife n. couteau (m.) à huîtres, ouvre-huîtres, m.
oyster-plant n. salsifis, m.

p

packing-case n. caisse, f.
page n. (of book) page, f.
painstaking adj. soigneux.
pair n. paire, f.
palate n. palais, m.
  delicate palate palais fin.
pale adj. pâle; (beer) blond.
palette n. palette, f.
palm-butter n. beurre (m.) de palmier.
palm-cabbage n. chou (m.) palmiste, palmiste, m.
palm-oil n. huile (f.) de palmier.
panada n. panade, f.

pastry panada   panade pâtissière.
pancake   n.   crêpe. f.
  filled pancake   crêpe fourrée.
  flamed pancake   crêpe flambée.
  savoury pancake   crêpe sans sucre.
  buckwheat pancakes   blinis, m.pl.
pancake-paste   n.   pâte (f.) à crêpes.
pancreas   n.   pancréas, m.
pancreatic   adj.   pancréatique.
panful   n.   poêlée, f.
panic-grass   n.   panic, m.
papaw   n.   papaye, f.
paper   n.   papier, m.
  butter paper   papier sulfurisé.
  buttered paper   papier beurré.
  greased paper   papier huilé.
  greaseproof paper   papier imperméable à la graisse, papier beurre, papier parcheminé.
  lace paper   papier dentelle.
paprika   n.   paprika, m.
paraffin   n.   paraffine, f.
to parboil   v.tr.   (faire) cuire à demi dans (de) l'eau.
to pare   v.tr.   éplucher, parer, rogner.
pared   adj.   épluché, paré, rogné.
parfait-mould   n.   moule (m.) à parfait.
parings   n.pl.   épluchures, f.pl., parures, f.pl., rognures, f.pl.
parr   n.   parr, m., tacon, m.
parrot-fish   n.   scare, m.
parsley   n.   persil, m.
  leaf parsley, picked parsley   persil en branches.
parsley-root   n.   racine (f.) de persil.
parsnip   n.   panais, m.
part   n.   partie, f.
  top part, upper part (esp. in butchery)   haut, m.
  equal parts   parties égales.
  in equal parts, into equal parts   en parties égales.
partridge   n.   perdrix, f.
  American partridge   caille (f.) d'Amérique, colin, m.
  Greek partridge   bartavelle, f.
  white partridge   arbenne, f.
  young partridge   perdreau m., pouillard, m.
party   n.   fête, f.
to pass   v.tr.   passer.
  to pass again (sauce)   repasser.

to pass through a cloth   passer à la serviette.
to pass through a cloth strainer   passer à l'étamine.
to pass with pressure   passer à la pression, passer avec pression, passer en pressant.
to pass with downward pressure   passer en foulant.
passed   adj.   passé.
  passed again (sauce)   repassé.
passion-flower   n.   passiflore, f.
  passion-flower fruit   barbadine, f.
paste   n.   pâte, f.; (glue) colle, f.
  cream-bun paste   pâte à chou.
  farinaceous paste   pâte farinacée.
  Genoese paste   génoise, f.
  marshmallow paste   pâte de guimauve.
  puff paste   pâte feuilletée.
  half-puff paste   pâte demi-feuilletée.
  raised paste   pâte levée.
  thinly rolled paste   abaisse, f.
  short paste   pâte brisée.
  smooth paste   pâte homogène.
  sweet paste   pâte sucrée.
  unsweetened paste   pâte non sucrée.
to paste   v.tr.   coller.
paste-cutter   n.   coupe-pâte, m., emporte-pièce, m.
pasted   adj.   collé.
pasteurization   n.   pasteurisation, f.
to pasteurize   v.tr.   pasteuriser.
pasteurized   adj.   pasteurisé.
pastille   n.   pastille, f.
pastry   n.   pâtisserie, f.
  pastry cream   crème (f.) pâtissière.
pastry-board   n.   planche (f.) à pâte, planche à pâtisserie.
pastry-brush   n.   pinceau (m.) à dorure, doroir, m.
(open) pastry-case   n.   flan, m.
pastry-cook   n.   pâtissier, m.
  head pastry-cook   chef pâtissier.
  young apprentice pastry-cook   patronnet, m.
pastry-cutter   n.   coupe-pâte, m., emporte-pièce, m.
  wheeled pastry-cutter   roulette, f.
pastry-tongs   n.   pince (f.) à pâte, pince à pâtisserie.
pastry-work   n.   pâtisserie, f.
patella   n.   patelle, f.
pawpaw   n.   papaye, f.

pay n. salaire, m.
to pay v.tr. & i. payer.
  to pay for payer.
pea n. pois, m.
  chick pea pois chiche, garbanzo, m.
  garden pea petit pois.
  marrowfat pea pois carré.
  split pea pois cassé.
  dried peas pois secs.
  fresh peas pois frais.
peach n. pêche, f.
  clingstone peach alberge, f.
peanut n. cacahouette, f., caca-huète, f., pistache (f.) de terre, arachide, f.
pea-pod n. cosse (f.) de pois.
  pea-pods cosses de pois.
pear n. poire, f.
  alligator pear, avocado pear avocat, m.
  marquise pear marquise, f.
  prickly pear figue (f.) de Barbarie.
  russet pear rousselet, m.
pearl n. perle, f.
  pearl barley orge (m.) perlé.
pearl-like adj. perlé.
pea-shuck n. cosse (f.) de pois.
  pea-shucks cosses de pois.
pebble n. caillou, m.
pecan n. pacane, f.
pecten n. peigne, m.
pectin n. pectine, f.
peel n. écorce, f., pelure, f.
  outer peel (of orange, lemon) zeste, m.
  candied peel zeste confit.
to peel v.tr. peler, écorcer, éplucher.
  to peel raw peler à vif.
peeled adj. pelé, écorcé, épluché.
  peeled raw pelé à vif.
peelings n.pl. pelures, f.pi., épluchures, f.pl.
peewit vanneau, m.
pennyroyal n. pouliot, m.
people n. gens, m.pl., occ. f.pl.
pepper n. poivre, m.
  black pepper poivre noir.
  Cayenne pepper cayenne, m.
  coarse-ground pepper mignonnette, f.
  ground pepper poivre moulu.
  Hungarian pepper paprika, m.
  Jamaica pepper poivron, m.
  long pepper poivre long.
  malaguetta pepper graines (f.) de paradis, malaguette, f., maniguette, f., poivre de Guinée.

mignonette pepper mignonnette, f.
  white pepper poivre blanc.
to pepper v.tr. poivrer.
peppercorn n. grain (m.) de poivre.
peppered adj. poivré.
pepper-mill n. moulin (m.) à poivre.
pepper-pot n. poivrière, f.
peptic adj. peptique.
perch n. perche, f.
percolator n. percolateur, m.
perfect adj. parfait.
to perfect v.tr. perfectionner.
perfected adj. perfectionné.
perfume n. parfum, m.
perfumed adj. parfumé.
perhaps adv. peut-être.
periphery n. pourtour, m.
periwinkle n. bigorneau, m., guignette, f., limaçon (m.) de mer, littorine, f., vigneau, m., vignot, m.
perry n. poiré, m.
persico(t) n. persicot, m.
persimmon n. kaki, m., figuecaque, f., plaquemine, f.
person n. personne, f.
personal adj. personnel.
personnel n. personnel, m.
pestle n. pilon, m.
  wooden pestle pilon en bois.
petal n. pétale, f.
pewter n. étain, m.
pheasant n. faisan, m.
  young pheasant faisandeau, m., pouillard, m.
pheasant-poult n. faisandeau, m., pouillard, m.
to pick up v.tr. ramasser.
picked up adj.phr. ramassé.
pickle n. marinade, f.
to pickle v.tr. mariner.
pickled adj. mariné.
pickling n. marinage, m.
pie n. pâté m.
  cold pie pâté froid.
  hot pie pâté chaud.
piece n. morceau, m., pièce, f.; (of string) bout, m.
  piece of crust croûton, m.
pie-crust n. chapeau, m.
pie-dish n. tourtière, f.
pie-mould n. moule (m.) à pâté.
pie-paste n. pâte (f.) à pâté.
to pierce v.tr. percer.
pierced adj. percé.
pig n. cochon, m., porc, m.

young pig cochonnet, m.
pigeon n. pigeon, m.
young pigeon pigeonneau, m.
piglet n. cochonnet, m., porcelet, m., goret, m.
pigment n. pigment, m.
pig-nut n. gland (m.) de terre, noix (f.) de terre, terre-noix, m.
pike n. brochet, m.
small pike, young pike brocheton, m.
pike-perch n. (of Central Europe) sandre, f., zandre, f.
pilaff n. pilaf, m., pilaff, m., pilau, m., pilaw, m.
pilchard n. pilchard, m., sardine, f.
pile n. tas, m.
to pile up v.tr. empiler, tasser, entasser.
piled up adj.phr. empilé, tassé, entassé.
pilfering n. petits vols, m.pl.
piling n. tassement, m.
piling up tassement.
pimento n. piment, m.
green pimento piment vert.
red pimento piment rouge.
sweet pimento piment doux.
pimpinella n. boucage, m.
pinch n. (of condiment) pincée, f., prise, f.
pineapple n. ananas, m.
pineapple-juice n. jus (m.) d'ananas, suc (m.) d'ananas.
pine-seed n pignon, m.
pink adj. rose; (wine) rosé.
n. (colour) rose, m.
pint n. pinte, f.
pintail n. pilet, m.
pipe n. tube, m.; (for gas, water) tuyau, m.
to pipe v.tr. (through piping-bag) pousser à la poche, coucher.
piped adj. (through piping-bag) poussé à la poche, couché.
piping-bag n. poche (f.) à douille, poche.
piping-tube n. douille, f., moule (m.) à douille.
pippin n. pomme (f.) reinette, reinette, f., rainette, f.
piquant adj. piquant.
piquant sauce sauce (f.) piquante.
pistachio n. pistache, f.
pith n. pulpe, f.
pithy adj. pulpeux.
place n. (space) place, f.; (locality) lieu, m., endroit, m.

to place v.tr. placer, poser, disposer.
placed adj. placé, posé, disposé.
plaice n. plie, f., carrelet, m.
plain adj. simple.
plane n. rabot, m.
plank n. planche, f.
plant n. plante, f.
cheese-rennet plant gaillet, m.
plate n. assiette, f.
silver plate argent (m.) orfévré.
plateful n. assiettée, f.
plate-hoist n. monte-plats, m.
platinum n. platine, m.
pleasant adj. agréable.
pleasant to look at agréable à l'œil.
please int. s'il vous plaît.
to please v.tr. plaire, v.ind.tr.
to please someone plaire à quelqu'un.
pleasure n. plaisir, m.
pledge n. parole, f.
plover n. pluvier, m.
golden plover pluvier doré.
great plover courlieu (m.) de terre, courlis (m.) de terre, œdicnème, m.
green plover vanneau, m.
ringed plover pluvier à collier.
plovers' eggs œufs (m.) de pluvier, œufs de vanneau.
pluck n. (of animal) fressure, f.
plug n. bonde, f.
plug-hole n. bonde, f.
plum n. prune, f.
mirabelle plum mirabelle, f.
sapodilla plum sapodille, f., nèfle (f.) d'Amérique.
plump adj. grassouillet, gras.
to poach v.tr. pocher.
poached adj. poché.
a poached egg un œuf poché.
poaching n. pochage, m.
pochard n. milouin, m.
pocket n. poche, f.
pod n. (of leguminous vegetable) cosse, f., écale, f., gousse, f.
point n. (in space) point, m.; (stage of operation) point; (tip) pointe, f.
point of the rump of beef pièce (f.) de bœuf, pointe de culotte, aiguillette, f.
pointed adj. aigu.
pointless adj. inutile.
poison n. poison, m.
poisonous adj. vénéneux.

poker n. pique-feu, m., tisonnier, m.
to polish v.tr. lustrer, polir.
polished adj. lustré, poli.
polite adj. poli.
politeness n. politesse, f.
pollack n. lieu, m., merlan (m.) jaune.
pomegranate n. grenade, f.
pomfret n. stromatée, m.
pompelmoose n. pamplemousse, m. or f.
poppy n. pavot, m.
  corn poppy coquelicot, m.
  red poppy coquelicot, m.
poppy-oil n. huile (f.) de pavot.
porcelain n. porcelaine, f.
  fire-proof porcelain porcelaine à feu.
pork n. porc, m.
  pickled pork petit salé, m.
  salt pork salé, m.
pork-butcher n. charcutier, m.
pork-butchery n. charcuterie, f.
pork-rind n. couenne, f.
port n. (wine) porto, m.
porter n. porteur, m.
pot n. pot, m.
potato n. pomme (f.) de terre.
  sweet potato patate, f., patate douce.
  match potatoes pommes allumettes.
potato-masher n. passe-purée, m.
potful n. potée, f.
poulterer n. volailleur, m.
poultry n. volaille, f.
pound n. livre, f.
to pound v.tr. piler, broyer.
  to pound in the mortar piler au mortier, égruger.
pounded adj. pilé, broyé.
  pounded in the mortar pilé au mortier, égrugé.
to pour v.tr. verser.
  to pour out (in a thin trickle) filer.
poured adj. versé.
  poured out (in a thin trickle) filé.
powder n. poudre, f.
powdered adj. pulvérisé; en poudre.
practical adj. pratique.
practice n. pratique, f.; usage, m.
to practise v.tr. & i. pratiquer.
prawn n. crevette (f.) rose, crevette rouge.

Dublin Bay prawn n. langoustine, f.
preceding adj. précédent.
to predominate v.i. dominer.
predominating adj. dominant.
to prefer v.tr. préférer.
preference n. préférence, f.
preferred adj. préféré.
preliminaries n.pl. préliminaires, f.pl.
preliminary adj. préliminaire.
preparation n. préparation, f.
  farinaceous preparation farinage, m.
  preparations (for the future) préparatifs, m.pl.
to prepare v.tr. préparer; (for cooking) marquer.
prepared adj. préparé; (for cooking) marqué.
present adj. (current) actuel; (opp. of absent) présent.
to present v.tr. présenter.
presentation n. présentation, f.
presented adj. présenté.
preserve n. confit, m.
  preserves conserves, f.pl.
preserved adj. confit.
preserving-pan n. marmite (f.) à conserves, bassine (f.) à confiture(s).
press n. presse, f.
to press v.tr. presser.
pressed adj. pressé.
pressure n. pression, f.
  high pressure forte pression.
  strong pressure forte pression.
pretty adj. joli.
to prevent v.tr. empêcher.
previous adj. précédent.
previously adv. à l'avance, auparavant, préalablement, précédemment.
price n. prix, m.
  retail price prix de détail.
  wholesale price prix de gros.
prickly adj. hérissé.
principal adj. principal.
principle n. principe, m.
privilege n. droit, m., privilège, m.
prize n. prix, m.
probationer n. stagiaire, m. or f.
to proceed v.i. procéder.
  "Proceed as for . . ." "Procéder comme pour . . ."
process n. procédé, m.
to produce v.tr. produire.
produced adj. produit.
product n. produit, m.; denrée, f.

food products denrées alimentaires.
profit n. bénéfice, m.
to profit v.i. profiter.
promotion n. avancement, m.
  promotion by selection avancement par choix.
  promotion by seniority avancement par ancienneté.
property n. proprieté, f.
proportion n. proportion, f.; raison, f.
  in proportion to à proportion de, en proportion de.
proprietor n. propriétaire, m., patron, m.
proprietress n. propriétaire, f., patronne, f.
protein n. protéine, f.
prudence n. prudence, f.
prudent adj. prudent.
prudently adv. prudemment.
prune n. pruneau, m.
ptarmigan n. perdrix (f.) de neige, ptarmigan, m., lagopède (m.) alpin, lagopède des Alpes.
pudding n. pouding, m.
  black pudding boudin (m.) noir.
  ice pudding bombe (f.) glacée.
to puff v.tr. (rice) gonfler.
puffed adj. (rice) gonflé.
  puffed rice riz (m.) gonflé.
pullet n. poulette, f.
pulp n. pulpe, f.
pulpy adj. pulpeux.
to pulverize v.tr. pulvériser.
pulverized adj. pulvérisé; en poudre.
pulverizer n. pulvérisateur, m.
pumice-stone n. ponce, f.
pumpkin n. potiron, m., citrouille, f.
punch n. grog, m.
pure adj. pur.
puree n. purée, f.
  apple puree marmelade (f.) de pommes.
puree-presser n. champignon, m.
purified adj. purifié, épuré.
to purify v.tr. purifier, épurer.
purse n. bourse, f.
purslane n. pourpier, m.
to push v.tr. pousser.
put adj. mis, placé, posé.
  put aside mis de côté.
  put away rangé.
  put back (again) remis.

put back into place replacé.
put to one side mis de côté.
to put v.tr. mettre, placer, poser.
  to put aside mettre de côté.
  to put away ranger.
  to put back (again) remettre.
  to put back into place replacer.
  to put to one side mettre de côté.
pyramid-shape n. pyramide, f.

q

quail n. caille, f.
quality n. qualité, f.
quantity n. qualité, f.
  desired quantity, required quantity quantité voulue.
quarter n. quart, m.; (of carcase) quartier, m.
  quarter of beef quartier de bœuf.
  quarter of lamb quartier d'agneau.
  a quarter of a litre un quart de litre.
quassia n. quassia, m.
queening n. calville, f.
question n. question, f.
quick adj. rapide.
quickly adv. rapidement, vite.
quince n. coing, m.
quince-blossom n. fleur (f.) de coing.
quinquina n. quinquina, m.
quite adv. assez; (followed by adjective or adverb) tout.
quoit-shape n. palet, m.

r

rabbit n. lapin, m.
  buck rabbit lapin mâle.
  tame rabbit lapin domestique, lapin de clapier.
  wild rabbit lapin de garenne, garenne, m.
  young rabbit lapereau, m.
rabbit-warren n. garenne, f.
radish n. radis, m.
rag n. chiffon, m.
rail n. (bird) râle, m.
to raise v.tr. lever.
raised v.tr. levé.
raisin n. raisin (m.) sec.
  Malaga raisin raisin de Malaga, raisin noir.

rake n. (for oven) tire-braise, m.
ram n. bélier, m.
ramekin n. ramequin, m.
rampion n. raiponce, f.
rank n. rang, m.
rape n. rave, f.
rapid adj. rapide.
rapidly adv. rapidement, vite.
raspberry n. framboise, f.
raspberry-flavoured adj. framboisé.
rather adv. assez, plutôt; (sooner) plutôt.
ratio n. proportion, f., raison, f.
ravioli n.pl. ravioli, m.pl.
raw adj. cru.
ray n. (fish) raie, f.
  common ray raie bouclée.
  small ray raiton, m.
to reabsorb v.tr. résorber.
reabsorbed adj. résorbé.
to read v.tr. & i. lire.
ready adj. prêt.
real adj. vrai.
reason n. raison, f.
to recall v.tr. rappeler.
to receive v.tr. recevoir.
received adj. reçu.
receptacle n. contenant, m.
recipe n. recette, f.
to recommend v.tr. recommander.
recommended adj. recommandé.
to reconstitute v.tr. reformer.
reconstituted adj. reformé.
to re-cook v.tr. recuire.
re-cooked adj. recuit.
rectangle n. rectangle, m.
rectangular adj. rectangulaire.
to rectify v.tr. rectifier, corriger.
rectified adj. rectifié, corrigé.
red adj. rouge.
  n. rouge, m.
  vegetable red rouge végétal.
red-currant n. groseille (f.) rouge.
red-eye n. rosette, f., rossette, f., rotengle, m.
reddish adj. rougeâtre.
redstart n. rouge-queue, m.
to reduce v.tr. diminuer; (liquid) réduire.
  to reduce by (a) half réduire de moitié.
  to reduce by a quarter réduire d'un quart.
  to reduce by a third réduire d'un tiers.
reduced adj. diminué; (liquid) réduit.

reduction n. réduction, f.
redwing n. mauvis, m.
to refine v.tr. raffiner.
refined adj. raffiné.
refining n. raffinage, m.
to reform v.tr. (to reshape) reformer.
reformed adj. (reshaped) reformé.
to refresh v.tr. rafraîchir.
refreshed adj. rafraîchi.
to refrigerate v.tr. réfrigérer.
refrigerated adj. réfrigéré.
refrigeration n. réfrigération, f.
refrigerator n. réfrigérateur, m.
regular adj. régulier.
regulation n. (rule) règlement, m.
to reheat v.tr. réchauffer.
reheated adj. réchauffé.
reindeer n. renne, m.
to relish v.tr. goûter.
to remain v.i. rester.
remainder n. restant, m., reste, m.
remaining adj. restant.
remains n.pl. restes, m.pl.; débris, m.pl
to remoisten v.tr. remouiller.
remoistened adj. remouillé.
remoistening n. remouillage, m.
remove n. relevé, m.
to remove v.tr. (from flame) retirer; (fillets, from fish) enlever; (garment) ôter.
  to remove from the fire, from the flame retirer du feu.
removed adj. (from flame) retiré; (fillets, from fish) enlevé; (garment) ôté.
to renew v.tr. renouveler.
renewed adj. renouvelé.
rennet n. caille-lait, m., présure, f.
  animal rennet présure animale.
  vegetable rennet présure végétale.
to repass v.tr. (sauce) repasser.
repassed adj. (sauce) repassé.
repertory n. répertoire, m.
to replace v.tr. (with something else) remplacer; (in place) replacer; (water, during soaking) renouveler.
replaced adj. (with something else) remplacé; (in place) replacé; (water, during soaking) renouvelé.
reply n. réponse, f.
to reply v.i. répondre.
to reproduce v.tr. réproduire.
request n. demande, f.; prière, f.

request for employment, request for work demande d'emploi.
to request v.tr. demander, prier.
requested adj. demandé.
to require v.tr. vouloir.
required adj. voulu.
  the required consistency la consistance voulue.
research n. recherche, f.
reserve n. réserve, f.
  held in reserve tenu en réserve.
to reserve v.tr. réserver, tenir en réserve, retenir.
reserved adj. réservé, tenu en réserve, retenu.
to reshape v.tr. reformer.
reshaped adj. reformé.
residue n. résidu, m.
resin n. résine, f.
restaurant n. restaurant, m.
  Kosher restaurant restaurant cachir.
result n. résultat, m.
  successful result réussite, f.
retail n. détail, m.
  retail price prix (m.) de détail.
to retain v.tr. garder, retenir.
reticulate adj. réticulé.
to re-tin v.tr. rétamer.
re-tinned adj. rétamé.
re-tinning n. rétamage, m.
return n. retour, m.
to return v.i. revenir; (home) rentrer.
  v.tr. retourner.
reunion n. réunion, f.
revive v.tr. rafraîchir, aviver.
revived adj. rafraîchi, avivé.
rhubarb n. rhubarbe, f.
rib n. côte, f.
  flat rib plate côte, plate-côte, f.
ribbon n. ruban, m.
to ribbon v.tr. rubaner.
ribboned adj. rubané.
rice n. riz, m.
  dry rice riz sec.
  polished rice riz glacé.
  puffed rice riz gonflé.
  separated rice riz en grains.
riddle n. crible, m.
right adj. (side) droit; (correct) exact.
  n. (side) droite, f.; (privilege) droit, m.
rim n. bord, m.
rind n. écorce, f.
ring n. anneau, m., bague, f.

ring-dove n. pigeon (m.) ramier, ramier, m., palombe, f.
ring-pigeon n. pigeon (m.) ramier, ramier, m., palombe, f.
ring-shape n. anneau, m., bague, f.
to rinse v.tr. rincer.
  to rinse out rincer.
rinsed adj. rincé.
  rinsed out rincé.
ripe adj. mûr.
to rise v.i. (pastry) (se) lever.
roach n. gardon, m.
roast adj. rôti.
  n. rôti, m., rôt, m.
to roast v.tr. rôtir; (almonds, coffee-beans) torréfier.
roast-cook n. rôtisseur, m.
  head roast-cook chef rôtisseur.
roasted adj. (almonds, coffee-beans) torréfié.
roasting n. rôtissage, m.
roasting-dish n. plat (m.) à rôtir.
  oval roasting-dish plat à rôtir ovale.
roasting-jack n. tournebroche, m.
roasting-tray n. plaque (f.) à rôtir.
rocambole n. rocambole, f.
rockling n. loche (f.) de mer, motelle, f., mostèle, f., mostelle, f., mustèle, f.
roe n.
  soft roe laitance, f., laite, f.
  hard roe œufs (m.) de poisson.
roebuck n. chevreuil, m.
  young roebuck faon, m.
roll n. (of bread) petit pain, m.; (of canvas, for knives) trousse, f.
to roll v.tr. rouler, enrouler.
  to roll thin (paste) abaisser.
  to roll up enrouler.
rolled adj. roulé, enroulé.
  rolled thin (paste) abaissé.
  rolled up enroulé.
roller n. rouleau, m.
rolling-pin n. rouleau (m.) à pâtisserie, rouleau de pâtissier.
room n. (space) place, f.
root n. racine, f.
  root vegetable racine.
rootlet n. (esp. of tuberous plant) radicelle, f.
rope n. corde, f.
rose n. rose, f.
rose-apple n. jambose, f., jamerose, f.
rosemary n. romarin, m.
rosette-shape n. rosace, f.
rosolio n. (cordial) rossolis, m.

roster n. tableau, m.
roughly adv. (coarsely) grossièrement; (approximately) environ, à peu près.
round adj. rond.
  n. rond, m.
  round of bread rond de pain.
  round of ham rond de jambon.
roundel n. rondelle, f.
royal adj. royal.
to rub v.tr. frotter.
  to rub with garlic frotter d'ail.
rubbed adj. frotté.
rudd n. rosette, f., rossette, f., rotengle, m.
ruff n. (fish) perche (f.) goujonnière, gremille, f.
to ruin v.tr. abîmer.
ruined adj. abîmé.
rule n. (principle) principe, m.; (regulation) règlement, m.
rum n. rhum, m.
  bay rum tafia (m.) de laurier.
  tafia rum tafia, m.
rump n. (of beef) culotte, f.
  point of the rump of beef pièce (f.) de bœuf, pointe (f.) de culotte, aiguillette, f.
rumpsteak n. romsteck, m.
ruscus n. fragon, m.
rush-nut n. souchet (m.) comestible.
rusk n. biscotte, f.
rust n. rouille, f.
to rust v.i. se rouiller, v.refl.
  v.tr. rouiller.
rusted adj. rouillé.
rustless adj. inoxydable.
rusty adj. rouillé.
rye n. seigle, m.

S

saccharin n. saccharine, f.
saccharometer n. pèse-sirop, m.
sack n. sac, m.
saddle n. selle, f.; (of hare, rabbit) râble, m.
  saddle of lamb selle d'agneau.
  saddle of mutton selle de mouton.
  saddle of hare râble de lièvre.
safflower n. safran (m.) bâtard.
saffron n. safran, m.
saffron-coloured adj. safrané.
sage n. sauge, f.
sago n. sagou, m.

salad n. salade, f.
  compound salad salade composée.
  fruit salad salade de fruits.
  lettuce salad salade de laitue.
  cos lettuce salad salade de romaine.
  mixed salad salade panachée.
  nasturtium salad salade de capucine(s).
  simple salad salade simple.
  sweet salad salade douce.
salad-bowl n. saladier, m.
salad-plate n. assiette (f.) à salade.
(wire) salad-washer n. panier (m.) à salade.
salangane n. salangane, f.
salep n. salep, m.
salmon n. saumon, m.
  smoked salmon saumon fumé.
  Scotch smoked salmon saumon d'Écosse fumé.
  young salmon saumoneau, m.
salmon-coloured adj. saumoné.
salmon-kettle n. saumonière, f.
salmon-trout n. truite (f.) saumonée.
salsify n. (white) salsifis, m.; (black) scorsonère, f., scorzonère, f., salsifis noir, salsifis d'Espagne.
salt adj. salé.
salt n. sel, m.
  celery salt sel de céleri.
  garlic salt sel d'ail.
  kitchen salt gros sel, sel gris, sel marin.
  table salt sel blanc.
to salt v.tr. saler.
salt-box n. boîte (f.) à sel.
salt-cellar n. salière, f.
salted adj. salé.
salting n. salage, m.
salting-tub n. saloir, m.
saltpetre n. salpêtre, m.
salt-spoon n. cuiller (f.) à sel, cuillère (f.) à sel; (spatula-shaped) pelle (f.) à sel.
salver n. plateau (m.) d'argent.
same adj. même.
  all the same adv.phr. quand même.
samphire n. casse-pierre(s), m.
  rock samphire criste-marine, f.
sample n. (taste, of food, wine) essai, m.
sand-eel n. équille, f., lançon, m.
sandpiper n. bécasseau, m., maubèche, f., totane, m., tringa, m.

sapidity n. sapidité, f.
sapodilla n. sapodille, f., nèfle (f.) d'Amérique.
sardine n. sardine, f., pilchard, m.
sargasso n. sargasse, f.
sarsaparilla n. salsepareille, f.
Saturday n. samedi, m.
sauce n. sauce, f.
  Béchamel sauce béchamel, f.
  cold sauce sauce froide.
  compound sauce sauce composée.
  egg-custard sauce sauce anglaise.
  made-up sauce sauce composée.
  Mornay sauce mornay, f.
  piquant sauce sauce piquante.
  required sauce sauce demandée.
  shallot sauce sauce échalote.
  small sauce petite sauce.
  Soubise sauce soubise, f.
  sweet sauce sauce douce.
  warm sauce sauce chaude.
  white sauce sauce blanche.
to sauce v.tr. saucer.
sauce-boat n. saucière, f.
sauce-cook n. saucier, m.
  head sauce-cook chef saucier.
sauced adj. saucé.
saucepan n. casserole, f.
saucepan-brush n. lavette, f.
saucepan-lid n. couvercle (m.) de casserole.
saucer n. soucoupe, f.
sauerkraut n. choucroute, f.
sausage n. saucisse, f.
  smoked sausage saucisson, m.
  white sausage boudin, m.
sausage-casing n. boyau, m.
sausage-filler n. poussoir, m.
sausage-funnel n. boudinière, f.
sausage-meat n. chair (f.) à saucisse.
sausage-skin n. peau (f.) à saucisse(s).
saveloy n. cervelas, m.
savory n. sarriette, f.
savour n. saveur, f.
savoury adj. (full of savour) sapide.
saw n. scie, f.
to saw v.tr. scier.
saxifrage n. saxifrage, f., casse-pierre(s), m.
  burnet saxifrage pied-de-bouc, m., pied-de-chèvre, m.
to say v.tr. dire.
scad n. saurel, m.
to scald v.tr. ébouillanter, échauder.

to scald out ébouillanter, échauder.
scalded adj. ébouillanté, échaudé.
  scalded out ébouillanté, échaudé.
scale n. (of fish) écaille, f.
  scales (for weighing) balance, f.
to scale v.tr. (fish) écailler.
scaled adj. (fish) écaillé.
scallion n. ciboule, f.
scaly adj. écailleux.
scampi n.pl. scampi, m.pl.
scarlet adj. écarlate.
  n. écarlate, f.
scent n. odeur, f.
school n. école, f.
  hotel school école hôtelière.
scissors n.pl. ciseaux, m.pl.
scollop n. (mollusc) coquille (f.) (de) Saint-Jacques, saint-jacques, m., peigne (m.) commun; (slice cut on the bias) escalope, f.
scollop-shell n. coquille (f.) (de) Saint-Jacques, saint-jacques, m., peigne (m.) commun.
scoop n. pelle, f.
to scoop out v.tr. évider.
scooped out adj.phr. évidé.
scorzonera n. scorsonère, f., scorzonère, f., salsifis (m.) noir, salsifis d'Espagne.
scoter n. macreuse, f.
scoter-duck n. macreuse, f.
to scour v.tr. récurer.
scoured adj. récuré.
scrag n. collet, m.; (esp. of veal, mutton) bout (m.) saigneux.
  scrag of veal collet de veau.
to scramble v.tr. brouiller.
scrambled adj. brouillé.
to scrape v.tr. (carrot) racler.
scraped adj. (carrot) raclé.
scraper n. curette, f.
  horn scraper corne (f.) de pâtissier.
scrapings n.pl. parures, f.pl.
scullery n. plonge, f.
sculleryman n. plongeur, m.
scullery-work n. plonge, f.
scullion n. marmiton, m.
scum n. écume, f.
to scum v.tr. écumer.
scummed adj. écumé.
scumming n. écumage, m.
sea n. mer, f.
sea-anemone n. anémone (f.) de mer, ortie (f.) de mer.
sea-bream n. pagel, m., pagelle, f., canthère, m.

sea-cock n. gal, m.
sea-cucumber n. holothurie, f.
sea-dace n. bar (m.) commun.
sea-kale n. chou (m.) de mer, chou marin, crambe, m., crambé, m.
to seal v.tr. (pie) souder; (aperture) obturer.
  to seal with a sealing-paste luter.
sealed adj. (pie) soudé; (aperture) obturé.
  sealed with a sealing-paste luté.
sealing-paste n. lut, m.
sea-perch n. bar, m., perche (f.) de mer, loup (m.) de mer.
season n. saison, f.
  in season en saison.
to season v.tr. assaisonner, condimenter, relever.
  to season highly assaisonner de haut goût.
seasoned adj. assaisonné, condimenté, relevé.
  assaisonné de haut goût, fortement assaisonné, très relevé.
seasoning n. assaisonnement, m.
sea-spider n. araignée (f.) de mer.
sea-swallow n. exocet, m.
sea-tench n. brème (f.) de mer.
sea-urchin n. oursin, m.
sea-wolf n. bar (m.) commun.
second adj. second, deuxième.
  n. seconde, f.
section n. partie, f., section, f.
sediment n. dépôt, m.
to see v.tr. & i. voir.
seed n. graine, f.; semence, f.
  caraway seeds graines de carvi.
  nasturtium seeds câpres (f.) capucines.
to seed v.tr. (raisins) épépiner.
seeded adj. (raisins) épépiné.
to seek v.tr. chercher.
segment n. segment, m.
to seize v.tr. saisir.
seized adj. saisi.
to sell v.tr. vendre.
semi-solid adj. demi-solide.
semi-sparkling adj. pétillant.
semolina n. semoule, f.
sempervivum n. artichaut (m.) des toits, joubarbe, f.
to send v.tr. envoyer.
  to send back retourner.
  to send up (from the kitchen) envoyer.
seniority n. ancienneté, f.
sense n. sens, m.

sense of smell odorat, m.
  common sense sens commun, bon sens.
to separate v.tr. séparer; (milk) écrémer.
separated adj. séparé; (milk) écrémé.
separately adv. à part.
separating n. (of milk) écrémage, m.
separation n. séparation, f.
separator n. écrémeuse, f.
September n. septembre, m.
series n. série, f.
to serrate v.tr. denteler.
serrated adj. dentelé.
to serve v.tr. & i. servir.
  to serve apart, separately servir à part.
  to serve as servir de.
service n. service, m.
service-dish n. plat (m.) de service.
  fire-proof service-dish plat de service allant au feu.
  long service-dish plat long.
service-lift n. monte-charge, m.
serviette n. serviette, f.
serving n. (of food) service, m.
set adj. fixé; (e.g. jelly) pris.
  set aside réservé.
  set in aspic aspiqué.
  set in place placé.
  set out étalé.
to set v.tr. fixer.
  v.i. (jelly) prendre.
  to set aside réserver.
  to set in aspic aspiquer.
  to set in place placer.
  to set on ice faire prendre sur glace.
  to set out étaler.
to sew v.tr. coudre.
  to sew up coudre.
sewn adj. cousu.
  sewn up cousu.
shad n. alose, f.
shad-berry n. amélanche, f.
shaddock n. pamplemousse, m. or f.
to shake v.tr. agiter, secouer.
  to shake up agiter, secouer.
shaken adj. agité, secoué.
  shaken up agité, secoué.
shallot n. échalote, f.
shallow adj. peu profond.
shandy n. bière (f.) panachée, panaché, m.
shape n. forme, f.

to shape v.tr. former; (vegetables) tourner.
  to shape like an olive tourner en olive.
shaped adj. formé; (vegetables) tourné.
  shaped like an olive tourné en olive.
share n. part, f.
to share v.tr. partager.
  to share out partager.
shared adj. partagé.
  shared out partagé.
sharp adj. (blade) tranchant; (point) aigu; (taste) aigre; (sauce) piquant.
  somewhat sharp (taste) aigrelet.
to sharpen v.tr. (blade) aiguiser.
sharpened adj. (blade) aiguisé.
sharpening-steel n. fusil, m.
sharpening-stone n. pierre (f.) à aiguiser.
shaving n. (of cheese) copeau, m.
sheet n. (of paper) feuille, f.; (of metal) plaque, f.
  sheet of gelatine feuille de gélatine.
  sheet of paper feuille de papier.
  small sheet of paper feuillet, m.
  metal sheet plaque en tôle.
sheldrake n. tadorne, m.
shelf n. planche, f.
shell n. (of egg) coque, f.; (of oyster, snail) coquille, f.
  deep shell (of oyster) coquille creuse.
  empty shell coquillage, m.
  meringue shell coquille de meringue.
shell-fish n. coquillage, m.
  crustacean shell-fish crustacé, m.
  mollusc shell-fish mollusque, m.
sherry n. xérès, m.
shield n. écu, m.
shield-shape n. écu, m.
shift n. (of work) service, m.
to shift v.tr. remuer.
shifted adj. remué.
shin n. (of beef) gîte, m.
to shine v.i. briller.
shoot n. (of plant) jet, m., pousse, f.
  hop shoots jets de houblon.
short adj. court; (in time) bref.
shortage n. manque, m.
to shorten v.tr. écourter.
shortened adj. écourté.

shoulder n. épaule, f.; (of mutton) éclanche, f.
shovel n. pelle, f.
shoveller n. rouge (m.) de rivière, souchet, m.
to show v.tr. montrer.
shred n. chiffon, m.
to shred v.tr. chiffonner; (almonds) effiler, effilocher.
  to shred coarsely ciseler.
shredded adj. chiffonné; (almonds) effilé, effiloché.
  coarsely shredded ciselé.
shrike n. pie-grièche, f., pigrièche, f.
shrimp n. crevette (f.) grise.
to shrink v.tr. (by cooking) pincer; (by heat) grésiller.
to shrivel v.tr. (by heat) gresiller.
shuck n. (of leguminous vegetable) cosse, f., écale, f., gousse, f.
to shuck v.tr. (leguminous vegetables) cosser, écaler, écosser.
shucked adj. (leguminous vegetables) cossé, écalé, écossé.
to shut v.tr. fermer.
shutting n. fermeture, f.
side n. côté, m.
  concave side (of flat fish) côté creux.
  convex side (of flat fish) côté bombé.
  dark side (of flat fish) côté gauche, côté peau noire.
  upper side dessus, m.
  white side (of flat fish) côté droit.
sideboard n. buffet, m.
sieve n. passoire, f., tamis, m.
  cloth sieve tamis de toile.
  coarse sieve passoire à gros trous.
  fine sieve passoire fine.
  hair sieve tamis de crin.
  silk sieve tamis de soie.
  wire sieve tamis de fer.
to sieve v.tr. tamiser.
sieved adj. tamisé.
silence n. silence, m.
silk n. soie, f.
silver n. argent, m.
  solid silver argent massif.
silverside n. (of beef) gîte (m.) à la noix.
similar adj. pareil.
to simmer v.i. (water) frémir; (on the side of the stove) mijoter; (in a closed container in the oven) mitonner.

v.tr. (on the side of the stove) faire mijoter, mijoter; (in a closed container in the oven) faire mitonner, mitonner.
to simmer gently v.i. frissonner.
simmered adj. (on the side of the stove) mijoté; (in a closed container in the oven) mitonné.
simmering adj. frémissant.
gently simmering (liquid) frissonnant.
simmering n. (esp. of water) frémissement, m.
simple adj. simple.
to simulate v.tr. simuler.
simulated adj. simulé.
sinew n. nerf, m., nervure, f., tendon, m.
to singe v.tr. flamber.
singed adj. flambé.
singeing n. flambage, m.
sip n. petite gorgée, f.
siphon n. siphon, m., vide-bouteille(s), m.
sippet n. croûton, m.
sirloin n. (of beef) aloyau, m.
boned sirloin contrefilet, m.
boned and trimmed sirloin faux-filet, m.
to sit (down) v.i. s'asseoir, v.refl.
situation n. situation, f.
"situations vacant" offres (f.) d'emploi.
"situations wanted" demandes (f.) d'emploi.
size n. dimension, f., grosseur, f., taille, f.
to sizzle v.i. grésiller.
skate n. raie, f.
small skate raiton, m.
skewer n. brochette, f.
metal skewer brochette en fer.
wooden skewer brochette en bois.
skilful adj. habile.
skill n. adresse, f., habileté, f.
to skim v.tr. (sauce) dépouiller; (to remove fat) dégraisser; (milk) écrémer.
skimmed adj. (sauce) dépouillé; (to remove fat) dégraissé; (milk) écrémé.
skimmer n. écumoire, f.
skim-milk n. lait (m.) écrémé.
skim-milk cheese recuite, f.
skimming n. (of sauce) dépouille-ment, m.; (to remove fat) dégraissage, m.; (of milk) écrémage, m.

skimmings (of stock-pot) n.pl. dégraissi(s), m.
skimming-ladle n. écumoire, f.
skin n. peau, f.; (of banana) pelure, f.; (of grape, or on boiled milk) pellicule, f.; (of eel) dépouille, f.
to skin v.tr. (banana) peler; (eel) dépouiller, écorcher; (broad beans) dérober; (by blanching) monder, émonder.
skinned adj. (banana) pelé; (eel) dépouillé, écorché; (broad beans) dérobé; (by blanching) mondé, émondé.
skinning n. (of eel) dépouillement, m.
skirt n. (of beef) bavette (f.) d'aloyau.
skull n. crâne, m.
to slacken v.tr. (consistency) détendre.
slackened adj. (consistency) détendu.
to slaughter v.tr. abattre.
slaughterer n. abatteur, m.
slaughterhouse n. abattoir, m.
sleepy adj. (pear) blet.
sleeve n. manche, f.
slice n. tranche, f.
fat slice tranche grasse.
fine slice lame, f.
rolled slice roulade, f.
round slice rouelle, f.
thick slice tranche épaisse.
thin slice tranche mince.
long thin slice (esp. of white flesh of chicken) aiguillette, f.
slice cut on the bias escalope, f.
slice of toast rôtie, f.
slices of equal thickness tranches régulières.
to slice v.tr. trancher.
to slice on the bias escaloper.
to slice thinly émincer.
sliced adj. tranché.
sliced on the bias escalopé.
thinly sliced émincé.
to slide v.tr. & i. glisser.
slight adj. léger.
slightly adv. légèrement.
to slip v.tr. & i. glisser.
sloe n. prunelle, f.
slow adj. lent.
slowly adv. lentement.
slowness n. lenteur, f.
small adj. petit; mignon; menu.
very small minuscule.
adv. menu.
to chop small hacher menu.

to smear v.tr. enduire.
   to smear with enduire de.
smeared adj. enduit.
   smeared with enduit de.
smell n. odeur, f.; arome, m.; parfum, m.; fumet, m.
to smell v.tr. & i. sentir.
   to smell of sentir.
   to smell of burnt fat sentir le graillon.
smelt n. éperlan, m.
smew n. harle (m.) piette.
smoke n. fumée, f.
to smoke v.tr. fumer.
smoked adj. fumé.
smoking adj. fumant.
   n. fumage, m., fumaison, f.
smolt n. tacon, m.
smooth adj. lisse; (esp. paste) homogène.
to smooth v.tr. lisser; (esp. paste) homogénéiser.
   to smooth with the knife lisser au couteau.
smoothed adj. lissé; (esp. paste) homogénéisé.
snack n. goûter, m.
   cocktail snack amuse-gueule, m.
   to have a snack goûter, v.i.
snail n. escargot, m.
   edible snail escargot comestible.
snail-dish n. escargotière, f.
snake-root n. bistorte, f.
snake-weed n. bistorte, f.
snipe n. bécassine, f.
   young snipe bécau, m.
snout n. museau, m.; (of pig) groin, m.
snow n. neige, f.
snowball n. boule (f.) de neige.
so adv. ainsi.
to soak v.tr. tremper.
   to soak in syrup siroper.
soaked adj. siropé.
   soaked in syrup siropé.
soaking n. trempage, m.
soap n. savon, m.
   cake of soap pain (m.) de savon.
soapy adj. savonneux.
washing-soda n. carbonate (m.) de soude.
soda-water n. eau (f.) de seltz, seltz, m.
soft adj. doux; (to the touch) mou.
   soft cheese fromage (m.) mou.
to soften v.tr. ramollir; (tissue) attendrir; (butter) manier.

softened adj. ramolli; (tissue) attendri; (butter) manié.
softening n. ramollissement, m.; (tissue) attendrissement, m.; (butter) maniement, m.
soft-roed adj. (fish) laité.
to soil v.tr. salir.
soiled adj. sali.
sole adj. seul.
   n. sole, f.
   lemon sole limande (f.) sole.
sole-knife n. couteau (m.) à filets de sole.
solid adj. solide.
solidification n. solidification, f.
solidified adj. solidifié.
to solidify v.tr. solidifier.
   v.i. se solidifier v.refl.
some adj. quelque.
somebody, someone pron. quelqu'un, m., quelqu'une, f.
something n. & pron. quelque chose, m.
   something else autre chose.
sometimes adv. quelquefois.
somewhere adv. quelque part.
soon adv. bientôt.
sophisticated adj. recherché.
sorb-apple n. sorbe, f.
sorghum n. sorg(h)o, m.
sorrel n. oseille, f.
   shredded sorrel chiffonnade (f.) d'oseille.
to sort v.tr. trier.
   to sort out trier.
sorted adj. trié.
   sorted out trié.
sorting n. triage, m.
sorting-out n. triage, m.
soufflé-tray n. plaque (f.) à soufflé.
soup n. (in general) potage, m.; consommé, m.; crème, f.; velouté, m.; purée, f.; soupe, f.; bisque, f. (see these entries in French–English section).
   bound soup potage lié.
   clarified soup consommé.
   clarified beef soup consommé de bœuf.
   clarified chicken soup consommé de volaille.
   cream soup potage crème, crème.
   thick passed soup potage purée, purée.
   thick shell-fish soup bisque.
   clear turtle soup tortue (f.) claire.
   mock turtle soup fausse tortue, f.

real turtle soup vraie tortue, f.
soup-ladle n. louche, f.
soup-machine n. presse-purée, m.
soup-plate n. assiette (f.) à potage, assiette creuse.
soup-spoon n. cuiller (f.) à soupe, cuiller à bouche.
soup-strainer n. passe-bouillon, m.
soup-tureen n. soupière, f.
sour adj. aigre.
source n. source, f., origine, f.
sourish adj. aigrelet.
sour-sop n. anone (f.) muriquée, anone réticulée, corossol (m.) hérissé.
southernwood n. aurone, f.
sow n. truie, f.
soya n. soja, m. soya, m.
soya-bean n. pois (m.) chinois.
space n. (room) place, f.; (empty) vide, m.
spaghetti n.pl. spaghetti, m.pl.
to sparkle v.i. (wine) pétiller.
sparkling adj. (wine) mousseux.
spatch-cocked adj. à la crapaudine, adj.phr.
spatch-cocked chicken poulet (m.) à la crapaudine.
spatula n. spatule, f.
metal spatula spatule en fer.
wooden spatula spatule en bois.
spawn n. frai, m.
spawning n. frai, m.
spawning-season n. frai, m., fraie, f., fraieson, f., fraye, f.
the spawning-season l'époque (f.) du frai.
to speak v.i. parler.
special adj. spécial.
speciality n. spécialité, f.
speciality of the house spécialité de la maison.
to spend v.tr. (money) dépenser; (time) passer.
spice n. épice, f.,; aromate, m.
to spice v.tr. épicer, relever.
spiced adj. épicé, relevé.
strongly spiced fortement épicé.
(wire) spider n. araignée, f.
spikenard n. nard, m., spicanard, m., spiquenard, m.
to spill v.tr. répandre.
spinach n. épinard, m.
bed of spinach lit (m.) d'épinards.
leaf spinach épinards en brenches, épinards en feuilles.
New Zealand spinach tétragone (f.) étalée.

spine n. échine, f.
spiral n. spirale, f.
spirit n. alcool, m., spiritueux, m.pl.
spirituous adj. spiritueux.
spit n. broche, f.
impaled on the spit embroché.
to spit v.i. cracher.
v.tr. embrocher.
spit-rack n. hâtier, m.
spitted adj. embroché.
spleen n. rate, f.
split adj. fendu.
n. fente, f.
to split v.tr. fendre.
to spoil v.tr. abîmer.
v.i. se corrompre v.refl.
spoiled adj. abîmé.
sponge n. éponge, f.
to sponge v.tr. éponger.
sponged adj. épongé.
spoon n. cuiller, f., cuillère, f.; (spatula-shaped) pelle, f.
spoonful n. cuillerée, f.
sprat n. sprat, m., esprot, m., harenguet, m., melet, m., melette, f., anchois (m.) de Norvège.
spread adj. répandu.
to spread v.tr. répandre.
v.i. se répandre, v.refl.
sprig n. bouquet, m.; brin, m.
sprig of sage brin de sauge.
sprig of thyme brin de thym.
small sprig brindille, f.
spring n. printemps, m.
in (the) spring au printemps.
of (the) spring adj.phr. printanier.
spring cabbage chou (m.) de printemps.
spring-like adj. printanier.
to sprinkle v.tr. (with liquid) arroser (de); (with powder or other solid) saupoudrer (de); asperger, semer, parsemer.
to sprinkle with (liquid) arroser de; (powder or other solid) saupoudrer de; asperger de, semer de, parsemer de.
to sprinkle with chopped parsley persiller.
sprinkled adj. (with liquid) arrosé; (with powder or other solid) saupoudré.
sprinkled with chopped parsley persillé.
sprinkling n. (with liquid) arrosage, m.; (with powder or other solid) saupoudrage, m.

Brussels sprout n. chou (m.) de Bruxelles.
   Brussels sprouts choux de Bruxelles.
sprue n. petites asperges, f.pl.
square adj. carré.
   n. carré, m.
square-shape n. carré, m.
squab n. pigeonneau, m.
to squash v.tr. écraser.
squashed adj. écrasé.
squash-melon n. pâtisson, m., artichaut (m.) d'Espagne, artichaut de Jérusalem.
to squeeze v.tr. presser; serrer.
   to squeeze in a cloth presser dans un linge.
   to squeeze out (lemon) exprimer.
squeezed adj. pressé; serré.
   squeezed out (lemon) exprimé.
squill-fish n. cigale (f.) de mer.
to stack v.tr. empiler.
stacked adj. empilé.
staff n. personnel, m.
   relief staff garde, f.
stag n. cerf, m.
   young stag hère, m.
stain n. tache, f.
to stain v.tr. tacher.
stained adj. taché.
stainless adj. inoxydable.
   stainless steel acier (m.) inoxydable.
stain-remover n. détacheur, m.
stair n. (of staircase) marche, f.
staircase n. escalier, m.
stale adj. (bread) rassis.
   stale bread pain (m.) rassis.
stalk n. tige, f., pédoncule, m.
to stalk v.tr. (grapes) égrapper, égrener; (strawberries) équeuter.
stalked adj. (grapes) égrappé, égrené; (strawberries) équeuté.
star n. étoile, f.
starch n. amidon, m.; fécule, f.
   potato starch fécule de pommes de terre.
starling n. sansonnet, m.
starred adj. étoile, f.
star-shape n. étoile, f.
star-shaped adj. étoilé.
to start v.tr. & i. commencer.
   to start again recommencer.
   to start off (cooking) faire partir.
status n. rang, m.
to stay v.i. rester.

steak n. steak, m.
   chuck steak paleron, m.
steam n. fumée, f., vapeur, f.; buée, f.
steaming adj. fumant.
stearin n. stéarine, f.
steel n. acier, m.
   stainless steel, rustless steel acier inoxydable.
stem n. tige, f., pédoncule, m.
step n. (movement) pas, m.; (of staircase) marche, f.
to sterilize v.tr. stériliser, pasteuriser.
sterilized adj. stérilisé, pasteurisé.
stick n. bâton, m.
   small stick bâtonnet, m.
to stick v.i. adhérer.
   v.tr. (with cloves, garlic) piquer.
   to stick with cloves piquer de clous.
   to stick with garlic piquer d'ail.
stick-shape n. bâton, m.
   small stick-shape bâtonnet, m.
still adv. toujours.
   adj. (wine) non mousseux.
   n. alambic, m.
still-room n. office, f.
to stir v.tr. (liquid) remuer.
stirred adj. (liquid) remué.
stirrer n. mouvette, f.
stock n. fonds, m.
   brown stock fonds brun.
   clear brown stock fonds brun clair.
   chicken stock fonds de volaille.
   fish stock fonds de poisson.
   game stock fonds de gibier.
   veal stock fonds de veau.
   white stock fonds blanc.
stock-list n. inventaire, m.
stock-pot n. marmite, f.
stomach n. estomac, m.
   first stomach (of ruminant) panse, f.
   second stomach (of ruminant) bonnet, m.
   third stomach (of ruminant) feuillet, m., mellier, m.
   fourth stomach (of ruminant) caillette, f.
stone n. pierre, f.; (kernel) noyau, m.
to stone v.tr. (fruit) dénoyauter.
(white) stonecrop n. triquemadame, f.
stoned adj. (fruit) dénoyauté.
stoneware n. faïence, f., grès, m.
   stoneware jug pot (m.) en grès.

stool n. tabouret, m.
to stop v.tr. arrêter; (aperture) obturer.
 v.i. cesser.
 to stop doing something cesser de faire quelque chose.
stopped adj. (aperture) obturé.
to stopper v.tr. boucher.
stoppered adj. bouché.
store n. économat, m.
storekeeper n. économe, m.
stout n. bière (f.) noire forte.
stove n. poêle, m.
straight adj. droit.
to strain v.tr. passer.
strained adj. passé.
strainer n. passoire, f.; tamis, m.
 coarse strainer gros tamis; passoire à gros trous.
 conical strainer chinois, m.
 fine conical strainer chinois fin.
 fine strainer passoire fine.
straw n. paille, f.; paillette, f.
 cheese straw paille au parmesan, paillette dorée, paillette d'or.
 small straw paillette.
strawberry n. fraise, f.
 wild strawberry fraise des bois.
strawberry-tree n. arbousier (m.) commun.
striated adj. strié.
striation n. strie, f.
to strike v.tr. frapper; (match) frotter.
 to strike a match frotter une allumette.
string n. ficelle, f.
 piece of string bout (m.) de ficelle.
 string of onions grappe (f.) d'oignon.
to string v.tr. (beans) effiler.
string-box n. boîte (f.) à ficelle.
stringy adj. (celery) cordé; (meat) filandreux.
 stringy celery céleri (m.) cordé.
strip n. aiguillette, f., lanière, f.
to strip v.tr. (of leaves) effeuiller.
stripped adj. (of leaves) effeuillé.
stromateus n. stromatée, m.
strong adj. fort.
strongly adv. fort; (followed by past participle) fortement.
 strongly seasoned fortement assaisonné.
stuck adj. (with cloves, garlic) piqué.
 stuck with cloves piqué de clous.

stuck with garlic piqué d'ail.
to stud v.tr. clouter.
studded adj. clouté.
student n. étudiant, m.; étudiante, f.
 catering student étudiant hôtelier; étudiante hôtelière.
to stuff v.tr. farcir.
 to stuff with farcir de.
stuffed adj. farci.
stuffing n. farce, f.
stump n. (of cabbage) trognon, m.; (of chicken-bone) moignon, m.
sturgeon n. esturgeon, m.
style n. style, m.; goût, m.
 in the Chinese style dans le goût chinois.
subject n. sujet, m.
 on the subject of au sujet de.
subject-matter n. matière, f.
to succeed v.i. réussir.
success n. réussite, f., succès, m.
successful adj. (kitchen operation) réussi.
succession n. suite, f.
 in succession de suite.
sucking-calf n. veau (m.) de lait.
sucking-pig n. cochon (m.) de lait.
suet n. graisse (f.) de rognon.
sufficient adj. suffisant.
sufficiently adv. assez, suffisamment.
sugar n. sucre, m.
 brown sugar cassonade, f.
 castor sugar sucre en poudre.
 Demerara sugar cassonade en gros cristaux.
 granulated sugar sucre cristallisé.
 lump sugar scure en morceaux, sucre en tablettes.
 maple sugar sucre d'érable.
 refined sugar raffinade, f.
 sugar candy sucre candi.
to sugar v.tr. sucrer.
 to sugar almonds lisser des amandes.
sugar-almond n. praline, f.
sugar-bean n. haricot (m.) de Lima.
sugared adj. sucré.
sugar-free adj. sans sucre, adj.phr.
sugar-icing n. glace, f.
sugarless adj. sans sucre, adj.phr.
sugar-pea n. mange-tout, m.
sugar-sifter n. passoire (f.) à sucre.
suitable adj. convenable.
suitably adv. convenablement.

sultana n. raisin (m.) de Smyrne.
summary n. relevé, m.
summer n. été, m.
sumptuous adj. luxueux.
Sunday n. dimanche, m.
sundew n. rossolis, m.
sun-fish n. poisson-soleil, m., perche
(f.) soleil; poisson-lune, m.
superior adj. supérieur.
to supervise v.tr. surveiller.
supper n. souper, m.
  to have supper souper, prendre
  le souper.
supplement n. supplément, m.
supplementary adj. supplémentaire.
sure adj. sûr, certain.
surmullet n. surmulet, m.
surplus n. surplus, m.
surprise n. surprise, f.
surround n. bordure, f.
to surround v.tr. entourer.
  to surround with entourer de.
surrounded adj. entouré.
  surrounded with entouré de.
swallow n. hirondelle, f.
to sweat v.i. suer.
  v.tr. faire suer.
swede n. navet (m.) de Suède,
navet suédois, navet jaune, chou-
navet, m., rutabaga, m.
sweet adj. doux.
  n. sweet (course) entremets, m.
sweetbreads n. ris (word seldom
used alone), m.; fagoue, f.
  calf's sweetbreads ris de veau.
  lamb's sweetbreads ris d'agneau.
to sweeten v.tr. édulcorer; (with
sugar) sucrer.
sweetened adj. édulcoré; (with
sugar) sucré.
sweetmeat n. bonbon, m.
sweet-sop n. anone (f.) écailleuse,
corossol (m.) écailleux.
sweet-spoon n. cuiller (f.) à
entremets, cuiller à dessert.
sweet-trolley n. voiture (f.) à
entremets.
to swell v.tr. gonfler.
  v.i. se gonfler.
swift adj. rapide.
swiftly adv. rapidement.
swill n. eaux (f.pl.) grasses.
to swill v.tr. laver à grande eau.
  to swill out laver à grande eau.
  to swill the floor laver le plancher
  à grande eau.
swimmeret n. patte (f.) natatoire.

swimming-bladder n. (of fish)
vessie (f.) natatoire.
swollen adj. gonflé.
swordfish n. espadon, m.
symmetrical adj. symétrique.
symmetrically adv. symétriquement.
syringe n. seringue, f.
syrup n. sirop, m.
  golden syrup sirop de sucre,
  mélasse (f.) raffinée.
  grenadine syrup grenadine, f.
  orgeat syrup orgeat, m.
syrupy adj. sirupeux.
system n. système, m.

t

table n. table, f.
table-cloth n. nappe, f.
table-knife n. couteau (m.) de
table.
table-spoon n. cuiller (f.) de
table, cuiller à bouche.
tablespoonful n. cuillerée (f.) à
bouche, cuillerée.
tafia n. (rum) tafia, m.
tag n. étiquette, f.
tail n. queue, f.; (of fish) bat, m.
  decorticated tail (e.g. of prawn)
  queue décortiquée.
to taint v.i. se corrompre, v.refl.
tainted adj. impur.
to take v.tr. & i. prendre.
  to take away retirer, enlever.
  to take care to do something
  avoir soin de faire quelque chose.
  to take off (remove) ôter.
  to take out (from oven) retirer;
  (from cupboard) sortir.
  to take place avoir lieu.
taken adj. pris.
to talk v.i. parler.
tallow n. suif, m.
tamarind n. tamarin, m.
tangerine n. mandarine, f.
tank n. (for live fish) vivier,
m.
tansy n. tanaisie, f., barbotine, f.
tap n. robinet, m.
tapioca n. tapioca, m.
tariff n. tariff, m.
tarragon n. estragon, m.
  chopped tarragon estragon
  haché.
  leaf tarragon estragon en
  branches.

tarragon-juice n. suc (m.) d'estragon.
tart n. tourte, f.
tartlet n. tartelette, f.
task n. tâche, f.
taste n. goût, m.
  sophisticated taste goût recherché.
  to taste adv.phr. au goût.
to taste v.tr. goûter; (before correcting seasoning) essayer. v.i. sentir.
  to taste of sentir.
  to taste greasy sentir le graillon.
tea n. thé, m.
  beef tea thé de viande.
  green tea thé vert.
  Paraguayan tea maté, m.
teal n. sarcelle (f.) (d'hiver), mercanette, f.
to tear v.tr. déchirer.
  to tear apart, to tear up déchirer.
tea-spoon n. cuiller (f.) à thé.
teaspoonful n. cuillerée (f.) à thé.
to tell v.tr. dire.
to temper v.tr. tempérer.
temperature n. température, f.
tempered adj. tempéré.
temporary adj. temporaire.
tench n. tanche, f.
tender adj. tendre.
to tenderize v.tr. attendrir; (by hanging) mortifier.
tenderized adj. attendri; (by hanging) mortifié.
tenderloin n. filet (m.) mignon.
tendon n. tendon, m., nervure, f.
tepid adj. tiède.
terrapin n. terrapène, m.
to test v.tr. essayer.
tetragonia n. tétragone, f.
to thaw v.tr. décongeler. v.i. se décongeler, v.refl.
thawed adj. décongelé.
thawing n. décongélation, f.
theft n. vol, m.
  petty theft larcin, m.
  petty thefts petits vols, pl.
then adv. ensuite.
theory n. théorie, f.
  in theory adv.phr. en principe.
thick adj. épais; gros.
to thicken v.tr. épaissir; (sauce) corser. v.i. (sauce) se corser, v.refl.
thickened adj. épaissi; (sauce) corsé.
thickening n. roux, m.

brown thickening roux brun.
fawn thickening roux blond.
white thickening roux blanc.
thickening-agent n. liaison, f.
thickness n. épaisseur, f.; (in cross-section) grosseur, f.
third adj. troisième. n. tiers, m.
thorax n. thorax, m.
thornback n. raie (f.) bouclée.
thorough adj. minutieux.
thread n. fil, m.
to thread v.tr. (needle) enfiler.
threaded adj. (needle) enfilé.
thrift n. économie, f.
thrifty adj. économe.
throat n. gorge, f.
to throw v.tr. jeter.
thrush n. grive, f.
Thursday n. jeudi, m.
thyme n. thym, m.
  wild thyme serpolet, m.
thymus(-gland) n. thymus, m.
tide n. marée, f.
tidiness n. propreté, f.
tidy adj. ordonné, rangé.
to tidy v.tr. ranger.
to tie v.tr. lier.
  to tie (up) with string ficeler.
tied adj. lié.
  tied (up) with string ficelé.
to tighten v.tr. (consistency) serrer; (sauce) corser. v.i. (sauce) se corser, v.refl.
tightened adj. (consistency) serré; (sauce) corsé.
time n. temps, m.; (by the clock) heure, f.; (occasion) fois, f.
  at the same time en même temps.
  the correct time, the right time l'heure exacte.
  to waste time perdre du temps.
  many times beaucoup de fois.
tin n. (metal) étain, m.; fer (m.) blanc, fer-blanc, m.; (can) boîte (f.) en fer blanc.
  tin of conserves boîte de conserves.
to tin v.tr. (copper) étamer.
tinamou n. tinamou, m.
tin-foil n. papier (m.) d'étain.
tinned adj. de conserve, adj.phr.; (copper) étamé.
  tinned copper cuivre (m.) étamé.
tinning n. (of copper) étamage, m.
tin-opener n. ouvre-boîtes, m.; couteau (m.) à conserves.

tint n. teinte, f.
tiny adj. minuscule.
tip n. (point) pointe, f.; (gratuity)
  pourboire, m.
  the tip of the knife la pointe du
  couteau.
  collecting-box for tips tronc, m.
to prep. à.
toad n. crapaud, m.
toast n. pain (m.) grillé, toast, m.
to toast v.tr. & i. griller.
toasted adj. grillé.
toasting n. grillage, m.
to-day adv. aujourd'hui.
toddy n. grog, m.
together adv. ensemble.
Tokay n. tokay, m., tokai, m.
tomato n. tomate, f.
  **canned tomatoes, tinned to-
  matoes** tomates de conserve.
tomato-pip n. graine (f.) de
  tomate.
(pair of) tongs, n. pince, f.
tongue n. langue, f.
  calf's tongue langue de veau.
  tongue coated with brown aspic
  langue à l'écarlate.
tongue-shape n. langue, f.
  small tongue-shape languette, f.
too adv. trop.
  too much trop.
tooth n. dent, f.
top n. (upper part) haut, m.;
  (upper side) dessus, m.
  top of leg (of chicken) gras (m.)
  de cuisse.
topic n. sujet, m.
topside n. (of beef) tende (m.) de
  tranche; (of flat fish) côté (m.)
  gauche, côté peau noire.
torn adj. déchiré.
  torn apart, torn up déchiré.
touch n. (of garlic) pointe, f.
tough adj. (meat) coriace, filandreux.
towards prep. vers.
toxic adj. toxique.
trade n. commerce, m.; (craft)
  métier, m.
trader n. marchand, m., commerçant, m., négociant, m.
tradition n. tradition, f.
traditional adj. traditionnel.
translucid adj. translucide.
transparent adj. transparent.
transversal adj. transversal.
transversally adj. transversalement.
tray n. plateau, m.

tray-cloth n. napperon, m.
treacle n. mélasse, f.
tread n. (of egg) germe, m.
to treat v.tr. traiter.
treated adj. traité.
treatment n. traitement, m.
tree n. arbre, m.
  bread-fruit tree artocarpe, m.
trefoil n. trèfle, m.
  bird's foot trefoil lotier, m.
trellis n. treillage, m.
trellis-pattern n. treillage, m.,
  grillage, m., grille, f.
  (arranged) in a trellis-pattern
  en grille.
trencher n. tailloir, m., tranchoir,
  m.
triangle n. triangle, m.
triangular adj. triangulaire.
to trim v.tr. parer, rogner; (by
  shortening) écourter.
trimmed adj. paré, rogné; (by
  shortening) écourté.
trimmings n.pl. parures, f.,
  rognures, f.
  mushroom trimmings parures
  de champignons.
tripe n. gras-double, m.; tripe(s),
  f.(pl.).
tripe-kettle n. tripière, f.
to triturate v.tr. triturer.
triturated adj. trituré.
trituration n. trituration, f.
triturator n. triturateur, m.
trivet n. trépied, m.
trolley n. voiture, f.
  cold trolley voiture à entremets.
  hot trolley voiture chaude.
tropic n. tropique, m.
tropical adj. (fruit) tropique.
trotter n. (of pig) pied, m.
trout n. truite, f.
  lake trout truite de lac.
  live trout truite vivante.
  river trout truite de rivière.
trout-kettle n. truitière, f.
trowel n. truelle, f.
true adj. vrai.
truffle n. true, f.
  black truffle truffe noire.
  white truffle truffe blanche.
trumpeter n. (bird) agami, m.
to truss v.tr. brider, trousser.
  **to truss (chicken) with the legs
  entered** brider en entrée.
trussed adj. bridé, troussé.
trussing n. bridage, m., troussage,
  m.

trussing-needle n. aiguille (f.) à brider.

to try v.tr. & i. essayer.
  to try to do something essayer de faire quelque chose.

tub n. baquet, m.

tube n. tube, m.

tuber n. tubercule, m.

Tuesday n. mardi, m.
  Shrove Tuesday mardi gras.

tufted adj. (bird) huppé.

tunny n. thon, m.

turban n. turban, m.

turban-mould n. moule (m.) à couronne.

turban-shape n. turban, m.

turbot n. turbot, m.
  young turbot turbotin, m.

turbot-kettle n. turbotière, f.

turkey n. dindon, m.
  young turkey dindonneau, m.

turkey-cock n. dindon, m.

turkey-hen n. dinde, f., poule (f.) d'Inde.

turmeric n. curcuma, m., saffron (m.) des Indes.

turn n. tour, m.
  turn of (the) pepper-mill tour de moulin.

to turn v.tr. tourner.
  to turn barrel-shaped tourner en baril.
  to turn inside out retourner.
  to turn olive-shaped tourner en olive.
  to turn over retourner.
  to turn yellow v.i. jaunir.

turned adj. tourné.
  turned barrel-shaped tourné en baril.
  turned olive-shaped tourné en olive.

turnip n. navet, m.
  Swedish turnip navet de Suède, navet suédois, navet jaune, chou-navet, m., rutabaga, m.

turnip-rooted adj. napiforme.

turnover n. chausson, m.

turtle n. tortue (f.) de mer; (on menu) tortue.
  green turtle tortue verte, chélonée (f.) franche.
  mock-turtle fausse tortue.
  real turtle vraie tortue.
  turtle herbs herbes (f.) à tortue.

turtle-dove n. tourterelle, f.

turtle-flipper n. nageoire (f.) de tortue.

twelfth-cake n. galette (f.) des Rois.

twice adv. deux fois.

twig n. branchillon, m.

to twist v.tr. tordre.

tying n. (with string) ficelage, m.

type n. type, m., genre, m.

U

udder n. tétine, f.

umber n. ombre, m., ombre commun, ombre de rivière.

umbrina n. ombrine, f., ombre (m.) de mer.

uncooked adj. cru.

to uncork v.tr. déboucher.

to uncover v.tr. découvrir.

uncovered adj. découvert.

under prep. sous.
  adv. dessous.

underdone adj. (steak) saignant; (not cooked enough) pas assez cuit.

underside n. dessous, m.; (of flat fish) côté (m.) droit.

to understand v.tr. comprendre.

understood adj. compris.
  understood! int. entendu!

to undo v.tr. défaire.

undone adj. défait.

to unfold v.tr. déplier, développer.

unfolded adj. déplié, développé.

uniform n. tenue, f.
  cook's uniform tenue de cuisine.

unimportant adj. petit.

unleavened adj. azyme.

unoccupied adj. libre.

unpack v.tr. déballer.

unsuccessful adj. manqué.

to untie v.tr. déballer.

until prep. jusqu'à.
  conj. jusqu'à ce que.

unused adj. neuf.

to unwrap v.tr. développer.

unwrapped adj. développé.

upon prep. sur.

to upset v.tr. répandre.

usable adj. utilisable.

usage n. uage, m., pratique, f.

use n. usage, m.; utilité, f.
  in use usité.

to use v.tr. utiliser, se servir de.
  to use up consommer, user.

used adj. utilisé, usité.
  used up consommé, usé.

useful adj. utile.

usefulness n. utilité, f.

useless adj. utile.
usual adj. habituel, usuel, ordinaire.
usually adv. d'habitude.
utensil n. ustensile, m.
   fire-proof utensil ustensile allant au feu.
   kitchen utensil ustensile de cuisine.
   oven-proof utensil ustensile allant au four.
   special utensil ustensile spécial.
utility n. utilité, f.
utilizable adj. utilisable.
to utilize v.tr. utiliser.
utilized adj. utilisé.

V

vacant adj. libre.
   "situations vacant" offres (f.) d'emploi.
vacation n. vacances, f.pl.
   on vacation en vacances.
valid adj. valable.
valuable adj. de valeur.
value n. valeur, f.
   of value adj.phr. de valeur.
vanilla n. vanille, f.
to vaporize v.tr. vaporiser.
vaporized adj. vaporisé.
vapour n. vapeur, f., buée, f.
variant n. variante, f.
variation n. (in recipe, method) variante, f.
varied adj. varié.
to variegate v.tr. panacher.
variegated adj. panaché.
variegation n. (of colours) panache, m.
various adj. varié; divers, pl.
to vary v.tr. varier.
veal n. veau, m.
vegetable n. légume, m.
   (any) early vegetable primeur, f.
   (any) forced vegetable primeur, f.
   pot vegetables légumes de (la) marmite.
   root vegetable racine, f.
   salad vegetable salade, f.
vegetable-cutter n. (for roots) taille-racines, m.
vegetable-dish n. légumier, m.
(small) vegetable-knife n. couteau (m.) d'office.
vegetable-mincer n. hache-légumes, m.

vegetable-peeler n. couteau (m.) (d')économe.
vegetable-slicer n. taille-légumes m.
vegetarian adj. végétarien.
   n. végétarien, m.; végétarienne, f.
vein n. veine, f.
velvet n. velours, m.
velvety adj. velouté.
venison n. venaison, f.
   large venison grosse venaison.
   small venison (hares and wild rabbits) basse venaison.
ventral adj. ventral.
venus n. vénus, f.
verbena n. verveine, f.
verjuice n. verjus, m.
vermicelli n.pl. vermicelli, m.pl.; vermicelle, m.sing.
vermouth n. vermout(h), m.
very adv. très, bien.
vetch n. gesse, f.
vine n. vigne, f.
vinegar n. vinaigre, m.
   elder-flower vinegar surard, m.
   tarragon vinegar vinaigre d'estragon.
   wine vinegar vinaigre de vin.
vine-leaf n. feuille (f.) de vigne.
vine-plant n. cep, m.
vine-shoot n. sarment, m.
vine-stock n. cep, m.
violet adj. violet.
   n. (colour) violet, m.; (flower) violette, f.
viscera n.pl. viscères, m.pl.
visceral adj. viscéral.
viscous adj. mucilagineux, visqueux.
visit n. visite, f.
to visit v.tr. visiter.
vitamin n. vitamine, f.
voucher n. bon, m.

W

wader n. échassier, m.
wafer n. gaufrette, f.
   cornet-shaped (rolled) wafer oublie, f., plaisir, m.
waffle n. gaufre, f.
waffle-iron n. gaufrier, m.
wage(s) n. salaire, m.
wage-earner n. salarié, m.; salariée, f.
wage-earning adj. salarié.
wagtail n. lavandière, f.
wait n. attente, f.

to wait v.i. attendre.
  to wait for v.tr. attendre.
waiter n. commis (m.) de restaurant.
  head waiter maître d'hôtel.
to walk v.i. marcher.
wall n. mur, m.; (of stomach) paroi, f.
wall-cupboard n. placard, m.
walnut n. noix, f.
  green walnut cerneau, m.
  pickled walnut cerneau confit au vinaigre.
want v.tr. vouloir.
wanted adj. voulu.
  "situations wanted" demandes (f.) d'emploi.
warden n. (pear) catillac, m., catillard, m.
warm adj. tiède; chaud.
  to keep warm tenir au chaud.
to warm v.tr. chauffer.
  to warm up again réchauffer.
warmed adj. chauffé.
  warmed up again réchauffé.
warming adj. chauffant.
wart-hog n. phacochère, m., sanglier (m.) d'Afrique.
to wash v.tr. laver.
  to wash (oneself) se laver, v.refl.
  to wash one's hands se laver les mains.
wash-basin n. lavabo, m.
washed adj. lavé.
  washed well bien lavé.
washer-up n. plongeur, m.; plongeuse, f.
washing n. lavage, m.
washing-up n. plonge, f.; (i.e. the articles to be washed up) vaisselle, f.
  to do the washing-up faire la vaisselle.
wash-room n. lavabo, m.
wastage n. gaspillage, m.
to waste v.tr. gaspiller.
wasted adj. gaspillé.
watch n. montre, f.
water n. eau, f.
  aerated water eau gazeuse.
  boiling water eau bouillante.
  cold water eau froide; eau fraîche.
  cool water eau fraîche.
  drinking water eau potable.
  fresh water (from river or lake) eau douce; (straight from tap) eau fraîche.
  hard water eau dure.

  hot water eau chaude.
  lukewarm water eau tiède.
  mineral water eau minérale.
  orange-flower eau de fleurs d'oranger.
  salt water eau salée.
  salted water eau salée.
  sea water eau de mer.
  soapy water eau savonneuse.
  soft water eau douce.
  tepid water eau tiède.
to water down v.tr. diluer.
water-biscuit n. biscuit (m.) à l'eau.
watercress n. cresson (m.) de fontaine.
watered down adj. dilué.
water-ice n. sorbet, m.
watering down n.phr. dilution, f.
water-jug n. carafe, f.
water-melon n. melon (m.) d'eau, pastèque, f.
water-paste n. pâte (f.) à l'eau.
water-pipe n. tuyau (m.) d'eau.
waterproof adj. imperméable à l'eau.
water-rail n. râle (m.) d'eau.
water-tap n. robinet, m.
water-vapour n. vapeur (f.) d'eau, vapeur.
watery adj. aqueux.
wattle n. (of cockerel) barbillon, m.; (of turkey) fraise, f.
way n. (fashion) façon, f.
  in the usual way à la façon ordinaire.
weak adj. (infusion) léger.
to wear v.tr. porter.
  to wear out v.tr. user.
webbed adj. (feet) membrané.
wedding n. noce(s), f.
Wednesday n. mercredi, m.
week n. semaine, f.
weekly adj. hebdomadaire.
weever n. vive, f., araignée (f.) de mer.
weight n. poids, m.
  gross weight poids brut.
  metal weight (to weigh down saucepan-lid) poids.
  net weight poids net.
well adv. bien.
  n. puits, m.
whale n. baleine, f.
what? pron. quoi?
wheat n. blé (m.) froment, froment, m.
wheatear n. motteux, m., cul-blanc, m.

when conj. quand, lorsque.
where adv. où.
  where? où?
whetstone, n. pierre (f.) à aiguiser.
whey n. petit lait, m., petit-lait, m., lait clair.
while conj. pendant que.
whip n. fouet, m.
to whip v.tr. fouetter.
whipped adj. fouetté.
whisk n. fouet, m., moussoir, m.
to whisk v.tr. fouetter.
whisked adj. fouetté.
whisky n. whisky, m.
white adj. blanc.
  n. blanc, m.
  pinkish white blanc rosé.
  white of egg blanc d'œuf.
  the white of an egg un blanc d'œuf.
  white of leek blanc de poireau.
whitebait n. blanchaille, f.
white-currant n. groseille (f.) blanche.
white-tail n. motteux, m., cul-blanc, m.
whiting n. merlan, m.
whiting-pout n. tacaud, m.
whitish adj. blanchâtre.
whole adj. entier.
  n. ensemble, m.
wholesale n. gros, m.
  wholesale price prix (m,) de gros.
wholly adv. entièrement.
whortleberry n. airelle (f.) myrtille.
why adv. & conj. pourquoi.
  why? pourquoi?
wicker-basket n. panier (m.) d'osier.
wide adj. large.
widgeon n. canard (m.) siffleur, maréca, m.
width n. largeur, f.
windpipe n. gosier, m.
wine n. vin, m.
  fortified wine vin viné.
  pink wine vin rosé.
  red wine vin rouge.
  Samian wine samos, m.
  semi-sparkling wine vin pétillant.
  sparkling wine vin mousseux.
  table wine vin de table.
  white wine vin blanc.
  wine at room-temperature vin chambré.

wing n. aile, f.
winglet n. aileron, m.
winkle n. bigorneau, m., guignette, f., limaçon (m.) de mer, littorine, f., vigneau, m., vignot, m.
winter n. hiver, m.
to wipe v.tr. essuyer.
  to wipe clean essuyer.
  to wipe dry essuyer.
to wish v.i. vouloir.
  to wish to vouloir.
wish-bone n. fourchette, f., lunette, f.
with prep. avec; à.
to withdraw v.tr. retirer.
within adv. dedans.
without prep. sans.
wood n. bois, m.
wood-ash n. cendre (f.) de bois.
  hot wood-ash cendre de bois chaude.
woodcock n. bécasse, f.
  young (of the) woodcock bécasseau, m.
wood-pigeon n. pigeon (m.) ramier, ramier, m., palombe, f.
  young wood-pigeon ramereau, m.
woodruff n. aspérule (f.) odorante.
wood-sorrel n. oxalide, f., oxalis, f., surelle, f., surette, f.
word n. mot, m.; (pledge) parole, f.
work n. travail, m.
to work v.tr. & i. travailler.
  to work v.i. (machine) marcher.
  to work v.tr. (butter) manier, malaxer, masser.
  to work with a spatula masser à la spatule.
worked adj. travaillé; (substance) manié, malaxé.
working n. (of butter) maniement, m.
worm n. ver, m.
worm-eaten adj. percé de vers.
wormwood n. absinthe, f.
worn adj. (clothes) porté; (worn out) usé.
to wrap up v.tr. envelopper, emballer.
wrapped up adj. enveloppé, emballé.
wrapping n. enveloppe, f.
wrasse n. labre, m., vieille (f.) de mer, vieille.
wrist-watch n. montre (f.) de poignet.
to write v.tr. écrire.

Y

yam n. igname, f.
yarrow n. achillée, f., millefeuille, f., mille-feuille, f.
yeast n. levure, f.
yellow adj. jaune.
  n. jaune, m.
yellowed adj. jauni.
yellowish adj. jaunâtre.
yes adv. oui.

yes, thank you oui, je vous remercie.
yesterday adv. hier.
yolk n. jaune, m.
  yolk of egg jaune d'œuf.
  the yolk of an egg un jaune d'œuf.

Z

zest n. (of orange) zeste, m.
zesting-knife n. couteau (m.) à zester.